Praise for
THE WISDOM OF YOGA

"Stephen Cope is a compassionate writer with a talent for bridging ancient wisdom and the modern mind. Artful, heartfelt and gracious, *The Wisdom of Yoga* leads the reader deep into yoga philosophy."
—Patricia Walden, international yoga teacher

"Absolutely masterful! Stephen Cope lays out the complete path of yoga with stunning clarity, and he does so in a narrative style that is as riveting to read as a good novel. I simply could not put it down."
—Sylvia Boorstein, author of *It's Easier Than You Think*

"Beautifully written, full of insight and compassion, and chock-full of stories . . . a life-enhancing and entertaining read."
—Amy Weintraub, author of *Yoga for Depression*

"Stephen Cope has done the impossible—turned the inscrutable *Yoga-Sūtra* into a page turner! His inspiring storytelling unfurls the mysterious, delicate threads of the *Yoga-Sūtra* and reveals the rich power of these teachings, showing us how truly alive they are for people like us, right here, right now.   —Cyndi Lee, author of *Yoga Body, Buddha Mind* and *OM Yoga*

"A tour de force of startling beauty and enthralling scholarship, *The Wisdom of Yoga* has the draw of a thriller novel, the depth of a sacred text, and an intriguing balance of information drawn from the sciences."
—Donna Farhi, author of *Bringing Yoga to Life:*
The Everyday Practice of Enlightened Living

"Stephen Cope continues to lead the way in developing and elucidating the future of yoga and meditation in America. I heartily recommend this beautiful new contribution to our wisdom tradition."
—Lama Surya Das, author of *Awakening the Buddha Within*
and *Letting Go of the Person You Used to Be*

"Written with depth, understanding, and compassion, *The Wisdom of Yoga* is a wonderful resource filled with profound teachings presented with clarity and wisdom. Its simple and thoughtful stories will remind you of who you are, while healing your life in the process."
—Sherri Baptiste, yoga teacher and founder of Baptiste Power of Yoga

"What a wonderful reminder that the benefit of yoga vastly exceeds the physical. This personal, very readable guide to understanding the wisdom of yoga is warm, engaging and inspiring."

—Sharon Salzberg, author of *Lovingkindness*

"A warm, masterful interweaving of key teachings from yoga, psychology, and Buddhism through personal stories and true-to-life examples; practical and esoteric at the same time."

—Rama Berch, C.S.Y.T., R.Y.T., Master Yoga Foundation

"Stephen Cope brilliantly unpacks the sage Patanjali's ancient blueprint for awakening, illuminating the teachings of classical yoga in the light of Western psychology, neuroscience, and Buddhist practice."

—Anne Cushman, contributing editor, *Yoga Journal*
and coauthor of *From Here to Nirvana*

"Stephen Cope's skills as a psychotherapist, scholar, and yogi are woven together with grace, insight and depth. This book is vivid, alive and immensely significant for practitioners of all schools of yoga."

—Larry Rosenberg, senior meditation teacher
and author of *Breath by Breath*

"Friendly, authoritative, and quite magical, *The Wisdom of Yoga* will help even experienced yogis discover what yoga is all about. This is not a how-to book, but a how-to-be, deep-yoga manual that should be in the library of anyone seriously interested in spirituality."

—Thomas Moore, author of *Care of the Soul* and *Dark Nights of the Soul*

"Stephen Cope brings to his subject matter the sharp sword of discrimination and wields it in a lucid, easy style. Any student of the nature of consciousness and its application to the human condition will greatly benefit."

—Swami Shivananda Sarasvati, D.Ay., R.Y.T.

"An unprecedented exploration of how yoga's timeless insights can be realized in one's own body, mind, and heart *right now*. This absorbing and compassionate book will be a prized compass for anyone setting out on a quest for the true self."

—Chip Hartranft, translator and editor of *The Yoga-Sūtra of Patanjali*

"*The Wisdom of Yoga* not only makes Patanjali's notoriously difficult *Yoga-Sūtra* intelligible but is also a real pleasure to read. Stephen Cope shows the relevance of this classic text to modern men and women and brings ancient yogic wisdom to life. Bravo!"

—Timothy McCall, M.D., medical editor, *Yoga Journal*,
and author of *Yoga as Medicine*

"Stephen is a rare voice in yoga today. While ever mindful of the sublime nature of yoga's tradition, *The Wisdom of Yoga* bravely and articulately conveys the very human and practical challenges we face in the process of becoming our best self."

—Rod Stryker, yoga teacher and author of *Exploits of a Sun Poet*

"*The Wisdom of Yoga* gently, accessibly shows how people with real issues can become spiritually mature and fully human. These are stories of people who learn to value the time-bound, limited, daily problems of practice equally to the timeless, the cosmic, and the transcendent."

—Victoria Austin, president, San Francisco Zen Center

"In these heartfelt stories, Stephen Cope shows us how Patanjali's ancient teachings provide sustenance and guidance that can steer our modern day lives into a course of clarity and action. I will enthusiastically recommend *The Wisdom of Yoga* to all my students."

—Richard Miller, author of *Yoga Nidra: The Meditative Heart of Yoga*

"Stephen Cope takes the complicated, ancient texts of Patanjali, and elegantly brings them to life. I found myself saying, 'Oh, *now* I understand!' after reading his wise insights and stories of friends and fellow yoga students as they struggle with today's dilemmas of living. Reading *The Wisdom of Yoga* has made me a more confident yoga teacher."

—Lilias Folan, author of *Lilias! Yoga Gets Better with Age*

"*The Wisdom of Yoga* is a must-read for yoga students, and a source book for how to bring your yoga practice into your daily life."

—Phillip Moffitt, founder of Life Balance Institute

"*The Wisdom of Yoga* offers a tremendous service to anyone on the path—it is an absolutely true to life, human, intimate expression of the wisdom of the *Yoga-Sūtra*. Another Cope classic has emerged that I will recommend to all."

—Shiva Rea, Yogini

"Stephen's Cope journey through the *Yoga-Sūtra* of Patanjali has the feel of Don Quixote and Sancho Panza's travels. Except this journey takes place in the midst of a 21st century humanity with its own halls of mirrors. It is an enchanting and sensitive rendering of human struggles that are all too familiar to each one of us."

—Mu Soeng, author of *Trust in Mind*

"Not only does Cope brilliantly map out the central means and milestones of the yoga journey, but—astonishingly—he does so by telling the intertwined stories of six fascinating contemporary characters. *The Wisdom of Yoga* is not just 'about' the yogic archetype of 'the fully alive human being.' It is a fully alive book."

—Marion Woodman, coauthor of *Coming Home to Myself*

ALSO BY STEPHEN COPE

Yoga and the Quest for the True Self
Published by Bantam Books

THE
WISDOM
OF

Yoga

A SEEKER'S GUIDE TO
EXTRAORDINARY LIVING

STEPHEN COPE

BANTAM BOOKS

THE WISDOM OF YOGA
A Bantam Book / July 2006

Published by Bantam Dell
A Division of Random House, Inc.
New York, New York

Book design by Susan Hood

Library of Congress Cataloging-in-Publication Data
Cope, Stephen.
The wisdom of yoga : a seeker's guide to extraordinary living / Stephen Cope.
p. cm.
ISBN-13: 978-0-553-80111-8
ISBN-10: 0-553-80111-2
Includes bibliographical references.
1. Yoga. II. Title.
BL1238.52 .C67 2006
181.'452 22   2006042656

Printed in the United States of America
Published simultaneously in Canada

www.bantamdell.com

10 9 8 7 6 5 4 3
BVG

FOR MU SOENG,

yogi, scholar, mentor, and cherished friend

CONTENTS

THERE were no formerly heroic times, and there was no formerly pure generation. There is no one here but us chickens, and so it has always been: a people busy and powerful, knowledgeable, ambivalent, important, fearful, and self-aware; a people who scheme, promote, deceive, and conquer; who pray for their loved ones, and long to flee misery and skip death. It is a weakening and discoloring idea, that rustic people knew God personally once upon a time—or even knew selflessness or courage or literature—but that it is too late for us. In fact, the absolute is available to everyone in every age. There never was a more holy age than ours, and never a less.

—Annie Dillard, *For the Time Being*

INTRODUCTION

Mircea eliade, one of the greatest students of religion in the twentieth century, once declared, "[We go] to the past only in order to learn about such authentic possibilities of human existence as may be repeatable in the present."[1]

This book is an inquiry into one such collection of possibilities—the three-thousand-year-old wisdom tradition called yoga.

In the pages that follow, we will direct our gaze backward to the fantastic possibilities for human existence discovered by this wisdom tradition. We will direct our gaze backward to an ancient series of discoveries about the human mind and body so remarkable that even the most sophisticated contemporary neuroscience is still at considerable pains to explain them—though their reality can hardly be denied. We will direct our gaze backward to a dazzling two-thousand-year-old treatise on yoga and meditation called the *Yoga-Sūtra*, a virtually anonymous tract that is one of the most brilliant pieces of spiritual and psychological writing known to humankind.

We will look backward, yes. But, as Eliade suggests, we will look back at this tradition only in order to see there the reflection of our own possibilities. We may be surprised to find that the ancient wisdom tradition of yoga speaks vividly, even urgently, to our present needs.

I first discovered yoga more than twenty years ago. Like most Americans, I came to it initially as a form of physical exercise. It didn't take me long to appreciate the enormous benefits of yoga postures and breathing exercises, and I found myself drawn into a regular practice that steadily increased my energy, stamina, concentration, resilience, and enjoyment of life. In the early years of my practice, however, I didn't appreciate that these physical practices are only one facet of a vast and extremely sophisticated wisdom tradition. I didn't realize that the yoga postures I was doing at my health club are part of a three-thousand-year-old science of extraordinary living that concerns itself with every aspect of human functioning—mental, physical, and spiritual.

As I discovered the larger wisdom tradition of yoga, I was intrigued: The practitioners of this science of extraordinary living have lived and thrived on the Indian subcontinent for at least the last three millennia. They have concerned themselves with a series of perennial questions—questions that are as challenging today as they were when scantily clad yogis first gathered in the forests and mountains of India: What is an optimal human life? What would it be like to function at the maximum potential of our minds and bodies?

For at least three thousand years, yogis have carried out experiments to investigate these questions. Their bold investigations have led to remarkable discoveries about human perception, attention, cognition, motivation, sensory integration, memory, intuition, and volition. These early yogis found that very few human beings live anywhere near the optimal range of human functioning. At the same time, they demonstrated that almost any of us could do so, with much less effort than we imagine. Surprisingly, extraordinary living does not require more native genius than most of us already have.

These yogis, too, have been interested in a second, related series of questions: What are the root sources of human suffering? Can these roots of suffering be cut? Can human beings learn to be happy and at ease in this difficult life?

Their answers to this second set of questions have also been surprising—and, frankly, for many Westerners, just plain unbelievable. Yogis studied the structure of ordinary human unhappiness, and found that the sources of everyday suffering could be entirely "extinguished"—leading to a kind of freedom we ordinarily think impossible. Yogis have called this "liberation." Liberation in this instance means freedom from all the sources of conditioning that bind us to small ways of thinking and being. Liberation means being entirely awake, and fully alive.

The most comprehensive exposition of the ancient wisdom tradition of yoga comes in the form of a two-thousand-year-old treatise called the *Yoga-Sutra*. Although its origins will probably always remain obscure, it is most likely that the *Yoga-Sutra* was written by a sage named Patanjali, in about the second century CE. The views and practices described by Patanjali in his *Yoga-Sutra* embody the genius of many centuries of yoga practice and investigation. Some scholars have come to call these views and practices classical yoga, but within the tradition itself they have most often been called *rāja-yoga*—meaning "the royal road of yoga," or "the exalted way," or "the noble way."

The wisdom tradition called *rāja-yoga* preceded the development of postures and breathing exercises (called *hatha-yoga*) by many centuries. In fact, most of the important treatises on *hatha-yoga*[2] were not written until the fourteenth century or later, and almost all of them refer back to Patanjali's *Yoga-Sutra*. Most of the greatest adepts of *hatha-yoga* have taught that postures and breathing practices should be practiced within the goals and context of the broader wisdom tradition. The *Yoga-Sutra* is a foundation stone of all later yoga practice—though (surprisingly enough for modern readers) this classic treatise involves almost no teaching about yoga postures as we know them.

What kind of yoga, then, does Patanjali teach if he does not teach postures? Usually, his text has been thought of as a meditation manual—and it is certainly one of the most sophisticated meditation manuals in the world. But it is more than that. Patanjali views every aspect of living as an opportunity for practicing wisdom. He is concerned with how we think and act, how we breathe, move, sleep, dream, and speak. Every aspect of our motivation, cognition, and behavior is of interest to Patanjali—and he harnesses them all as part of the path of yoga.

Patanjali's treatise comes with a notorious challenge. The *Yoga-Sūtra* was clearly written for advanced practitioners. As a result, many of us contemporary yogis (who have not yet experienced the dazzling possibilities described in the *Yoga-Sūtra*) find it difficult to read, its meanings often frustratingly elusive.

This has been a problem for me and for many of my friends who practice yoga and who wish to understand its deeper practices. My first copy of the *Yoga-Sūtra* sat for almost five years on my bedside table gathering dust. Occasionally it called out to me just before sleep, reminding me of my obligations as a yoga student. *Read me!* Because I am a Presbyterian by upbringing, I guess, and an over-achiever by nature, this eventually worked. I picked it up.

I'm glad I did. For a decade and a half now, I've been pondering small and digestible portions of the *Yoga-Sūtra*. It's been challenging at times. But compelling—because a little bit of study reveals a stunningly clear exposition of the structure of human consciousness, and the path of optimal living. (Early students of the *Yoga-Sūtra* have made extravagant claims about studying the *Yoga-Sūtra*. One tradition—about which I remain skeptical—claims that the internal architecture of this treatise is in itself so mind-altering that simply memorizing and repeatedly chanting its lines will lead to complete liberation.)

There is reassuring news about the challenges of this treatise: we contemporary yogis are not as alone with its difficulties as we might imagine. For two thousand years, this complex document has intrigued, inspired, and befuddled practitioners of yoga. As a result, it has spawned countless translations, commentaries, and verbal and written wrestling matches of every sort. Each new generation of yoga practitioners struggles with this treatise, and leaves behind the helpful traces of that struggle.

It seems certain that most of Patanjali's students, and peers, were renunciates and ascetics who devoted their lives to rigorous training—like Olympic athletes of the spirit. They were willing and able to invest the tens of thousands of hours usually required to master the forms of mental training detailed in the *Yoga-Sūtra*. Patanjali was clearly writing for these yogi athletes. Much of what he writes presumes a direct experience of the various stages of yoga which he describes.

Alas, most of us contemporary Western yogis are not ascetics, or monks or nuns. And though we may aspire to be Olympic athletes of the spirit, most of us do not have so much time on our hands. We're lucky to practice for half an hour a day, between getting meals for the kids, doing the laundry, and working the extra shifts to pay for the new roof.

Does it make any sense, then, for us to study this ancient wisdom tradition of yoga? Perhaps we should just stick with our once or twice weekly dose of downward-facing dog pose and cobra pose at the YMCA. Does it make any sense for us to meddle in a tradition originally prescribed for wandering renunciates and mystics?

I think it does. For when we pare Patanjali's treatise down to its bare bones, we will find that at its heart lies some very simple principles—principles and practices virtually anyone can understand and use. Indeed, in many cases they are principles and practices we can use *while* we're getting meals for the kids, and doing the laundry, and getting to work. They are principles and practices we can use in conjunction with our twice-a-week yoga classes, or our daily practice of Ashtanga yoga, or Kripalu, Iyengar, or Bikram yoga.

And it is my experience that we can discover a great deal of freedom in the process. To be honest, though, this freedom will

almost certainly not include "extinguishment" of all the roots of suffering—achieved by the great yogi athletes of ancient India. It will
almost certainly not include the fantastic supernormal powers of
which Patanjali writes in his great treatise. But it might, just might,
include liberation of a sort, nonetheless.

For the last fifteen years, I've been studying and teaching the principles of the *Yoga-Sūtra*. Throughout most of that time, I've been a
teacher at Kripalu Center for Yoga and Health, in the Berkshire Hills
of western Massachusetts, the largest residential yoga center in
America. I've taught these principles and practices to every sort and
condition of modern yogi. Sometimes with results that surprise even
the most skeptical among us.

I am a psychotherapist by training, and schooled in Sigmund
Freud's ironic declaration of the goals of Western-style psychotherapy: "Psychoanalysis," said Freud, "frees the patient from neurotic
misery, so that he can return to ordinary unhappiness."[3] The ancient
yoga practitioners were not nearly so interested in neurotic misery as
we have been. But they were very interested in what we might call
"ordinary unhappiness." Yogis believed there might actually be an antidote for ordinary suffering. My experience with thousands of students over the past fifteen years—and in my own life—leads me to
believe that this is not esoteric hyperbole. Regular study and practice
of the principles of yoga does in most cases lead to a life with less suffering. It does free us to live more fully. In some cases (and I've seen
more than one), it even leads to profound changes in character.

In the pages that follow I'll attempt to bring to life the bare bones of
this fascinating tradition of *rāja-yoga*—as they are laid out in the
Yoga-Sūtra, and as they are embodied in the lives of my friends, students, fellow yogis, and teachers on the path. As our story unfolds, the
reader will meet six contemporary yogis who have given the broader

principles of Patanjali a serious try: Jake O'Brien, a lawyer struggling at midlife with seemingly intractable relationship issues; Maggie Winslow, a sixty-two-year-old aspiring novelist, seeking to discover her own authentic voice; Susan Goldstein, a popular interior designer, wife, and mother, who suffers from compulsive eating; Kate Johannson, a professional dancer, now retired because of injury, and separated from her wealthy husband; Rudi Sawyer, a local Berkshires handyman, gardener, and yoga adept; and myself, a middle-aged, sometimes neurotic, and possibly overeducated WASP, trying to have a useful and happy life—and struggling to write a book very much like this one.

My narrative unfolds at or near Kripalu Center for Yoga and Health, in Lenox, Massachusetts. The characters are composite portraits based on real people and all the stories in this book reflect real events. However, names, dates, and circumstances have been significantly altered to honor the obligations of friendship, confidentiality, and decency.

It will become apparent to the reader that each character in this book struggles with some particular aspect of living. It is not fashionable in so-called spiritual circles these days to talk of struggle. But the ancient yogis did not hesitate to acknowledge that life is full of struggle and pain. And yet, these early practitioners found that struggle itself could be transmuted into the most noble characteristics of the human being. Indeed, an optimal life is not possible without struggle. Liberation and struggle are two sides of the same coin.

Occasionally in these pages, the words of an intriguing character will appear—a character who was particularly interested in struggle and its relationship to liberation. His name was Swami Kripalu (1913–1981). He was the most recent lineage holder of an ancient yoga lineage that stretches back to mythic Indian time—back to Vishvamitra, an Indian Seer who was one of the founders of Vedic Hinduism. Kripalu Center is named for Swami Kripalu, who visited and lived with the community for four years before his death in 1981. Swami Kripalu was a highly accomplished hatha yogi. He was also a devoted adherent of the larger wisdom tradition of *rāja-yoga*. He was a prolific writer, poet, classical musician, athlete, actor, and speaker. He was dauntingly learned. At the same time, he was a sweet and down-to-earth man—very grandfatherly. He also had a warrior side—and was relentlessly honest about the reality of struggle. He said:

> In the entire world, there is not one human being who is free from pain. Even in favorable conditions, a person encounters struggle. The external form of struggle appears to be cruel. Some describe it as a horrible demon, but its nature is not malicious. In fact, it is proper to welcome struggle, for its arrival is always auspicious. Struggle keeps us from growing sluggish. It changes an animal into an ideal person. It transforms an ordinary human into a spiritually-awake person respected by the world ... It is alright if we cannot receive struggle with love, but struggle should never be discarded. To discard struggle is to discard God's grace.[4]

Struggle and liberation live side-by-side in the life of a practitioner of yoga. My hope is that the stories of struggle and liberation that follow will inspire the reader to look carefully into the possibilities of transmuting ordinary struggle into a quietly extraordinary life. And that our gaze backward into the discoveries of the ancient yogis will also be a gaze inward—a gaze that will, as Eliade suggests, unlock our own authentic possibilities for living.

Lenox, Massachusetts
2005

PROLOGUE

Seekers, Then and Now

Seek not to follow in the footsteps of the wise ones of old;
seek what they sought.

—*adapted from Matsuo Basho*
(1644–1694)

CONTEMPORARY SEEKERS, MILDLY NEUROTIC

I sat at the highest point of the old orchard with my back leaning against the gnarly bark of an apple tree. The massive brick structure of Kripalu Center lay a hundred yards below, down a steep hill now covered with August wildflowers. In the distance, the Berkshire Hills receded into the late summer morning in waves of green and distant purple. The lawn crews had been at work again the afternoon before, and the sweet smell of newly mown grass mixed with the cool morning air. I let my whole weight drop back against the tree.

Shortly, Maggie and Jake would join me for a hike to the ridge, where we would meet Kate, and our friends Rudi and Susan for a picnic. I had arrived early at our meeting place in the orchard, hoping for a quiet moment to myself. I was feeling cranky. On edge. This day marked the end of a six month writing sabbatical. Tomorrow I would go back to work full-time—teaching yoga.

For the previous six months, I had been working on a beginner's guide to Patanjali's *Yoga-Sūtra*. This morning I felt defeated. In six months, I had barely scratched the surface of this complex treatise. For much of the sabbatical, I'd found myself caught up in reading various commentaries and translations, both ancient and modern. My desk was stacked with yellowing esoteric scriptures and books on Sanskrit. If anything, I was more confused about the ancient path than when I began.

Recently, I had considered giving up the project altogether. Certainly the world did not need another amateur examination of Patanjali. But something about this scripture—this tradition—had snagged me, lodged itself under my skin. Part of me wished that it had left me alone. But there was something here for me—though I wasn't yet even sure what it was. I sensed that my gropings around this enigmatic tradition had already changed the way I looked at the world.

I let out a sigh as I rested in the shade of the tree. There was probably no way out of the task I had set for myself. I had a contract with a publisher, and my editor, Robert, was expecting a completed manuscript in about a year. I supposed I would have to plow ahead with the manuscript, poking away at it in what little spare time I had.

For a moment my eye caught a hawk circling overhead. The late August sky was crystal blue, more like the high blue sky of a July day. But the air was dry and cool. Just a hint of color was already appearing in the trees, and there was in the air the kind of whiff of autumn that so delighted our New England poet-philosopher Henry David Thoreau.

It was utterly still in the orchard, and for a few delightful moments I was absorbed in the quiet.

My reverie was interrupted by the early approach of Maggie Winslow (who perhaps had also anticipated a moment alone). I raised my head and watched as she crossed the last stretch of lawn to join me. As always, Maggie carried herself with a kind of natural elegance. She was sixty-two years old this month.

Maggie had inherited the best of her high-WASP family genes. She was tall—almost stately. I'm sure that her regular yoga practice over the last twelve years had contributed to the lithe quality of her movements. (The many tweedy skeptics among her friends in Lenox would say it was, rather, a lifetime of tennis and swimming that had lent her movements such grace.) Her face was long and distinguished. Her high cheekbones, which could have been severe on another face, were softened by large brown eyes. Her hair was cut—and had been for the last forty-five years—in what used to be called a pageboy. Simple and somewhat severe. But perfectly Maggie.

Maggie sat down on the grass next to me. She said nothing, but reached out for my hand and held it as she looked at me—then kissed the back of it. Her white skin had the sweet smell of lavender soap.

We had become immediate friends when I bought the little cottage next to her family's collapsing Tudor manse. The houses (just two miles down the road from where we now sat) were positioned such that I could see directly through my kitchen window into hers. She had invited me to tea the week after I moved in, and before long I was a regular visitor. Most days during the summer, I would wander over for tea, or to help in her herb and flower garden.

"Well, my dear, I will miss you terribly," said Maggie with a sigh.

And I would miss her. Throughout the six months of my sabbatical, Maggie, too, had been holed up with a writing project. Maggie was writing a novel. (When asked, Maggie described herself as "an invisible writer" and I suppose in some sense this was true. She was certainly invisible to the world of New York publishing houses. She had three unpublished novels on her shelf now, and was writing another that would most likely never see a publisher's list.)

Maggie and I had developed a joint routine: we would both study and/or write in the early hours of the morning, then break at ten thirty. I would go to her house for tea, either in her big timbered parlor or in the garden. And then we would take a walk up to the orchard where we now sat. Sometimes we would walk all the way to the ridge, a mile up the winding path through the woods behind us. We both did our yoga postures in the afternoon, between four and six, and sometimes meditated together for half an hour after that.

We sat together now for a moment, in silence.

Finally, Maggie lifted her chin.

"Well come on. At least now you can get your head out of those old books and rejoin the world of real people."

I looked at her sideways. There was truth in what she said. But I knew that Maggie felt as driven by the writing life as I did—and she must have known that it was more complicated than that.

Maggie and I both heard Jake arrive before we actually saw him. We turned our heads.

"Run, Cope!" Jake had thrown a Frisbee, and it was now soaring out over the young trees at the front of the orchard. Frisbee had become our favorite game throughout this short but unusually warm Berkshire summer. I stumbled to my feet and raced to catch it, but missed by a body length.

Jake O'Brien appeared over the crest of the hill, having entered the orchard from a different direction than Maggie. He was smiling broadly, and wearing his usual three-day growth of beard. Jake was a lawyer from Boston, who had become a fixture in our world earlier that summer. He was tall and lean, with a long face and high brow, and a thick mane of red-brown hair.

Jake approached us and hugged Maggie, practically picking her up off her feet. Maggie resisted—outwardly—but clearly loved the attentions of this handsome younger man.

Jake pulled a small figure out of his knapsack. "And this is for you, Miss Maggie—as a corrective for your stuffed-shirt pilgrim ancestors."

Jake had brought Maggie a small bronze statue of the dancing Shiva—or *Shiva nataraja,* the yogi's god of transformation. He placed it carefully on the edge of the big wicker picnic basket that Maggie had carried up to the orchard.

Maggie feigned horror. What would her devout Episcopalian ancestors think?

Shiva sat happily on the brown wicker basket, dancing in his bronze ring of fire. Jake had been passing out these little statues for the past month, sharing the bounty from a box of them he'd found at a flea market in Manhattan.

After some catching up, we pulled together our gear for the picnic, and headed up the narrow path behind the orchard, single file—bound for the ridge at the top of the mountain, where we would meet our friends and spend the day hiking, exploring, and eating. The day would celebrate the end of my sabbatical, and the end of the remarkable summer we had shared.

I brought up the rear, carrying the picnic basket full of sandwiches. Jake bounded ahead of me. He was tanned from a summer of camping and cycling, and he looked wiry and healthy. It was hard to imagine that this was the same guy who had arrived so bewildered and depressed at my door just four months before, after "messing up badly" (his words) at his white-shoe Boston law firm. In retrospect, it was clear that Jake's summer break from the law (and from the city) had turned out to be an excellent idea.

As we made our way up the sun-spotted path, I thought of our yogi forebears in the forests and mountains of ancient India. I thought of the great teacher Patanjali, and the students he must have gathered around him. I wondered: Were these early yogis really any different from us? Were they as conflicted? As neurotic? As ordinary? Was their seeking, in fact, very much like ours? Did they also lurch and stumble from one discovery to another? Or were they some other strain of human being altogether?

THE SPIRIT OF THE STRIVERS

The wisdom of classical yoga has its roots in the social and spiritual crucible of what is now India, during the sixth, fifth, and fourth centuries BCE. During these centuries, the traditional social and religious hierarchies of parts of the Indian subcontinent were being transformed. Village structure was challenged by the increasing social and economic importance of cities. The rigidities of the ancient caste system were increasingly interrupted by independent thinkers and seekers.

It was a time of questioning, and the ferment of the age gave rise to some of the world's greatest spiritual teachers—including Siddhartha Gautama, the Buddha (563–483 BCE), and Mahavira, a founder of the Jains (599–527 BCE). It was the time of some of the most brilliant mystical writing of the Upanishads.[1] Thousands of seekers and wandering philosophers and ascetics examined the meaning of life, and the possibilities of being human.

As early as the sixth century BCE, the spiritual inquiries of these lively seekers began to take place outside established religious hierarchies in an unruly tradition scholars now call the *sramanic* stream. *Sramana* means, literally, "striver."[2] Indian *sramanas* were practical mystics who had become disillusioned with the ritual practices of the Vedic religion. They renounced the complex hierarchies of priests, rituals, and castes and became dropouts from the mainstream religious culture. They were seeking the state of "living liberation" or "the soul awake in this lifetime," and in order to find it, they turned to a series of brilliant teachers who insisted that realization of the true Self could be developed, not through external religious ritual, but through direct and persistent inner investigation of the body and mind. The best of these teachers insisted upon the power of self-reliance, self-examination, and self-development.

"Strivers" dedicated their lives to spiritual and psychological experimentation—practicing both in small groups and in solitude, living quietly at the edge of mainstream society, in caves or in forests. They investigated diet, breath control, physical exercises, ethical behavior, sense restraint, prayer, meditation, magic, chanting, and worship of every conceivable god and goddess. Their lives were almost always characterized by asceticism, renunciation, and internal sacrifice.

These seekers rejected doctrine and dogma, and did not particularly favor codification of their ideas and practices. For this reason the results of their personal investigations went largely unrecorded. Their growing body of wisdom was passed along primarily by word of mouth. In its earliest stages, much of the strivers' experimentation was probably highly shamanistic,[3] concerned with what we might even call magic—black, white, and otherwise. Some of their work, of course, led to dead ends—endless metaphysical speculation, or practices that were downright harmful. But over the course of hundreds of years, and with the efforts of thousands of highly motivated seekers, some headway was made in discovering a reliable path to the fully alive human being. A loose tradition was born—an esoteric tradition that combined the best powers of shamanism with some remarkably sophisticated psychological discoveries. A set of reliable principles and practices emerged. At some point, this tradition became known as yoga—a word that means literally "to yoke" or to bring into union—and its practitioners as "yogis."

Yogis used their own minds and bodies as laboratories for experiments in living. They arrived over and over again at a series of stunning insights into the human condition:

~ The ordinary reality in which most human beings live is merely an elaborate construction based on subtle but important errors in perception.

~ These chronic errors and inadequacies in perception become "fetters" which obscure a clear view of reality, and lead us to act in ways which are counterproductive. The unskillful actions which result from a fettered mind create suffering for ourselves and others.

~ The "fetters" become learning disabilities which make it impossible for us to bring to fruition the deepest capacities of the body, mind, and heart—capacities which lie within the reach of all human beings, but are beyond the comprehension of the ordinary mind.

~ It is possible to become gradually disentangled from these unskillful habits of body and mind, and as we do, to see more clearly, and to experience less suffering.

~ The process of disentanglement is not easy. It requires a considerable amount of effort, and the cultivation of insight and subtle mental and physical skillfulness. It is, nonetheless, within the reach of virtually every human being.

~ As we become disentangled from unskillful habits, we discover that the mind at its subtlest levels—what yogis called illumined mind—follows different laws than the ordinary mind out of which we routinely function.

~ When the fetters have been attenuated, only the deepest, most illumined functioning of the mind remains. Freed from the fetters, we learn to be guided by the luminous wisdom of awakened mind, making choices that create happiness for ourselves, others, and the world.

These are radical views, to be sure. Strivers found the human being to be caught in a subtle web of delusion. Their investigations revealed this web to be tenacious in its grasp. And yogis found the process of extracting ourselves from this mesh an extraordinarily complex one.

The extraction process (which yogis came to call "introversion") is difficult for us because the skills we rely upon to do the job simply do not work. Throughout history we human beings (always and everywhere encountering this same set of problems) have tried to think our way out of the fetters. Or fight our way, or will our way, or power our way. Yogis found that none of these strategies can succeed. More often than not, in fact, thinking ensnares us more deeply. Willpower, too, is of limited value. And force is positively counterproductive.

How, then, shall we confront the tangle? This was the principal question of the *sramanas*. Whereas Western cultures from early on became obsessed with knowledge and philosophy as forms of transcendence and mastery, the *sramanas* found knowledge for its own sake to be of limited value. As the Buddha, one of the most famous of these *sramanas*, said about metaphysics, "These philosophical conversations do not lead to edification!"[4]

Sramanas became more concerned with what we might call wisdom. Wisdom is a knowledge or understanding that we gain as a result of having seen or perceived the world directly. It is understanding gained through careful examination of direct experience. Above all, wisdom is a practical knowledge about how things work—how life works. It is the kind of knowledge that makes us more skillful in living.

(This view of wisdom seems universal. The Indo-European root of the word "wisdom" is *ueid-* which means "perceiving" or "seeing." In Latin, the root is *videre*, "to see." The ancient Akkadian word for a wise person—borrowed from Sumerian—meant "master craftsman." Wisdom is the kind of knowledge that makes us master craftspersons at life.[5])

In the final analysis, then, strivers found that it is not what you know, but how you live that counts. Strivers might have been the world's first existentialists.

At some point during the second or third century CE, a great yogi philosopher-practitioner (probably named Patanjali) wrote down the central principles of this evolving wisdom tradition. The text produced by this mysterious sage—called the *Yoga-Sūtra*—has stood for almost two thousand years as the definitive statement of the philosophy and practice of the yogis. It brilliantly captured the core discoveries of many centuries of experimentation.

(At this point, the interested reader might wish to turn briefly to the back of the book and leaf through an English translation of Patanjali's *Yoga-Sūtra*—just to get an initial feel for this fascinating document. Even a cursory perusal will reveal some important characteristics: its division into four "chapters"; the remarkable concision of Patanjali's writing; the stunning breadth, depth, and sophistication of the ideas; and, of course, the inscrutability to which I have already alluded.)

Patanjali's treatise is written in an elegant and highly condensed literary form called *sūtra*—which means, literally, "thread." His writing is lean and compact. In his text, there is no compelling development of a central spiritual character—no Moses, Buddha, Mohammed, or Christ. Rather, in the course of 196 *sūtras*, Patanjali gives us a spare but brilliant description of the traps into which we have become ensnared, and the path out of the snares.

The author of the *Yoga-Sūtra* makes no claim to be undertaking ordinary spiritual writing. He is not interested in founding a new religion. He is not interested in entertaining us, or drawing on the deepest archetypes of the human religious imagination. Patanjali seems to say that what mature human beings require is not another religion. What we require is not more theology, but a reliable practice: a training program that may help the highly motivated student to realize the full potential of being human.

As we begin to understand Patanjali's view of things, we discover something surprising: the views and practices of the strivers are not unique to second century India. Versions of this same view of human transformation appear over and over again in diverse times and cultures. The Buddha—teaching some seven hundred years before Patanjali—articulated a similar training program. (Interested readers will find a short essay on the relationship between yoga and Buddhism in Appendix A.) Students of Christianity will hear strong echoes of the sixteenth century Spanish saint Ignatius of Loyola's program. Some will detect the views of St. Augustine, and of Meister Eckhart, the thirteenth century mystic. Students of philosophy may think of Plotinus, who codified the teachings of Plato. Others will hear resonant strains of Nietzsche, Schleiermacher, and Goethe.

My own awakening to the views of the strivers came first through the bold stream of *sramanism* in American spiritual life—particularly through the incandescent spiritual explorations of Emerson, Thoreau, and the Transcendentalists. These Transcendentalist voices will be heard often in the pages to come, along with other vivid American *sramanic* voices—especially those of Thomas Merton, Annie Dillard (an acknowledged heir of the Transcendentalists), and anthropologist and seeker Carlos Castaneda and his *sramanic* (and shamanic) teacher, Don Juan.

The wisdom of the strivers emerges wherever seekers accept the radical responsibility for confronting reality directly. Above all, strivers insist upon a persistent, direct, and authentic investigation of the experience of being human—and this always includes a careful examination of the ways in which misperception leads to distorted thinking and an unrealistic view of the world. Marcel Proust, the French author who lived and wrote very much in the investigative spirit of yoga, wrote, "The real voyage of discovery consists not in seeking new landscapes, but in having new eyes."[6] In the yoga tradition, it's the seeking that matters, because it is the seeking itself that transforms our vision of things. Secondhand answers have no power in them. This view led generations of *sramanas* to be exceedingly wary of formulas of all kinds, and to insist on direct investigation. "Seek not to follow in the footsteps of the elders," declared the Zen poet Matsuo Basho. "Rather, seek what they sought."

The Transcendentalists insisted upon this principle. Ralph Waldo Emerson said it elegantly:

> You think in your idle hours that there is literature, history, science behind you so accumulated as to exhaust thought and prescribe your own future. In your sane hour, you shall see that not a line has yet been written; that for all the poetry that is in the world your first sensation on entering a wood or standing on the shore of a lake has not been charted yet. It remains for you; so does all thought, all objects, all life remain unwritten still.[7]

All wisdom traditions insist upon a healthy mistrust of other people's answers—or even the revealed experience of others. Yoga, at its truest, insists upon giving us not answers, but a way to find our own answers. Wherever this view is held (and it is not easy to hold), we might say that it is connected to the great *sramanic* stream of practice and inquiry. Our own Thomas Jefferson was, in this light, very much a *sramana*. In what was considered by many a blasphemous act, he rewrote the Christian Bible in a way that faithfully represented his own experience of God.

The tradition of the strivers points us not backward toward ancient answers, but toward the immediacy and urgency of our own inquiry. To be heirs of the tradition of the strivers, we must each finally write our own scriptures. Of eternal fulfillment, the theologian Paul Tillich said, "If it is not seen in the present, it cannot be seen at all."[8]

SHIVA'S DANCE

Jake, Maggie, and I finally arrived on the ridge, where we found our triumvirate of friends. Susan, Kate, and Rudi were sitting on a rock, in the partial shade of a scrub oak, deep in conversation.

The day was already warm, and the sun was still moving higher in the sky. We spent the next hour exploring the outcroppings at the top of the ridge and admiring the spectacular view of the Berkshire Hills. The sun laid a shimmering path of light on Lake Mahkeenac, and the sky was so clear that we could see surrounding ranges of mountains and hills, off into New York to the west, and Connecticut to the south. Rudi gave us a riveting description of the geology of the Mahkeenac Bowl—a circular formation of hills that surrounds the pristine mountain lake over which we looked.

As we gathered into a loose grouping on the granite overlook, Kate and Jake paired off and sat with their legs dangling over the ridge, looking south toward Connecticut. Susan, Maggie, Rudi, and I sat at the other end of the outcrop. As we talked, I noticed the call-and-response of Kate's long blonde hair to the midday sun.

Jake and Kate had become fast friends over the course of the summer. They had both arrived at Kripalu almost four months earlier, seeking a refuge from confusion, depression, and disillusionment. In spite of vastly different personalities, both Kate and Jake had seemed to be hitting their heads against life—somehow always coming to life at right angles. Maggie said it succinctly: "Those kids are just trying too hard." I secretly identified with them both, and wondered that Maggie hadn't also made the same observation about me.

Kate had been a professional dancer until her thirty-fourth birthday, two years earlier, when a serious foot injury forced her retirement. At about the time her dancing career melted down, her relationship with her husband encountered some serious trouble. She and Ward, her husband of six years, were now in a period of trial separation. Ward was spending the year as a cardiology research fellow at a New York medical school, while Kate was deepening her study and practice of yoga and meditation.

Susan—with characteristic drama—began to unpack the sandwiches she had carefully stacked in Maggie's wicker basket early that morning, proudly announcing each offering as she pulled it out: there were coriander chutney sandwiches on homemade whole wheat bread, grilled eggplant and sweet pepper sandwiches on sourdough, and avocado, sprout, and vegetable spinach-wraps. The group uttered a sigh from all corners of the rocks. Talk abated as everyone savored Susan's masterpieces. This feast, I knew from experience, would lead to naps on the cool granite outcrops.

The sun was beginning to burn hot as it neared its zenith in the blue sky. As I surveyed the line of purple mountains in the distance, shading my eyes with my hand, something caught my eye on the ledge to my right. I looked closely. Jake had placed another little bronze Shiva at the top of the highest boulder on the ridge, and the statuette was alive with the sun's fire. Jake, positioned with his back to the sun, and halfway through a sandwich, observed my discovery. For a moment we caught each other's eye.

Shiva is an embodiment of the central discovery of the strivers: the world is not as it appears to be. Hidden beneath the veil of our ordinary lives lie astonishing potentials of mind and body. Nowhere is this view of hidden realities more highly refined than in the views and practices of *rāja-yoga*. Though we did not know it that sunny afternoon, each of us in this band of friends (and each in our own way) would soon have an encounter with Shiva—and with the hidden realities toward which yoga points.

Though the picnic had been planned as a celebration of endings, we would later see that it was also a beginning. In the months that followed, our group of friends would become even more of a tribe—bonded together by surprising crises and challenges. The addition of Kate and Jake would give the group a kind of critical mass. Over the course of the next two years, we would meet regularly as an informal study group, investigating the ways in which yoga was unsettling and challenging each of us. My wrestling match with the *Yoga-Sūtra* would continue, and I would use this group of friends as a sounding board for what they would remind me were my "endless questions" about the views and practices of *rāja-yoga*. The group read and commented on chapters of my fledgling *Beginner's Guide to the Yoga-Sūtra* as they appeared in various drafts.

When Kate finally left to return to the Midwest, almost exactly two years later, I realized that out of our interactions, our practice, our crises, and our growing regard (and even love) for one another had emerged a living truth of yoga more powerful than anything I could find in ancient scriptures.

Part One

THE PROBLEM
OF
ORDINARY
UNHAPPINESS

THE mass of men lead lives of quiet desperation. What is called resignation is confirmed desperation. From the desperate city you go into the desperate country, and have to console yourself with the bravery of minks and muskrats. A stereotyped but unconscious despair is concealed even under what are called the games and amusements of mankind. There is no play in them, for this comes after work. But it is a characteristic of wisdom not to do desperate things.

—Henry David Thoreau, *Walden*

JAKE

The Quest for the Firebird

JAKE O'BRIEN was a lawyer from Boston—a litigator, as he liked to remind us. His chiseled face was softened by a thick and often unruly shock of hair, and his blue eyes were clear. He was cavalier about his lean good looks, and this added to his charm. Jake looked the way you want your litigator to look: like a wild cat, restrained and canny, with the capacity to pounce at any moment.

Jake had been one of thirty students in a two-week *hatha-yoga* intensive I had taught ten years earlier. Throughout the course, I had been impressed by the intensity and focus he brought to his posture practice. Jake wasn't the most flexible yogi in the room. But I admired the methodical way he worked with himself. His tenacity and patience gave his posture practice real beauty.

After the intensive, Jake and I had become friends. In those early years of our friendship, Jake seemed to me to have an enviable life. In fact, at times I coveted its apparent glamour. Several of my students from that first class admitted to the same feelings. They told me that they wished they could be more like Jake: confident, well-spoken, successful. Jake's image triggered deep cravings in those around him. His ease with his own success aroused our longing for "the ideal" and fed our sense that this ideal could really be manifest—if not for us, well, at least for some lucky souls. Jake was aware of the envy he aroused, and he seemed to get some satisfaction from it.

As I came to know Jake better, I discovered, much to my surprise, that underneath his sleek exterior, he was suffering. It was this suffering that had now brought him to the deeper practices of yoga. Jake derived no true satisfaction from his accomplishments. It gradually became apparent that he felt constantly driven to prove himself. Happiness, for Jake, seemed always just out of reach, around the next corner. It would, perhaps, come with the next legal triumph. He looked for happiness everywhere—but always outside himself. Finally, Jake had been forced to settle for the image of happiness and success—unable as he was to attain the genuine article.

It was difficult for me, at first, to bear seeing beneath Jake's glossy exterior to the troubled man underneath. But, finally, knowing Jake's real conflicts drew me closer to him. Indeed, when I looked closer, I found that I identified with him. I had so often felt driven in some of the same ways—driven to succeed at my work, to look good, even to risk posing at times as glamorous. I knew how phony this posing felt from the inside, and how inevitably it all fell apart.

At midlife, Jake was visibly troubled. Most disturbing to him was the fact that he couldn't maintain a satisfying relationship with a woman. Every time he got close to a woman, Jake became terrified and would inevitably create a chasm of emotional distance. It was only a matter of time until every new girlfriend left him. Though he initially felt relieved after she decamped, he soon became depressed and lonely, and began the hunt all over again.

By the time he reached forty, Jake was chronically heartbroken. He longed for love. Or, more accurately, he longed for his idea of what love might be like. Jake had an image in his mind of how he should look in a relationship: a faithful and loving partner, a good father, the proud founder of a new branch of his tribe. The problem was that Jake simply did not have the inner skills to live up to this image. Early on in relationships, Jake promised what he wanted and deeply hoped to receive. But finally he could only deliver what had been delivered to him in the struggling, sometimes impoverished and often overwhelmed family in which he had grown up. In relationships, Jake was selfish, frightened, unsure of himself, and sometimes rageful. These feelings were intolerable to him because they were at odds with his sense of how he *should* show up.

Late on the night after his forty-first birthday party (just two years before he arrived at Kripalu for the summer), Jake and I ended up at a little bar in Lenox. Here, absentmindedly twirling a swizzle stick around in a tumbler of expensive whiskey, Jake acknowledged to me the extent to which he was living a life of quiet desperation. Judging by the obvious relief this conversation prompted in him, I imagined he had been wanting to tell me this for a long time.

Shortly afterward, Jake launched himself into a newly energized quest to get to the root of his malaise. Once again I had the opportunity to witness his tenacity: he treated his exploration much like he might have treated a big case at work—methodically, and with a mixture of passion and resolve. Jake was a creature of will. He had no doubt that he would crack this case, just as he cracked cases at his law firm. To that end, Jake began a lifestyle of internal exploration—psychotherapy, "The Forum," more intensive yoga, rebirthing, meditation.

Jake's quest was driven by a clear intention: he would discover the deeply buried key to his "character flaws" (his words). He would re-live the moment when his development had been derailed by trauma. As a result, he would experience a profound catharsis. Then, he thought, he would be the way he should be. He would be happy. He would experience lasting satisfaction from his many successes. He would be able to sustain a relationship with a woman for more than six months. He would have love as he imagined it should be.

At first I found the intensity of Jake's quest compelling, and I tried to join him in it as best I could. I even accompanied him on some weekend intensive yoga excursions. When Jake visited Kripalu, our long dinners were dominated by talk about the nature of life and the human heart. He hammered away at his questions in endless walks with me on the east drive, and up into the woods behind the orchard. He attended a number of my programs and classes, and became an ever-more accomplished practitioner of yoga postures.

Eventually, however, Jake's Search for Truth turned strangely sour.

His obsession with the "why" questions—why am I like this? Why don't women want me?—had left him in an obsessive thought-loop that never seemed to close on a satisfying answer. Though preoccupied with himself, he was strangely dissociated from a direct experience of his pain. Oddly, Jake seemed more committed to the Search than he was to happiness. In this period, he seemed to be somehow slipping emotionally out of reach, and this often left me feeling powerless to help. It was as though his boat had slid off its mooring and begun to drift silently out to sea.

Throughout this time, it took some restraint for me to remain in the role of Jake's friend and not veer into the role of psychotherapist. And, in truth, I wasn't always successful at holding the boundary. The therapist side of me could not help but notice: what appeared to be Jake's quest for healing was really a complex defense against suffering.

Finally, in his early forties, with years of struggle behind him, and things not getting any better, I watched as Jake slipped into a quiet form of self-hatred. I noticed that he began to talk snidely and sarcastically about himself. In front of my eyes, Jake began to die. It was subtle at first, but over time I watched as Jake fell into a classic trap of midlife. As he got older and failed to meet his own high aspirations, he began to turn against himself.

Jake's psychological situation was perilous but common. The vital aspirations of Jake's deeply held internal ideals had been thwarted by life. And when this happens—as it surely will for each of us—it creates a crisis in the personality. There are only two possible outcomes from this crisis: either the unrealistic ideals will be modified to align more closely with reality (we'll have to change those ideas in our minds about how we "should" show up), or there will almost certainly be a turning against the self, and a concomitant deterioration in the character, leading to self-loathing and passive forms of suicide. Jake was veering toward this second option—unwilling as he was to change his ideas about himself. As a friend, this grieved me.

———

By the time he took a sabbatical from his law practice, Jake was entering a crossroads to which we all come sooner or later. For each of us is driven by these same kinds of unconscious ideals—fixed ideas about who we are and who we should be. These ideas come from a well of motivations, volitions, and drives of which we're almost entirely unaware. Nonetheless, this web of thoughts, feelings, and images drives most everything we do—including spiritual practice and psychotherapy. Our unconscious ideals cause us to sacrifice our true lives to a beautiful chimera, a haunting dream, a compelling illusion.

Imagine a bird hunter on the loose in a magnificent rain forest, searching for the mythical Yellow-Crested Firebird. The hunter is relentless in his search for this bird, a mythic bird that, unfortunately, exists only in pictures, and in our own supercharged imaginations. This is Jake's story: in the desperation of his search, he ignores the magnificence of the real birds all around him—the real vegetation, the real mysteries of the rain forest. He misses the immediate experience of life—focused as he is on a beautiful fiction.

From the sidelines, from the audience, we can see the hunter's mistake. We can see his delusion. And we want to call out, "No. There, right there, is a beautiful *real* bird. A magnificent *real* palm tree. A spectacular insect. Stop the search. Stop the insanity." Nonetheless, we conduct our own lives in much the same way Jake did. Each of us has our own Yellow-Crested Firebird—our own pictures that we paint on reality, pictures that become more powerful than reality itself.

Contemporary psychologists, recognizing the importance of these mysterious internal ideals, have stretched to make maps and models of them. Ego psychologists have suggested that there are two very distinct facets of the Firebird. One has sometimes been called the ego ideal. The other the ideal ego. Their manifestations, and their interactions, will be at the heart of the struggle of each character in this book.[1]

The ego ideal is a kind of internal "felt sense" of the ideal state for which we long. This ego ideal is made up of fragments of images and feelings that we've collected throughout life—highly charged images connected with internal states of happiness and well-being that we've fleetingly experienced. Some of these internalized representations were no doubt formed during our early experience of symbiosis—or merger—with mother. Aspects of this ego ideal manifested themselves for Jake (at least in part) as the longing to be safely held and soothed in a trusted relationship. And also as the longing to be deeply admired in an important career.

The highly charged internal representations of the ego ideal drive us to want to "merge, fuse, and unite"[2] with the objects of our longing. These longings can become attached to a person (as they were so often for Jake, connected to his latest girlfriend) or to a career or a beloved project or quest (like my writing project, for example). These longings may become attached to any object that we unconsciously imagine might help us find again the lost states of perfection in which we were once held and contained.

The longings generated by the ego ideal are extraordinarily powerful—but because they are mostly unconscious, we have the experience (just as Jake did) of being compelled by a force we do not see and do not understand. Nonetheless, inscrutable as they are, these ineffable strivings feel like they exist at the very center of "us." They seem at the very center of our being. For most of us, these internal ideal representations are experienced as the best part of us. We will sacrifice anything for them—happiness, peace of mind, even sanity itself. Our various quests are driven by these longings, and we feel these quests to be the most noble aspect of our selves.

Curiously, though, because our quests are driven by such unconscious motivations, their imperious and often delusory demands all too often lead us to founder on the shoals of life (just as Jake's quest for the perfect mate left him often bereft, depressed, abandoned). Our best literature, of course, is replete with stories of such quests. And of course, we all identify with them. We feel a sense of their nobility, however hopeless they may be: Male or female, we are Don Quixote fighting windmills for the Queen. We are Romeo in pursuit of Juliet. We are Parsifal on the quest for the Holy Grail. We are Scott in search of the South Pole. Religious or spiritual quests, of course, are not exempt from complex motivations and disastrous outcomes: they almost always begin with the most noble of intentions and all too often end in personal, social, or cultural disaster.

Is it inevitable that these noble longings should lead us to destruction? Is the ego ideal inherently leading us over the cataract? Not at all. The problem is that allied with the ego ideal is a set of unrealistic ideas about the self that cause endless problems with "steering" our various quests—and often leave us deluded, flying blind, and questing after any number of versions of the illusory Firebird. Ego psychologists sometimes call these unrealistic ideas the ideal ego, to distinguish them from the ego ideal.

The ideal ego is quite a different set of internal representations from the ego ideal, and is, if anything, even more hidden and slippery. The ideal ego is composed of those unconscious ideas we have about who we *already are.* If the ego ideal contains the felt sense of longing—the heat and passion—that motivates us to spend our lives in pursuit of the Firebird, the ideal ego is the secretly held belief that we actually already are the Firebird. We are searching for nothing less than our magnificent lost selves. These hidden ideas—the ideal ego—make us out to be secret kings and queens, held captive in the heart of our own interior castle. They imagine us to be solid, permanent, immortal, powerful, and perfect.

The central problem with the ideal ego is this: the internalized representations of the ideal ego push us to deny certain important realities—like the mortality, transience, and relative insignificance that each one of us eventually must face. But the ideal ego defends itself against intimations of impermanence and mortality at all costs. It keeps our view of difficult realities obscured—hidden behind a wall of internal defenses. Their delusional nature makes these ideas particularly deadly: They block any real inquiry into the true nature of our being. It is these ideas that make the Hunter turn away from the real birds, toward the siren song of the illusory Firebird.

As we shall see in coming chapters, yogis identified these same clusters of internalized images—though of course they did not call them ego ideal and ideal ego. Yogis found that the interactions between these two collections of internalized representations of a "self" are the root causes of unhappiness and delusion. But they also discovered some good news: through contemplative practice, the unrealistic representations of the ideal ego can be seen through—and finally completely deconstructed. They found that as a result, the longings of the ego ideal can be harnessed to a newly effective steering mechanism (and a windshield cleaned of obscuring idea-debris) that will take consciousness all the way to the outer boundaries of human freedom and happiness.

This is tricky territory. Many modern students of contemplative practice believe that the so-called death of the ego is one of the requirements for liberation. In my experience, this is not so. Rather, in the process of practice and personal inquiry, the delusive aspects of the ego are seen through—seen to be what they always were. The longing that drives the Search for the Firebird, however, is not killed. It is, rather, transmuted into something finer, something more subtle, and also something more realistic. The strivings and longings at the heart of the ego ideal are not lost, but are harnessed in such a way that they become the driving force for entirely new and authentic possibilities for being human.

But I am getting ahead of my story. It will take many chapters to unpack the mysteries at the heart of the Search for the Firebird. And quite a bit of struggle. And even significant psychological meltdown. It seems, alas, that we only give up our wishful concepts of ourselves after they have been repeatedly battered by life. "Struggle," says Swami Kripalu, "changes an ordinary human into a spiritually awake person."

The spring of Jake's forty-third year went badly. Jake had another relationship breakup (Anne-Marie)—a particularly difficult one. In addition, and perhaps more disastrously, Jake had a major failure at work. In April, he dramatically lost an important case that his firm had worked on for three years. The loss was due to a serious error on Jake's part. "A momentary loss of concentration," he had rationalized initially to his boss, due to his depression over the stormy breakup with Anne-Marie.

But Jake had seriously minimized the extent of his role in the debacle. The managing partners of the law firm had taken him aside and put it to him in no uncertain terms: his future with the firm was no longer assured. His salary would be significantly cut. "Sitting through that meeting was like being in a dream," Jake said later. "Like being in an automobile accident. Everything happened in slow motion.

"But the strange thing was that it was almost as if I had set it all up intentionally. Something had to give. It was like I was an animal caught in a trap, and I knew I had to gnaw my own paw off in order to escape. When it happened, I felt strangely exhilarated."

Jake had had losses before. Many of them. But this one was different. This time, Jake quietly folded his cards and left the table. No one was more surprised than his law partners, who expected him to fight. Somewhere, the backbone of Jake's unrealistic internal representations had been broken. At least temporarily, the energy drained out of his unrealistic strivings like air out of a helium balloon. Jake took a six-month leave of absence from his firm and came to Kripalu. He spent most of the months of May, June, July, and August out in the woods, wandering the vast tract of land from Stockbridge to the Bird Sanctuary. Some nights, he slept up on the ridge, without a tent. He wandered. He wrote in his journal. He made drawings of small plants and animals that he saw. His face seemed always to be in three days' growth of beard, as it was on the day of the picnic, and his dark hair bushy—no longer stylishly mussed and gelled. His regular life in the city, previously so well-ordered, collapsed. Bills went unpaid. He didn't care. In a matter of a couple of months, he had become like an Old Testament hermit and wanderer.

Jake's Boston friends—even many of his friends at Kripalu—thought he was clinically depressed. "You're depressed, regressed, and you should be on medication," our friend Susan Goldstein had told him. He had just looked at her. "Goldstein, you're not getting this at all," he said.

Jake did not feel depressed. In fact, he felt free, perhaps for the first time. Free of the constraints of his self-image. Free of the relentless but delusive Search for the Firebird. He had failed at last. Dramatically. And now he was relieved. Here was a state of mind whose possibilities he had never even imagined—though I believe his soul had been driving him toward it for the previous four years.

It was alarming for many of Jake's friends to see his personality melt down in this way. But his internal experience of it was quite different. It was a meltdown with something immensely radiant and alive cooking right at its center. Somebody altogether new was trying to get out of the trap of Jake's old self. Something beyond his own will seemed bent on immolating his old life, ideas, concepts, even to some extent his personality.

Jake was disillusioned, disorganized, and exhausted by his various strivings. But he was also surprisingly excited, inspired, and energized for a search whose dimensions he did not yet understand. In the yoga tradition, the kind of breakdown which Jake faced was auspicious. At its core blazes an urgent concern with authenticity, self-realization, self-responsibility, as well as a concern for the overall meaning of life. It involves a curious combination of depression and a quiet vehemence for renewal. I recognized it. As Jake's friend, I knew that it was excellent news. It was the classic portal into the deeper practices of yoga.

Chapter 1

THE SECRET STRENGTH
OF DISILLUSIONMENT

SAMVEGA: TURNING AWAY FROM THE BONE

During the summer of his "breakdown," all Jake knew was that he couldn't go backward, and apparently he wouldn't go forward. The experience of direct involvement with the present moment was just the place in which he had previously been unable to dwell. He was determined now to stay put. He knew that, paradoxically, some great success was buried within his failure. He sensed that he had had some kind of awakening. But what was it?

Yogis call this state *samvega*—a complex state involving a kind of disillusionment with mundane life, and a wholehearted longing for a deeper investigation into the inner workings of the mind and the self.[1] *Samvega*, as described by the contemporary Buddhist monk Thanissaro Bhikkhu, involves "at least three clusters of feelings at once":

> the oppressive sense of shock, dismay, and alienation that come with realizing the futility and meaninglessness of life as it's normally lived; a chastening sense of our own complacency and foolishness in having let ourselves live so blindly; and an anxious sense of urgency in trying to find a way out of the meaningless cycle.[2]

Samvega is a developmental state not mentioned in Western psychological texts. It brings with it a realization that objects of grasping (money, fine things, titles, fame, even people—when seen as objects) cannot supply any true satisfaction. It involves a radical realization that all objects are intrinsically empty of the capacity to feed us in the way we really want—or need—to be fed.

A classic Buddhist teaching story describes this realization:

> A dog stumbles across a bone that has been exposed to the elements for many months, and is therefore bleached of any residual flesh or marrow. The dog gnaws on it for some time before he finally determines that he is "not finding" any satisfaction in the bone, and he thus turns away from it in disgust. It is not that the bone is intrinsically disgusting; it is rather the case that the dog's raging desire for meat just will not be satisfied by the bone ... when he wakes up to the truth that the bone is empty of anything that will offer him satisfaction, he becomes disenchanted, and spits it out in disgust.[3]

Of course, the symptoms of *samvega* arise only after extensive experimentation with "the bone." Tibetan teacher Chögyam Trungpa Rinpoche says it elegantly: "The shoe of ego is only worn out by walking on it."[4] For many of us, objects of longing gradually reveal themselves to offer no real happiness. No matter how hard we gnaw on them, we find no meat on the bone. *Samvega* then arises with a linked complex of symptoms, many of which Jake was now experiencing. These can include:

~ A puzzling failure of previous sources of satisfaction
~ A heightened concern with authenticity
~ A deepening pull toward an intuited interior world
~ A sense of urgency about realizing deeply hidden gifts and talents
~ A global and diffuse sense of internal disorganization—equal parts psychological and spiritual

~ A deeply felt internal imperative to stop business as usual—or, as Jake said, to "get quiet"

~ A call to explore a path that might give transcendent meaning to the enigmas of life

One of the harbingers of the developmental imperative of *samvega* is that we—like Jake—begin to hear ourselves muttering about our Old Life and our New Life. Out of the blue, we begin to feel like captives in our lives—lives which may have fit comfortably for years. Our well-known world begins to feel stale and dead. Gradually we start hankering to leave for the New World. We begin to feel imbued with the spirit of our Seeker ancestors. We want nothing more than to leave the Old Country. This internal movement presages a profound reorganization of the psyche, a redirection of the energy of longing, and a completely new relationship with the world of people, places, and things.

Even though this developmental stage is as common in human life as adolescence, one will search Western psychology books in vain for a clear description of its causes and trajectory. We ordinarily attempt to fit the complexities of *samvega* into our old, usually pathological, categories. We trivialize it as "midlife crisis," or we wonder if it is not really just neurotic depression, or regression—as Susan Goldstein did when encountering Jake's version of *samvega*.

But contrary to the typical Western view, the kind of "breakdown" in which Jake found himself is not a regression into the past. It is not a pathological state. It is not a move backward at all. It is, rather, a step toward the possibility of a vastly expanded way of living in the world.

In yogic texts, the word *samvega* is often translated as "vehemence," because it brings with it an unshakeable resolve to develop into a fully alive human being. Patanjali introduces the term *samvega* in the first chapter of the *Yoga-Sūtra*—using the word to indicate a "wholehearted" (or "vehement") determination to find a way out of suffering.

For those who seek liberation wholeheartedly, realization is near. How near depends on whether the practice is mild, moderate, or intense. (1.21–22)

Yogis found that even though this state of "vehemence" carries with it a tremendous amount of feeling and power, it does not disturb the mind—rather it calms the mind. (In the summer of his breakthrough, everyone noticed that Jake was not disturbed. He was calm and profoundly "resolved.") *Samvega* is a kind of passion that does not create suffering—but, rather, generates the happiness that comes with the sure knowledge of freedom. Because the state of *samvega* is so full of possibilities, it is often referred to as a state of "emergence." Through the practice of yoga, says Patanjali, we can emerge from the traps of ordinary suffering. How quickly this emergence takes place depends on the intensity and persistence of our practice.

NIRODHA: STOP THE WORLD

When *samvega* emerges, it brings with it an altogether new hunger: the hunger for internal quiet. We seek this quiet not just because we're exhausted by living at right angles to life—as Jake certainly was—but also so that we can see more clearly. It becomes obvious that in order to know our true nature, we will have to stop the world. Stop the world! The Native American shaman Don Juan gives precisely this advice to his student Carlos Castaneda. "In order to become a man of knowledge, a warrior-traveler, you will first have to learn to stop the world."[5]

What does this mean? In order to see clearly, to examine how things work, we will have to stop our lives, slow things down, look carefully—like the person who has suddenly discovered she has created the mother of all knots in the shoelace of her boot. We must stop. Slow down. Look. Examine. How did this happen? How does this work? How can I reverse this? We will have to deconstruct the very way we perceive and rebuild it again from the ground up.

Stop the world. The impulse toward stillness is the central movement of the contemplative life. Monastics through the ages have described it: One intuits some precious new interior self. One sneaks off into the woods like an animal, builds a nest for the birth. Guards it ferociously. And waits in silence.

Says Thomas Merton, one of the great Catholic contemplatives of the twentieth century:

> The true contemplative is not one who prepares his mind for a particular message that he wants or expects to hear, but is one who remains empty because he knows that he can never expect to anticipate the words that will transform his darkness into light. He does not even anticipate a special kind of transformation. He does not demand light instead of darkness. He waits on the Word of God in silence, and, when he is answered it is not so much by a word that bursts into his silence. It is by his silence itself, suddenly, inexplicably revealing itself to him as a word of great power, full of the voice of God.[6]

Jake had an urgent need to stop the world. And he discovered, as all strivers do, that when the mind is still, our true nature begins to reveal itself. Out of stillness, like the early morning mist on the lake, emerges a thinking that is not thinking—a wisdom beyond thought. Out of stillness emerges, effortlessly, a subtle world of experience for which we had only longed until now. It is real. It rolls itself out in waves as we get still, quiet, concentrated, and settled.

The path of classical yoga is organized around the relationship between inner stillness and wisdom. The first two *sūtras* in Patanjali's *Yoga-Sūtra* are:

> *Now, the teachings of yoga.*
> *Yoga is to still the patterning of consciousness.* (1.1–2)

The Sanskrit word *nirodha*, which Patanjali uses in the second *sūtra*, means "stilling, cessation, or restriction." This stilling is both the path and the goal of yoga. Its appearance at the beginning of the treatise signals its centrality in Patanjali's technique.

"Yoga is to still the patterning of consciousness." Yoga is to still the thought waves of the mind. Yoga is to bring a natural quiet to the mind and body—so that we can, for the first time, see clearly. And in this stillness—miraculously, outrageously—the knots undo themselves. Inner realities emerge.

As both Merton and Don Juan understood, inner stillness opens a doorway in the mind. A little trapdoor we have rarely noticed. A secret escape hatch for the mind that is not even in the Western psychological user's manual. Merton's prayer suggests that in order to be found, we must first acknowledge the radical degree to which we're lost. Then, as the poet David Wagoner suggests, we must pay very close attention:

> Stand still. The trees ahead and the bushes beside you
> Are not lost. Wherever you are is called Here,
> And you must treat it as a powerful stranger,
> Must ask permission to know it and be known.
> The forest breathes. Listen. It answers,
> I have made this place around you.
> If you leave it you may come back again, saying Here.
> No two trees are the same to Raven.
> No two branches are the same to Wren.
> If what a tree or a bush does is lost on you,
> You are surely lost. Stand still. The forest knows
> Where you are. You must let it find you.[7]

This teaching captures the essence of the yogic view: what we are searching for is also searching for us. The way is to stop. To let ourselves be found. Stand still.

The Sanskrit word *marga* means "the way" or "the path." It is often used to refer to the yogic system for uncovering Reality. But interestingly, the word originally referred to "the hunter's path." This image of the hunter underlies much of the practice of yoga. Practice is seen as a kind of hunt for the real—for the lurking wild game of our true nature. Author and Zen practitioner David Chadwick suggests that hunting is one of the experiential origins of contemplative practice. "Hunters," he points out, "have had to sit and wait motionless, even for days at a time. The course is unknown ahead of time to the hunter, who must sniff and look for signs and watch and wait."[8]

In order to understand the path of the strivers, we will have to convince ourselves of the necessity, the magic, the absolute brilliance of stillness. Over and over again we will have to do this. We will forget. Farther down the path, tomorrow, or perhaps later today, we will forget about stillness. And when we do, we will have lost the thread. Without this central practice, none of it will make any sense.

In the wisdom of the strivers, we find an answer for those of us overheated by the search for the elusive Firebird. Stop. Become still and quiet. Stop the world. Stand perfectly still and listen. Kafka said it so well:

> You don't need to leave your room. Remain sitting at your table and listen. Don't even listen, simply wait. Don't even wait. Be quite still and solitary. The world will freely offer itself to you. It has no choice. It will roll in ecstasy at your feet.[9]

During the summer of his breakdown, Jake sought true contemplative stillness for the first time in his life. His resolve astonished me. Some days he would sit on a bench behind the old colonial church on the hill in Lenox, gazing at the eighteenth century graveyard. For Jake, experiencing the state of *samvega*, the cemetery seemed just the place to be—an excellent vantage point from which to ponder the meaning of life.

Jake and I spent a lot of time together that summer. He had

become to me a newly fascinating human being. We met regularly in the cemetery behind the church—which was just across the street from my house (and Maggie's). When wandering the cemetery Jake and I spoke a lot about death. I recalled for him the teaching that Yaqui shaman Don Juan had given to his student, anthropologist Carlos Castaneda: "The thing to do when you're confused," instructed the shaman, "is to turn to your left and ask advice from your death. An immense amount of pettiness is dropped if your death makes a gesture to you, or if you catch a glimpse of it, or if you just have the feeling that your companion is watching you."[10]

Jake wandered among the stones sometimes for hours at a time, perhaps hoping to get a glimpse of his own death. Or a longer perspective on his life. And so, that summer, Jake sat and peered and wandered and prayed and listened—like a hunter who wasn't sure if he was hunting or being hunted. Looking to his left.

Chapter 2

CLOSE ENCOUNTERS
WITH MIND

WILD PUPPY OF MIND

"OK. Remember your posture for meditation. Stable. Upright. Relaxed belly." I looked directly at Jake as I spoke, because he was slouching dramatically and looked as though he might fall asleep at any moment.

It was Jake's first meditation retreat. For the first time since I'd known him, Jake was really interested in sitting still, and in learning to meditate. Motivated as he was, however, it was still not a smooth ride.

For two days, I had been teaching a group of twenty beginning meditation students. Over and over again, I'd given the class a simple assignment: "Let your awareness rest in the sensations of the breath. Let the mind become absorbed in the rising and falling sensations of the breath."

This was my first class since returning to work from my writing sabbatical. I was enjoying it immensely and wondered, now, why I had been so reluctant to return to teaching.

This afternoon, I was instructing the group in the simplest of so-called concentration techniques—a mainstay of all meditative practice. In concentration techniques, we train attention to aim at an object—either an internal object, like the breath, or an external object, like an icon—and to stay on the object, or continually bring awareness back to the object.

It's not as easy as it sounds.

Jake was struggling. He couldn't get comfortable. He sat with his eyes open, and a defeated look on his face, eyeing the silent whooshing of the overhead fan. His eyes met mine, imploring. I could read the look: can't we turn it off? By this point in the retreat, Jake had already adjusted the windows several times, turned off the fan next to him, and asked the grounds crew not to mow the lawn near the building. I had talked to him several times about how to handle his aversion to sound (explore the aversion itself, and let go of trying to perfect the environment), but he still struggled. He was bumping up against the major obstacle with which he would wrestle for the next year.

All of this is to be expected. As a meditation instructor, I know that most beginning meditators don't really meditate—in any technical sense of the term. It is a law of the universe: at first, we just begin to get accustomed to negotiating the extreme strangeness of the inner world.

"Just let your body breathe normally," I coached, in response to some weird sounds coming from the back of the room. These were the same instructions that I had already given over and over again through the last two days. "And now let your awareness rest in the sensations of breath. Wherever you feel the sensations. Belly, chest, tip of the nostrils. Awareness resting right there."

At about fifteen minutes into the "sit" everyone had finally settled down, and quiet suffused the room. Eventually, it was so silent that I could hear only the subtle rising and falling of the breath. The aroma of freshly mown lawn infused the room with a subtle sweetness, and the almost imperceptible movement of air on my face and bare arms and legs felt sublime.

It was a clear September afternoon. The big windows in the Sunrise Room at Kripalu were thrown open to the vast expanse of emerald lawn sloping gently off to the west. The direct afternoon sun was filtered through a graceful stand of elms at the end of the lawn. The faint strains of a motorboat rose from Lake Mahkeenac below.

I settled into a concentrated state, and even the distant drone of the boat receded completely.

Thirty minutes later, I lifted the little mallet and hit the gong softly. The sound reverberated off the stucco walls and out onto the lawn in front. At first no one moved. Finally Jake took a big loud stretch and let out a kind of growl—signaling, I thought, his relief.

After a short break and a little stretching, the group reconvened to discuss our experience of meditation.

"How did it go?" I asked the group.

Jake threw up his hands. "I'm a total meditation moron.

"I can't do it. Can't do it," he said. "My mind is everywhere. But most of the time it's, well, it just ain't here."

He looked around at the faces of the group. "Well, all right. *All* of the time it's not here. Never here. Never. The whole time. I was faking it."

Everyone had a laugh, because, naturally—the mind being what it is—everyone had had some version of this experience.

"Welcome to the reality of your mind, Jake. And not just *your* mind. *The* mind. The *nature* of ordinary mind."

I explained to the class that the Eastern contemplative traditions have many words and phrases to describe the restlessness of this ordinary mind: monkey mind, wild elephant mind, raging river mind, crazy puppy mind.

Our first experiment with a meditation technique of this kind inevitably brings us face-to-face with an alarming discovery: we cannot do the technique at all! We cannot let awareness rest in the breath for even *a few seconds together* without it slipping off and thinking about dinner tonight, or that irritating snoring sound coming from our neighbor. We've given awareness a very simple object—the breath. And such a simple directive: Stay!! Stay, Lassie, stay. Stay on the breath. But Lassie just keeps romping off to play in the woods.

I sometimes call this discovery "the Noble Failure." It is certainly a failure—because we discover that the mind will simply not rest on the object. But it is also noble, because it gives us (perhaps for the first time) a vantage point from which to observe the nature of ordinary mind.

All early attempts at contemplative practice present us with this Noble Failure. *Samvega* inevitably draws us into an investigation of the ways of the mind. But when we begin to explore, when we finally lift the lid of the mind, we discover that we're in complicated and difficult new territory.

I continued to probe. "Did any of you notice exactly where your awareness went when it slipped off the object of the breath?"

A rush of answers: The pain in my knee. The project at work. What I'm going to cook for dinner when I get home.

Where does the mind go? The past. The future. Our dreams. Our fantasies. Mind flits happily everywhere. But it cannot stay with the present moment.

When we use a meditation technique to examine our minds' activities, most of us are shocked to find out what's going on in there. It's a torrent of disconnected thoughts—reactions to sensations, memories, fantasies. It seems out of control. At any moment when we dip into the stream of ordinary discursive thought, we'll find a ceaseless, churning river of activity.

The discovery that it is impossible for us to maintain a fixed awareness on the breath—or on any object—for more than a few seconds at a time is a powerful and important one. Mircea Eliade, one of the twentieth century's most distinguished yoga scholars, comments eloquently on this phenomenon:

The mere act of trying to hold the mind to a single point, an act with which higher forms of meditation all begin, teaches the beginner in a radically concrete and experiential way, that he or she has little or no control over the mental flow. All attentional training starts with this failure. Thus, when the Christian is asked to concentrate his attention solely upon God, when the Muslim attempts to link his attention solely to the names of God, when the Tibetan Buddhist attempts with massive attention to construct elaborate images of Tara on the screen of consciousness, the first lesson these practitioners learn is that they cannot do it.[1]

Just so. The experience in beginning meditation is that the attention constantly *slips off the object* and follows an associational stream.

I remember how disconcerting this discovery was to me as a beginning meditator. Like Jake, I was sure that everyone else on the meditation cushions around me was doing the technique better than I was—and that I was actually a meditation imposter of sorts.

Yet in spite of this undeniable failure—which I shared with all novice meditators—I found my early experiences remarkably freeing. Even remembering to bring my attention back to breath for a few seconds every minute seemed to have a profound effect. Why?

The answer goes to the heart of the transformation wrought by meditation. When one notices that the attention has slipped off the object, there is an opportunity for the observing mind to witness just exactly where this crazy puppy of mind has been: "Oh, I was just fantasizing, or daydreaming, or thinking about the past, or dreaming about the future. Now I can return to the breath." And with practice, this fledgling witness, this incipient observing self, cannot fail to notice some pattern in the train of associations that one follows away from the still point.

One of the first things the beginning meditator gets to see, then, is precisely what her mind is occupied with—what, presumably, her mind is doing day in and day out when she's not paying attention. We become a witness to the internal chatter that is unconsciously driving our behavior in every moment. Transpersonal psychologist and author Michael Washburn describes this discovery succinctly: "In attempting to be a silent witness, the mental ego realizes what a nonstop talker it is."[2]

But what is this "mental ego," this ordinary discursive mind, talking *about*? This is not good news. In fact, it can be downright dismaying. I remember on my first meditation retreat being shocked as I stood in the lunch line waiting for my turn to dish up the one solid meal of the day. As I hovered over the food with my stomach grumbling, watching my mind, I couldn't believe what I witnessed: A plethora of nasty, anxiety-driven grumbling: "Why doesn't that person move more quickly?" Plenty of judgmental, homicidal thoughts: "Oh my God, look how much food that guy is putting on his plate. He is a real pig. I'm glad I'm not such a hog." And an abundance of greed and aversion: "If that woman takes the last piece of coffee cake, there won't be any for me. I hate her."

Were these thoughts really me? Egad. When I watched my thoughts in that first retreat, I discovered that they were full of concerns about food, sex, comfort, and aggression. Was Sigmund Freud right? It appears so. Many of our thoughts are driven by craving and aversion of the most primitive kind. Decades of social polishing and the various finishing schools of life create only a thin veneer over this activity. Ordinary mind is more like our three-year-old nephew than we would like to think. As Joseph Goldstein, the American Buddhist teacher, has said, "The mind has absolutely no pride."[3]

Paradoxically, there is good news here: the very discovery of the primitive quality of this internal dialogue—and the concomitant discovery of our inability to control it—is itself the first, and most important, lesson to be learned from the technique. In order to learn it, we must simply be willing to continually bring attention back to the object of awareness—however infrequently it seems we can do so. This repeated action *provides a new point of view for the observing self—* some solid ground to which we can return again and again, giving us an entirely new observational base for what is called in yoga "the Witness." In the process, we get to see how tiny this observing self really is—especially at the beginning of our practice. Then we get to see how this still, silent Witness actually gets bigger, stronger, with practice. Eventually, we'll discover that that little Witness is the seed of Illumined Mind—the very kernel around which will develop all the remarkable fruit of practice.

DIS-IDENTIFICATION

The Noble Failure teaches us many interesting lessons. Among them is this: through watching the flow of our thoughts, we see, perhaps for the first time, how very identified we are with those driven, primitive, grasping thoughts. Lacking any other perspective, we have naturally assumed *until now* that our thoughts are who we are.

The second lesson of the beginning meditator is simply that this is not so. *We are not our thoughts.* We are not our internal chatter.

At the end of the second day of the retreat, I walked Jake home to Rudi's cabin—Acorn Cottage—where Jake had been renting a small upstairs bedroom. Acorn Cottage was a tumbledown Italianate cottage, built originally as a caretaker's cottage on an isolated part of Maggie's old family estate. (It was about a two-mile walk from Kripalu, and also about two miles through the woods from my house and the neighboring Tudor manse where Maggie now lived.) The old cottage—named Acorn Cottage by Maggie's grandmother—perfectly suited our friend Rudi, who had it stacked around with gardening equipment, tools, and neat piles of firewood for the winter.

It was a soft evening, just at dusk. Crickets still hummed loudly, and the leaves rustled as we shuffled down the dark path to the cottage. Jake was quiet. I had rarely experienced him like this. He was present. Not leaning into the next moment. Not trying to devour this moment with his usual obsessive examination. Jake's silence was full of presence. I mused to myself about the way in which seeing through thoughts gives us this little distance. A little breathing room.

Later, as the moon rose, we sat in big green Adirondack chairs and sipped tea on the porch of Acorn Cottage. We talked about Jake's experience of meditation over the previous two days, and about the power of dis-identifying with thoughts.

"A meditation teacher of mine used to have a wonderful drawing of this dis-identification with thoughts," I said. I drew the little diagram for him on a crumpled piece of paper I fished out of my pocket.

My teacher would draw a rectangle of pure blue, framed with a line.

"What is that?" my teacher would ask me. Well, of course, who knew what it was? Anybody's guess. Maybe it was the deep blue sea. Maybe it was just blue.

Then he would put a little triangle of green in the bottom right-hand corner of the picture, just above the frame.

This little patch of green in the corner, this teeny patch of ground, gave context to the blue. Suddenly it was clear: "Oh, of course I see now. It's sky." This little bit of ground allows us to see our thoughts for what they are: Oh, this blue is just the sky of mind. Maybe crystal blue, maybe cloudy and stormy. But sky.

A regular meditation practice is just like this, my teacher would say. "It gives you a small patch of ground to stand on, every day. So you know where you are, and what's what."

To know that we are not our thoughts is the first step toward freedom. Eliade makes this important point in his essay on meditation: "As long as we are unconsciously and automatically identifying with the changing contents of consciousness, we never suspect that our true nature remains hidden from us. Contemplative traditions affirm in one metaphor or another that our true identity lies not in the changing contents of consciousness but in a deeper layer of the self, mind or soul. To reach this deeper layer one must slowly disentangle oneself from automatic identification with the contents of consciousness."[4]

While the first confrontations with the stream of thoughts can create some anxiety, there may arise, even quite early in meditation practice, a sense of the spaciousness that comes from this dis-identification—a sense of relief in not having to react to thoughts. The meditative self simply has a more spacious world in which to be.

I remember noticing early on in my practice that with the daily anchor of meditation, the chaos in my external life calmed down noticeably. As I brought my mind and body back to the meditation cushion every day, I grew less identified with Puppy Mind, and acted less frequently on its promptings.

Ego psychologists like Michael Washburn sometimes refer to this as "uncramping." Eliade calls it the "interruption of automatized behavior." But in many religious traditions it is referred to simply as "emptying." "God cannot fill a heart or mind that is already full," says Thomas Merton. There are images in every contemplative tradition that point toward this kind of self-emptying: One finds them in John of the Cross, in Teresa of Avila, and in the work of the anonymous author of the *Cloud of Unknowing*—who calls it "self-forgetting." The beginning meditator sees just how full the mind actually is, and how we're constantly bounced hither and yon by our automatic identification with this tumultuous river of thoughts.

The first step in crossing this river is discovering the nature of its process, and appreciating its vastness and depth. The "wedge" of dis-identification that happens early in our experience of meditation begins to give us perspective on the mind's nature. Eliade reminds us of the importance of awaking to this reality: "Without this realization no progress can be made, for one must first know one is in prison in order to work intelligently to escape."[5]

In the first phase of meditation, this insight creates a new sense of spaciousness, of freedom, and of equanimity. And with this comes a first glimpse of an altogether new kind of mind. Deeper levels of the mind are revealed to lie underneath the flow of ordinary discursive thought. What yogis call "awake mind" emerges to the forefront of our experience. Our intuition, our knowing, and our discernment are heightened.

There is one more fruit of the Noble Failure available to the beginning meditator: Once we have begun to dis-identify with the current of thoughts on the surface of the mind, concentration automatically deepens. We can allow ourselves to stay with the object (the breath) precisely because we realize the ultimate futility of following the stray dog of discursive thought. This insight begins a process of ever-deepening cycles of concentration paired with the emergence of new, and often astounding, discoveries. The simple process of resting in the object, as we shall see, will eventually accomplish nothing less than the restructuring of the mind itself.

DRASHTRI: THE "SEEING" WITHOUT A "SEER"

The meditation class was circled together in the center of the Sunset Room at Kripalu. Jake was sitting near the back, looking relaxed (finally) and at ease. It was the morning of the last day of our retreat, and we had just sat again for thirty minutes (after an hour and a half of practicing yoga postures). The day had dawned brilliant, blue and still—and the air was cooler and drier than the previous day.

In our final discussion, I wanted to draw the class's attention to a small but very persistent piece of good news in their experience of meditation—and one of the central pillars of Patanjali's view.

I asked them to go with me to that endlessly repeating moment in concentration meditation when we notice that awareness has slipped off the object. When Lassie has wandered off to play in the fields.

"Relive this moment with me," I said. "You've noticed that attention has slipped off the object, and you've brought awareness back to the breath. Here's the question: Who was it that noticed mind had wandered? Who was it that brought mind back?

This gets them to thinking.

What part of the mind is this? Is this also Puppy Mind?

Slowly the truth dawns.

"There is someone watching," said a tentative voice from the front row.

"Exactly!" I said. "There is someone watching the whole thing—the whole storm of thoughts, feelings, and sensations. We're not constantly aware of this, but every now and then we're aware that We, or Some One or Some Thing or Some Alien Force, is watching, witnessing, seeing the whole bloody mess."

And now, of course, the fascinating question posed itself to the class: Who? Who is watching? And who is being watched? Are these two different parts of our mind? Seer and Seen?

The mysterious presence of this Seer is good news to those of us first encountering the Noble Failure. The storm clouds of wild mind lift for a moment. And there it is: a little island of presence. An island of solid land in the stormy seas. A still point that seems to be unmoving. Bali Hai! The ghostly but undeniable presence of this Seer is extremely reassuring. This silent Witness is always present. Even in the worst storm—a reliable presence.

Yogis have called this silent Witness *drashtri:* the Seer, or Pure Awareness. We know that *drashtri*, this Seer, will be an important part of Patanjali's treatise, because he puts it at the very beginning of his first chapter—in the third *sūtra*: "Then, Pure Awareness [*drashtri*] can abide in its very nature," he says.

> *Now, the teachings of yoga.*
> *Yoga is to still the patterning of consciousness.*
> *Then pure awareness can abide in its very nature.* (1.1–3)

The nature of this Pure Awareness, of this *drashtri*, is hard for us, at first, to comprehend. Early on in our understanding of Patanjali's teaching, we may find ourselves referring to Pure Awareness as a Seer or a Witness—as if it were a person. At first, this personification of the Seer must stand in for a more subtle and difficult truth. For by the end of his treatise, Patanjali will have taught us that Pure Awareness is not a thing or a person or even an "it" of any kind. Pure Awareness is without form, time, change, location, or mass. It does not even behave. But not until the end of the path will we fully know the nature of this *drashtri* to which Patanjali alludes at the outset of his teaching. For now, we have no choice but to let it remain something of a mystery.

Almost all transformational psychologies begin by imagining some kind of Observer: an "observing ego." A Witness. A Seer. Carl Jung struggled to describe the function of witnessing. Marion Woodman, one of his students, and now a great feminist Jungian analyst and writer, describes it in a helpful graphic form. She draws a line across a big white sheet of newsprint. And then she draws a teeny little circle just in the center of the line.

Beneath the line (because Woodman is a Jungian) is the dark sea of the unconscious—completely unavailable to our awareness most of the time. Above the line is the conscious mind. Available to awareness. (But Puppy, nonetheless.) And right at the center of the line is the little seeing eye of the Witness. The still point at the center of the storm. Small. But maybe getting bigger as we practice. And no matter how small, always, always there.

The presence of the Witness is a source of reassurance and comfort for meditators and Jungians alike. A companion on the path. But is witnessing really always present? Can this be true? Sometimes ordinary mind becomes so entirely chaotic that it seems that the Witness is gone. Lost at sea. Entirely absent. Completely off the radar screen. But yogis discovered a deeper truth: the Witness IS the radar screen.

Ram Dass (the former Harvard professor Richard Alpert) often told a wonderful story about the ever-present Witness. Throughout his years as a spiritual teacher, he had a great number of friends and students all over the world who stayed in touch with him by phone. One evening while he was at home on the East Coast, he received a desperate call from one such student in California. She was apparently "wrecked" on LSD—she was psychotic, hallucinating, hearing voices. Terrified. In the storm of her drug-induced psychosis, she was having a great deal of trouble being coherent. (Wild mind times ten—with chemical intervention.) Ram Dass couldn't connect with her.

Finally, he said to her, "I'd like to speak to the person who dialed the phone." This was brilliant. I'd like to speak to the person who picked up the receiver and dialed an eleven-digit phone number from memory. He knew that she had called him. He knew that it was the Witness that had made the phone call. The seed of a Witness was in there somewhere. And this was precisely the part of her mind with which he had to connect in order to help her.[6]

Our first experiments with meditation are often more difficult than we hope they will be, but they are also wonderfully productive and important. Very often, they yield all of the raw information we need to explain the entire path of yoga. In the first three days of practice, with some luck and a bit of perseverance, our beginning meditation class had directly experienced the three central building blocks of *rāja-yoga*:

1. The problem of Puppy Mind
2. A few mind-altering seconds of stillness
3. The presence of the Witness

These are precisely the three components with which Patanjali begins his terse description of the path of yoga.

As our morning session drew to a close, the class seemed settled, re-assured. A cool breeze wafted through the Sunset Room. No one seemed eager to move. To end, I read the first three *sūtras* to the class, using the translation and commentary I had come to prefer—that of yoga teacher and scholar Chip Hartranft's *The Yoga-Sūtra of Patanjali*.

Now, the teachings of yoga. "Now" refers to the moment when we're finally willing to lift the lid and look inside. Now means, per-haps, the moment when we've finally had enough pain and insanity and suffering—when we're tired of being driven hither and yon by that crazy stray dog of mind. Our puppies have gnawed enough on the meatless bone. We're ready to sit down in a room and negotiate. Now, the teachings of yoga will have some meaning.

Yoga is to still the patterning of consciousness. There's a promise in this *sūtra*. Wild mind can be tamed. Stilled. And this stillness sounds good. It sounds like rest. Like happiness. Like an afternoon in the hammock. Like we could stop living at right angles to life.

Then pure awareness can abide in its very nature. Then the Witness abides in its very nature. Just seeing. Just knowing. Just Bali Hai and calm seas all around.

When consciousness is disturbed, Pure Awareness cannot be distin-guished from the waves of mind. The restlessness of the mind, like a choppy pond, fractures the reflection.

When consciousness is stilled, however, a great mystery is re-vealed: *Pure Awareness abides in its very nature.* And what is this nature? This consciousness, when stilled, has two remarkable characteristics: it is *reflective,* reflecting Pure Awareness back to itself; and it is *transparent,* allowing itself to be completely seen and penetrated.

It is one of the glories of this technique that the end of the path is present even in the beginning. For even from the first days of practice, the meditator begins to "know" and "be known." And to understand that knowing and seeing is what it is all about.

Chapter 3

QUIET DESPERATION

DUHKHA: PERVASIVE UNSATISFACTORINESS

The instant we begin investigating the mind through meditation, we have joined the great river of yogi-scientists—from the ancient strivers of the time of the Buddha and Mahavira all the way down to my own little band of friends and seekers. And because the nature of the human mind is everywhere the same, the seeker of today and the *sramana* of three thousand years ago has a remarkably similar experience.

The meditator's first investigations reveal a subtle but disconcerting struggle going on deep in the mind and body—a kind of conflict which colors all experience with a vague sense of unsatisfactoriness. No amount of reading about this can replace the direct, immediate experience of it. The yogi's first task is to closely examine the nature of this unhappiness.

How does this investigation proceed? We have seen that the beginning meditator finds an object and lets awareness simply rest in that object. We have seen, too, that the mind cannot rest on that object for more than mere nanoseconds before it goes zipping off, unbidden, into memories of the past, or fantasies of the future.

When we examine this process closely, we will discover the nature of the problem: the mind seems to be profoundly ill at ease with the present moment. Mind cannot seem to rest with "how it is" right now. Indeed, the mind seems to be always conducting a sub-threshold war with "right now"—using every strategy available to avoid it. I sometimes call this the War With Reality.

Most of us, even before we begin to meditate, have had some awareness of this war with the present moment. In order to bear sitting at our desk for eight hours a day, we have spent the last three months dreaming about our upcoming trip to England with our beloved. We've anticipated exactly how it will be. We've pored over the pictures of the quaint hotel in which we'll be staying, and secretly put the brochure in the top drawer of our desk so that we can look at the images throughout the workday. It will be ten days of heaven. All of this fantasizing serves as a distraction from the strangely difficult "present moment."

OK. But then, when we get to our dream destination, everything is not quite the way we had pictured it. As we arrive, we try not to notice that the quaint guesthouse for which we're paying a fortune is next to what must be London's version of a crack house. When we check into the room, we discover that the mattress is too soft, and there is an annoying musty smell that might trigger our allergies. A hard rain falls all night.

In the morning, we discover that breakfasts in England are just not right. Too much fat. Too many eggs. Where's the granola? The fresh fruit? After breakfast, we have a fight with our so-called beloved. Suddenly, we're in the nightmare vacation. Inside, the drumbeat begins: "NO! I don't want it to be like this! I won't have it be like this." We're at war with How It Is.

This is a dramatic example, of course. But the very same process goes on in more subtle ways in every instant of mental experience. Most of us do not see this until we attempt to examine the moment-by-moment flow of thoughts and sensations in the mind and body through meditation. Then, we cannot avoid it. Aaarrrggghh. This war is going on all the time. How did we miss it?

At almost any point in my day when I stop and check down inside, I will find some version of my silent *mantra*—this moment should be different!—going on. I dislike how it is right now. It's not so pleasant. I want it to be like it was the other day, last week, last year. Or, I love how it is right now. It's very pleasant. I want it to stay. How can I make this pleasant feeling stay? How can I keep the flow of experience from snatching it away? Oh, don't let it go.

Each of us has our own silent War With Reality. And whatever our particular War With Reality is, its result is always a pervasive sense of the *unsatisfactoriness of the moment*. Yogis came to call this *duhkha*. *Duhkha* means, literally, "suffering," "pain," or "distress." (It seems that the word *duhkha* originally meant "having a bad axle hole," which must have been distressing indeed.)[1]

When we explore the mind-state of *duhkha*, we find that it is created by a deep aversion to being with How It Is right now. This silent, unconscious war with How It Is unwittingly drives much of our behavior: We reach for the pleasant. We hate the unpleasant. We try to arrange the world so that we have only pleasant mind-states, and not unpleasant ones. We try to get rid of this pervasive state of unsatisfactoriness in whatever way we can—by changing things "out there." By changing the world. By changing England, if we have to.

Thoreau, through his close investigation of his own mental states in the quiet at Walden Pond, discovered this very same phenomenon of underlying unsatisfactoriness. He called it "desperation." "The mass of men lead lives of quiet desperation," he said. "A stereotyped but unconscious despair is concealed even under what are called the games and amusements of mankind."

Thoreau's quiet desperation is precisely *duhkha*. He saw that ordinary mind seems chronically ill at ease with How It Is. We simply cannot say, "This is the way things are. This is how things are here in England, at least at this particular guesthouse." Instead, mind does not hesitate to try to change the entire country of England. After a few days we get tired of trying to change England, and perhaps we surrender just the littlest bit to how England is. But we don't surrender to how we are. To *exactly* how we are. We're plagued by shoulds: *I should be happy. I should be in heaven. I paid three thousand dollars for this trip, and it's wrong, wrong, wrong. I should be able to fix my beloved, who is acting weird and distant. Something exciting should be happening to me. I shouldn't be so bored.*

Thoreau understood that this *duhkha*, this quiet desperation, is the water in which we swim. He saw that we mostly lead our lives blithely unaware of it. We simply don't see it. In fact, it is quite common for new meditation students to raise their hands and object strenuously: "I have no suffering. I have no *duhkha*. We have no real suffering in this wealthy culture of ours—do we? I think this notion is sheer self-indulgence."

The yogi's response to this blindness is always the same: look more closely.

KLESHA: THE DISCOVERY OF AFFLICTED MIND

The ancient yogis did look more closely. They explored the experience of *duhkha* like an ancient science project—practicing meditation for years on end, in solitary caves, forests, in small groups of dedicated seekers. They persisted in their questioning: Why is it so difficult for our minds to rest in the present moment? What are the causes of pervasive unsatisfactoriness? What are its roots? Is there a cure?

Over the course of many centuries, their investigations kept coming up with precisely the same answer: the causes of this unhappiness are the forces of grasping, aversion, and delusion buried deep in the mind. Patanjali called these forces *kleshas*—literally "afflictions" or "troubles" or "poisons."

> *... unwholesome thoughts may arise from greed, anger, or delusion; they may be mild, moderate, or extreme; but they never cease to ripen into ignorance and suffering...* (2.34)

39

The mapping out of these forces in the mind is one of the great discoveries of yoga. Patanjali and his tradition came to believe that these "afflictions" only arise because of our ignorance of our true nature (or, "not seeing things as they are"—*avidyā*), and that once we know our true nature they evaporate from the mind. His complete description of the roots of affliction comes early on in the second section of the *Yoga-Sūtra:*

> *The causes of suffering [klesha] are not seeing things as they are, the sense of "I," attachment, aversion, and clinging to life.* (2.3)

Later on in this book, I'll examine the subtle and complex meanings of "not seeing things as they are" *(avidyā)* and "the sense of 'I'" *(asmitā)*. In teaching the *Yoga-Sūtra,* however, I've found it most useful to begin by discussing the immediate, visceral ways in which we experience *duhkha*. Patanjali names three of them: *rāga*—craving, clinging, and greed; *dvesha*—aversion, hatred, and avoidance; and *moha*, delusion.[2]

Rāga—attraction—is the tendency to lean forward out of the way it is right now toward the fantasized next moment, or toward any moment in the hoped-for future (England!), or the fondly remembered past. It involves reaching, clinging, craving. *Rāga* has a grabby, anxious kind of energy. I want. I want. I must have. Mommy, give me that cookie before I die. In some of the contemplative traditions this quality is called "thirst" *(tanha)* or "hunger."

Dvesha—aversion—is the tendency to lean backward, dig in our heels, and say, Whoa, Nellie. We may say, Stop! Get me out of here! We may say, Yuck. Aversion is a big NO to the experience of the moment. Imagine the face of a child—a picky eater—who has just eaten her first bite of the dreaded turnip. Some of the contemplative traditions identify this aversive state as hatred or fear.

Moha—delusion—is the quality in the mind that wants us to disappear entirely from the moment. Like the child in the theater who, when she sees something shocking, just covers her eyes, as if this will make everything go away. "I cannot bear to look. Tell me when it's over."

We lean forward out of the present moment. Or we dig in our heels and lean backward. Or we twist away from the naked truth of the moment. All three experiences keep us from being present with How It Is just now. This war with the present moment keeps us almost continually uncomfortable in our own skin. And the sense of unsatisfactoriness that results, though usually beneath the threshold of our awareness, nonetheless drives much of our experience, and many of our decisions, in an unconscious, reactive way.

In attempting to understand the nature of afflicted mind-states, most of us early on will encounter a problem: Is all longing afflicted? Is all desire really afflicted? What about the longing for God? For love? What about the longing for my beloved? Is all aversion, all anger, afflicted by its very nature? What about the anger in response to life's horrendous injustices—to violence and aggression of all kinds? What about the anger that serves me by setting a clear boundary for those who might harm me? And what about delusion? Aren't there times when a dollop of delusion serves us—when we are not yet ready, perhaps, to bear the full brunt of grief or loss?

So, it is important to say at the outset that all longing is not necessarily afflicted. Indeed, even anger is not necessarily afflicted. What, then, precisely, does mark certain mind-states as "troubled" or "poisoned"? What distinguishes some states as afflicted and others as non-afflicted?

Yogis mapped out this territory with great precision. All of the so-called afflicted mental states have three primary distinguishing characteristics in common:

~ Afflictive states are disturbing.
~ Afflictive states are obscuring.
~ Afflictive states are separative.

First, *afflictive states are disturbing*. When experiencing craving or aversion, we lose the mind's natural equanimity. We lose the balance of the mind. States of grasping keep ordinary mind roiled, restless, agitated, ill at ease—the surface of the pond broken up. And as a result of this disturbance of mind, we feel *uncomfortable with the experience of being itself*.

Second, *afflictive states are obscuring*. They obscure the true nature of reality. They seriously distort what Western psychologists call "reality testing." Aversion, for example, makes things appear worse than they are (wholly bad). Jake felt aversive to the "airheads" in his law firm (especially after some of them forced his embarrassing departure), and this aversion so colored his perception of these men and women that he was unable to see their many positive characteristics. Conversely, our attraction to and craving for certain objects of desire may so color our perception that their deleterious effects may become invisible to us, and we may see them as better than they are (wholly good). So, assessments of reality based on afflicted mind are not accurate. Thus, they are said to be "obscured."

And thirdly, *afflictive states are separative*. They separate us from a direct experience of bare reality. They are mental states not supported by a direct experience of How It Is, but rather by our *idealized notions about how things should be*—our hopes or wishes about how things might be. They separate us from a real, direct, and complete experience of the phenomena of life. Afflicted states drive us to believe that objects—love objects, material objects, or success objects—will make us happy. When under the thrall of these afflicted states, we're left feeling fundamentally separate from our own happiness, craving for the object (and the object is always "out there"—like the trip to England) that will complete us.

RĀGA, DVESHA, AND *MOHA*

Now we might call to mind once again the central principle of yoga practice: the mind is transformed only by direct, systematic, and careful personal investigation of experience. Not by concepts about reality. Not by metaphysical constructs. Alas, there is no way to understand the afflicted mind-state of craving, aversion, and delusion without exploring our own immediate experience of them.

Of course, as always, there is good news: for any of us willing to pay attention, we do not have to search far afield for a confrontation with these states. They are with us in practically every moment of life.

And what does a direct investigation of these states yield? Let's look more closely at each one of the three afflicted states, beginning with craving, or greed.

In our culture, it is particularly hard to see craving and clinging as forms of unhappiness. We exalt the drive for bigger and better. Indeed, we practically regard ambition and consumption as social duties. But what happens when we investigate the mind-states that so often drive our craving?

On my very first long meditation retreat (with a well-known Buddhist meditation teacher), my teacher challenged me to do just that. During an interview, he asked me a question: "Have you ever allowed yourself to fully experience a moment of craving? I mean, fully experience? Have you ever just stopped? Stopped, when you desperately wanted something? Stopped to feel the heat of craving?"

An honest answer to him would have been "certainly not." Why would I have? Only a meditation teacher would ask one to do such an unnatural thing.

On the other hand, what an intriguing idea. I tried it that same day—in the lunch line at the retreat. We had already had six days of sitting and walking meditation. Sitting and walking, sitting and walking—thirteen hours a day. There was no entertainment at all.

Indeed, the only thing that came close to entertainment was lunch. Lunch created a huge excitement in my mind. In this context, it was a virtual trip to Las Vegas.

For six days we had eaten adzuki beans and rice for lunch. On the seventh day, a miracle occurred. Blueberry cobbler appeared on the lunch line. (Perhaps a Christian had been smuggled into the kitchen.) I could see the cobbler from my position toward the back of the line. I could practically taste it on my tongue—its big, fat blueberries bursting with tangy pulp.

The line moved, oh, so slowly. First, of course, the frustratingly serene kitchen staff rang the little bell. We had to stand for what seemed like an age in just-pretend meditation. As I observed the blueberry cobbler from across the room, I felt the saliva fill my mouth. The inner wolf began to emerge, and I knew that my fangs had come out and my pink tongue was lolling down around my neck like a dog on a hot day.

As the line moved, I watched the blueberry cobbler disappear. Then there were only five pieces left, and eleven people in front of me. Were there reinforcements coming from the kitchen? I feared not.

When it became clear that I was not going to get the cobbler, I decided at the very least to get the lesson. I decided to try the technique I had been learning all week: Bring awareness to the breath, the sensations in the body. Move toward the feelings—the feelings in the body. Examine the texture and movement of the sensations there.

Well, OK. The sensations started deep in my belly and moved in a straight line up to my diaphragm, where they wrapped like a rope around my body and cinched tighter and tighter, stopping my breath. Talk about unsatisfactory. It was painful.

What a surprise. Craving is painful. The wolf wanted to howl. To keen. Who knew? Wanting, fully experienced, is almost unbearable. Wailing seems the appropriate response.

Later that afternoon, an insight stole in like the weather: all of that compulsive eating and sexing and consuming and shopping I've done. All of that stuff *I do* all the time. It's all an attempt to *get rid* of this feeling of craving. It's not a celebration of craving at all. It's a way to avoid feeling it.

Aversion creates almost exactly the same feeling in the body as greed. Let's go back to the lunch line at the meditation retreat. On day eight there is no blueberry cobbler. Only adzuki beans and rice.

Aarrgghhh!! No. Not again. This can't possibly be. Tell me I'm dreaming. The mind simply rebels. This is beyond the bounds of all decency. Eight days of adzuki beans and rice. A fantasy comes unbidden to the mind: pick up a freshly opened five-pound bag of adzuki beans, look directly into the face of the cook, and empty the entire boring contents onto the floor.

But no. Stop. Feel. Track the sensations. (This technique is getting on my nerves now, too.) It's somewhere at the top of my chest and up in my throat. It is heavy—like lead. Tight. There is a slight choking sensation in my throat.

As I stay with the sensations, I feel the nascent scream that wants to emerge. This sensation of aversion, when I actually feel it, is terribly like the sensation of greed. It's the wolf wanting to howl again. It hurts deep inside. For a split second I'm actually with the pain of aversion. It begins to feel a lot like sadness.

And now the miracle: as soon as we've felt it fully, aversion begins to move off toward the horizon like a big thunder boomer. It moves through like a spell of bad weather—intense for a while, but soon gone. Once it's seen through, aversion begins to evaporate.

At the beginning of meditation practice, it is helpful to start examining the most gross manifestations of aversion. It's helpful to get some practice noticing what the big stone in your shoe feels like before trying to apprehend the little pebble between your sock and the ball of your foot—the one that has made you walk funny all morning but you don't know why. The one that made that whole morning walk through the woods "unsatisfactory."

When we become more skillful in our internal sleuthing, we may find craving and aversion in their subtle, insidious form dusting the insides of our guts, painting our entire lives with unsatisfactoriness. Eventually, we'll have to experience the craving or aversion itself. We'll have to sit on the moldy bed in England and cry, cry, cry, cry. Perhaps we'll throw open the window and howl.

How about delusion?

I grew up in a family that preferred delusion above all other afflicted mind-states. When my first book was published, there was a naked young man on the cover, in a beautiful yoga pose. (The photo was shot in an appropriate way. His genital area was completely shadowed out, but nevertheless he was definitely naked.) When my elderly Aunt Caroline first saw the book, she called me right away on the phone. There was anxiety in her voice. "Stephen, when I first saw your book, I thought that young man was naked." Pause. "But then I realized he had shorts on."

Well, of course, he didn't have shorts on at all. She put them on him. In her mind. This was not a stretch for Aunt Caroline, nor would it have been much of a stretch for anyone from my tribe.

Delusion reflects our commitment to our notions of how life should be. And in my family we had strong ideas about how life should go. Unfortunately this commitment to How It Should Be is always accompanied by a fatal indifference to How It Is. Psychologists have a name for the everyday version of this defensive structure: the False Self. We all know it to some degree: the False Self that emerges when our perceptions and behaviors are driven by unconscious ideas about how reality should look. About how our family should only look magnificent and functional, never neurotic and weird and sometimes smelly as they really are; ideas we have about that special heart-filled corporation we work for—as if it loves us, and as if it will never, ever call us in to the boss's office the week before Christmas and ask us (and our paper box full of family photos) to be out of the building by sundown.

I've told the Aunt Caroline story in talks, and usually someone raises his hand and says, "But if Aunt Caroline needed to believe that he had shorts on, why not? At least it will keep her comfortable. After all, she's so old." This is the ignorance-is-bliss theory. Alas, ignorance does not actually create happiness, or anything real whatsoever. There is a saying in yoga circles: "not seeing *duhkha* is *duhkha*."

Not seeing suffering is suffering. This is the *sramanic* view. And the correct one, I think. As a psychotherapist, I know it well. When clients can't bear the truth, they twist away from it. They twist away from painful feelings in the body and mind. They twist away from the truth of what's just happened at home under their very noses. Twisting away is in some ways the deepest pain. Even if you cannot see the twisting in the face, you can see it in the soul. Not seeing *duhkha* is *duhkha*.

SUKHA: EVERYTHING IS ALREADY OK

"I don't know, it was like a flash of insight or something," said Jake.

"I was just standing in the shower, hot water pounding on my head. I looked up. And all of a sudden *I saw* the new tiles." Jake was shaking his head in disbelief.

"You know, I'd helped Rudi renovate that shower four months ago, when I first arrived at Acorn Cottage. But in that moment, I realized I had never really *seen* those damned new blue tiles we put in. Even though I've been in that shower every friggin' morning for four months. I've never seen them. Never looked at them! Then, in a flash I realized something: in that moment, I was actually there. Just there. Damn."

Several weeks after his first meditation retreat, Jake was relating a "post-meditation" experience—a moment of happiness. For a few sweet moments, he had been "just there," and going nowhere else—not leaning forward or backward. Not covering his eyes. "It was as if I had fallen out of the sky and landed on the earth after having been away a long, long time." He shook his head again.

Jake had been practicing meditation regularly since the retreat, and he suspected that this moment of happiness was the fruit of his practice. I think he was right.

The sense of well-being Jake experienced was categorically different from any he could remember. In those moments when there is no clinging, no craving, no aversion, no delusion, we are entirely free. We experience *sukha,* or "sweetness." *Sukha* is the happiness that is not colored by craving or aversion.

Jake's discovery paralleled one of the Buddha's great discoveries. After he left his father's palace in search of enlightenment, Siddhartha Gautama (the Buddha-to-be) studied with many of the greatest yogis of his day. When he felt he had mastered everything they had to teach, he went to the forest to practice severe austerities with a group of other wandering *sramanas*. By the end of this period, he was eating only one grain of rice a day. He had become the world's most severe ascetic. He found, however, that these austerities did not seem to be awakening his mind. Eventually he renounced them, and in a famous gesture, accepted a bowl of milk from a young girl.

Just after doing so, he had a life-changing memory. He remembered sitting as a young boy in the shade of a rose apple tree, watching his father's farmers plow the fields. His parents and family were nearby. In that moment, he wanted nothing. Disliked nothing. He was perfectly happy with things as they were. His mind was balanced and at ease. He was able to embrace both joy and sorrow—without clinging to or pushing away any particular mind-state. He realized, reliving this experience in memory, that *this* was the state of enlightenment. Furthermore, he realized that it was a *naturally arising state*. And if it arose naturally, could it not, then, be systematically cultivated?

In that moment, Siddhartha understood the central issue: When the afflictions are absent, we are enlightened. When the afflictions are absent, the mind stops. Patanjali has given us this insight at the very beginning of his treatise: "Yoga is to still the patterning of consciousness. Then pure awareness can abide in its very nature." When the fluctuations of the mind are at rest, the Seer is established. Pure Awareness shines forth.

Bhagwan Shree Rajneesh—the late, controversial "crazy-wisdom" guru, and prolific writer about the *Yoga-Sūtra*—has said it well:

> When you can simply look without being identified with the mind, without judging, without appreciating, without choosing—you simply look and the mind flows, a time comes when by itself, of itself, the mind stops. When there is no mind, you are established in your witnessing. Then you have become a witness—just a seer—a *drakshta*, a *sakchhi*. Then you are not a doer, then you are not a thinker. Then you are simply being—pure being. Then the witness is established in itself.[3]

Mind, consciousness itself, arises and passes away moment-by-moment along with the objects of attachment. When we dis-identify with craving and aversion, the subtle afflictions that create *duhkha* do not continue to arise. There is, then, only witnessing. Only seeing. These are moments in which there is no suffering. And in which we see the world clearly: Jake in the shower.

In practice, we penetrate these moments of enlightenment again and again. Sometimes they happen in the shower, sometimes on the yoga mat or meditation cushion. We're sitting at the breakfast table, and we experience a moment in which time slows down and we feel completely "here." Everything feels entirely OK. Everything is a source of delight—the smell of the coffee, the thought of our family sleeping upstairs, even the thought of our day at work. At first these moments occur as strange but delightful altered states, as Jake's experience in the shower had occurred to him—a fleeting visit to a foreign country. But as practice proceeds, these moments occur more frequently. After a while, we get to know them. And finally, having visited many times, we begin to find ourselves living there.

When the afflictions are extinguished (even momentarily), consciousness naturally reveals two remarkable characteristics: it is transparent and it is reflective. In these moments, consciousness is often described as being "a still forest pool." Its surface is calm. The waters underneath are calm. There is no reactivity anywhere. Consciousness is reflective, like a mirror. Looking into it, one can see one's own reflection. It is also transparent. On a sunny day, one can see the colors of the polished granite stones on the bottom. There are no eddies, no undertows. All of the mud has settled to the bottom.

In the state of *sukha*, as Jake discovered:

~ Mind is undisturbed—quiet
~ Mind is unobscured—seeing clearly, and perceiving bare reality rather than ideas about reality
~ Experience is unitive, rather than separative: we feel a sense of oneness with and relatedness to all beings

In these moments, we become acquainted with a new kind of pleasure—the pleasure of savoring experience. The pleasure of a happiness that is not saturated with grasping. In coming chapters, we will see how this capacity to know experience in an entirely unafflicted fashion is a major theme of the *Yoga-Sūtra*.

As they familiarized themselves with the mechanics of afflicted mind, yogis developed a remarkable point of view. Their experience taught them that *craving and aversion do not exist in the deeper, luminous parts of the mind.* The implications of this discovery are momentous: The afflictions are not essential components of the mind. They are just visitors.

As meditation practice proceeds, we make a wonderful discovery: We do not have to learn how to be happy. We already know. Happiness is not an alien land. It is our homeland. Furthermore, we do not need to "get rid" of Puppy Mind in order to be happy. Indeed, there is no getting rid of Puppy Mind. Puppy Mind is simply the nature of the ordinary, discursive part of the mind. Puppy Mind is not the problem. Puppy Mind is not the affliction. The affliction is our *reactivity* to the puppy—and to the ever-changing weather of the mind.

The good news of meditation is that this reactivity of *duhkha* can be seen through and profoundly attenuated through practice. We are still assaulted by storms (and this is true of even the most adept meditators) but we do not suffer as much from them. We discover that *sukha*, or happiness, can arise even in the most difficult of circumstances. We can make room for any kind of weather. There is no need to force happiness. It is right here all along. It is an essential ingredient of our true nature.

Part Two

ILLUMINED MIND
IN
EVERYDAY LIFE

*I*NSIDE this clay jug, there are canyons and pine mountains, and the maker of canyons and pine mountains!

All seven oceans are inside, and hundreds of millions of stars.

The acid that tests gold is there, and the one who judges jewels.

And the music from the strings no one touches, and the source of all water.

If you want the truth, I will tell you the truth:

Friend, listen: the God whom I love is inside.

—Kabir

(Translation: Robert Bly)

MAGGIE

The Search for Authentic Self-Expression

MAGGIE WINSLOW was from a long line of New England Winslows who had inhabited the Berkshire Hills since at least the early decades of the eighteenth century. The first known Winslow in these parts—Nathaniel—had been a clergyman, and a colleague of the famed preacher Jonathan Edwards. Maggie's branch of the family had lost their fortune and their lands during the Great Depression, and Maggie herself was left with a meager inheritance. She lived in the increasingly tattered remains of one of the family's houses—the old Tudor-style manse next door to my small clapboard cottage.

I loved Maggie almost from our first meeting—a friendly chat over the picket fence separating our houses. In that short conversation, Maggie's intelligent face wore an expression of penetrating interest. Her large brown eyes were soft, but sturdy. She evinced a kind of tweedy self-reliance and resourcefulness. I liked her no-frills haircut, her sensible clothes, and her battered old Subaru wagon.

I soon became a regular visitor to Maggie's house—which was always in a barely controlled state of chaos. Two cats and a dog had the run of the place. A profusion of houseplants exploded under fading wallpaper and threadbare damask-covered sofas. Oil portraits of eighteenth century ancestors stared down from aging gilt frames—now darkened with dust.

Over the course of many quiet afternoon teas, Maggie had revealed to me (in often irreverent tales) the story of her life. She described her upbringing by her grandparents, Georgiana and Carrington Winslow—who as children had seen the twilight of the great golden age of the Berkshires. Maggie's parents had both been killed in the crash of a commercial airliner in 1946. Maggie had been just three years old, and so had almost no memory of her parents. She called Georgiana, Gammy; Carrington she called Daddy. They had been the only parents she had really known.

Maggie told me, too, of her mundane, and finally deadening, marriage to a local banker; of their three children; and of her husband's untimely death of a heart attack at forty-eight. She commented (in remarkably even tones) about the difficult financial straits that faced the family after his loss. Throughout her life, it seems, she had accommodated to living in refined poverty.

It appeared, though, that I knew Maggie in what was a kind of second incarnation. After her husband's death, Maggie took a part-time job at the local library—and quickly became a pillar of that institution. In her free time, however, she turned her energy to her great—and long suppressed—passion: writing. She had always been fascinated with the combination of beauty and deadness in the old social hierarchies of the wealthy—a suffering which she had seen up close. Now she turned her writer's gaze on these, and in eight years she produced three novels investigating this glamorous but disturbed world.

Maggie's cousin Geoffrey, a New York writer who had acted as her mentor, complained that her novels, somewhat Wharton-esque, were too plodding and predictable. He had made only halfhearted attempts to interest his own agent in them—and finally had declared to Maggie that they were unlikely to find a publisher. Nonetheless, I found them fascinating—and a wonderful introduction to Maggie. There were moments of brilliance and flashing insight in her books, when the reader could feel Maggie reaching down for deeper truth. These moments in her prose were exciting. They spoke of a Maggie still trying to find her real life, her voice.

Curiously, Maggie's writing gave her the freedom to live more fully in middle age than she had ever imagined. She was passionate about her art—more so than about anything else. She was not a mother who clung to her children. (Some would say this was an understatement.) To the consternation of family and friends, she sometimes wrote straight through holidays without making any plans. Christmas. Easter. They would simply come and go. She knew that some in Lenox had designated her eccentric—and worse: a bad mother. But her grown children adored her, and doted on her when she let them.

Maggie had her own rhythms. She didn't care that neighbors gossiped about her peculiarities. She could give up writing for weeks on end—spending her spare time gardening, and hanging out with me and the cats and dog. Then, wham, she would disappear into her second-floor study. I began to realize that there would be times when I would see little of her. In those periods, she seemed possessed. She had now retired from her library job, and was able to devote herself completely to writing. The one other place she always seemed to show up, however, was yoga class. And even more so during her periods of heightened creativity.

A year or so into our friendship, Maggie began to take me increasingly into her confidence. One afternoon, when I stopped for tea, Maggie acknowledged that she was depressed. As we sat on tattered wicker chairs in the garden, she recounted her problem. "I'm getting old, Steve. And I fear that my life has been a waste," she said with an air of resignation, watching the cat swat a bee. "I feel, I don't know, just so unsatisfied. As if there were something I was supposed to accomplish, but didn't."

I was astonished. I had no idea Maggie felt this way—though it did account, perhaps, for the drivenness of her writing.

Maggie looked up. "There is something in here," she said, touching her fingers to her chest, "that must be expressed. Something that's trapped. Something excellent. I know it. I just haven't been able to get to it."

Over the ensuing months, during the leisurely afternoons of my sabbatical, the story spilled out in more detail. At sixty-two, Maggie was terrified that she had not lived up to her potential. Memory, she said, often took her back to the days of her childhood (which she recalled now as a happy one) at Bellewood, the Winslows' old estate and farm. (Bellewood, now in ruins, was just two miles through the woods from the house Maggie now inhabited. When we visited Rudi at Acorn Cottage, we could see it through the trees.)

Maggie remembered her grandparents, who raised her, as particularly noble people. Not noble by birth, exactly, but by character. She had seen the nobility of their struggle, as they built a life on the ruins of their past, with little money, and only fading memories of prestige and power. She had seen her grandmother's struggle with her art (Georgiana had become an accomplished painter of landscapes). She had watched as her grandfather, Carrington Winslow, became a farmer so that the family could survive.

Maggie said to me, "I have seen profound things in my life. Important things. I feel that I have to speak them. Write them."

Maggie sensed that these important things, "these fine things," were in her, also. This same Winslow character was in her, was it not? Or perhaps these extraordinary things that she sensed—this capacity to love and to endure hardship and loss—were in everyone. Perhaps this nobility was part of being human?

Maggie insisted that she did not need admiration, or praise, or even commercial success from her writing. She said that she needed only the satisfaction of expressing the best of her. But I was not sure. Her writing quest was driven by more than one deep hunger—and I thought she was too quickly disavowing the hunger for recognition. I wondered if, perhaps, she did not really feel the need to bring prestige back into the family—after the failures and collapses of the past. Perhaps this hoped-for success would be her tribute to her grandparents.

Whatever her precise needs, it was clear that they had now overtaken her. She felt driven, she told me, and increasingly distracted.

She didn't feel the cat in her lap, because she was thinking about her book. She didn't wash the dishes or clean up the house because she was composing a line. She was consumed by this one final shot at something fine.

Maggie's quest for the Firebird was different from Jake's. It was more ineffable—less defined by outward success. It was made up of images of Georgiana: her high spirits and her beauty, her flashing honesty and temper, the discipline she brought to her painting, her power to be who she was in an age when it was not fashionable for women of her ilk to do so. It was made up of images of Carrington: his sturdiness and impeccability, his softness of speech, his large and capable hands, his beautiful restraint, his love of fine music.

Maggie's internal representations of her "self" were dominated by these images—and others from the rich mine of her youth. She felt that she would be a failure unless she somehow manifested these qualities in her own generation. Her search was driven by the ego ideal, of course—the wish to be held again in that state of perfection that she once knew. But even more so by the ideal ego—the unconscious belief in her magnificence and power, and the magnificence, sturdiness, and brilliance of her internalized family.

I sensed that Maggie's search for the Firebird did, indeed, contain much of the best of her—much of the true genius and actual nobility of her family. Indeed, there seemed to be aspects of this particular Firebird that were quite real. And, yet, there was illusion (or delusion), as well.

I began to see the suffering in Maggie's drivenness. There was so much will in it, so much craving, so much grasping. And finally, so much disappointment. The older she got, the more desperate she felt about the situation. Her grasping for the golden ring was surely colored with *duhkha*. There was disturbance, there was obscuration, and there was separation.

But there was one piece of very good news in the picture. Maggie had begun to bring some of her craving into her yoga practice. Out of desperation, perhaps, Maggie began to bring her longing to her yoga mat, and to the *mantra* and meditation practice she and I did together with Rudi every Friday night. Maggie did these practices with great resolve. She was capable of tremendous discipline (something she had perhaps learned from Georgiana and Carrington). I noticed over the course of my six month sabbatical, when Maggie and I were practicing together almost every day, that her practice had begun to develop in altogether new ways: there was more precision, more energy, more fire. She began to hold postures longer. She went deeper into triangle pose, and warrior, and down dog. There was some new spirit of strong determination at the heart of her yoga practice.

I could see it, too, in our *mantra* and meditation sessions. I saw the budding of something fresh in Maggie, something I could not yet quite define. A quiet confidence had begun to emerge. A new little island of sanity—of what the psychotherapist in me would call "observing ego"—and of equanimity in the midst of her drive for excellence. There was a new center.

She felt it, too. She acknowledged as much to me one Friday evening before our *mantra* practice with Rudi: "I feel, after these sessions," she said, "as though I had landed back home on earth."

TYING THE PUPPY TO A POST

MANTRA AND THE UNIFIED MIND

*"tat savitur varenyam bargo devasya dhimahi dhyiyo yo nah
pracodayāt..."*

Rudi sat on his meditation cushion, across from Maggie and me, his
resonant baritone voice intoning the words of an ancient *mantra.*[1] His
big blue eyes were closed now, and as he methodically fingered
his black beads, the words of the *mantra* became one with his breath.

It was just past seven on a crisp October evening. Maggie, Rudi,
and I had gathered, as always, at Acorn Cottage, for our Friday night
mantra practice. (Jake was in Boston, setting himself up for his move
back to work at his law firm four days a week.) I let my eyes drift
around the room before closing them to begin my own practice. The
one big room was spare but orderly, paneled in now-bronzed pine,
and smelling of wood smoke. Books lined every wall, and a big har-
vest table sat in the middle of the room, surrounded by a dozen mismatched chairs. Candles burned everywhere tonight. At one side,
near the woodstove, Rudi had created an altar with a swath of Indian
silk. On it stood a brass statue of Shiva, a small wooden Virgin Mary, a
golden Burmese Buddha, and various small icons of Hindu gods.

61

There, in front of an icon of Krishna, stood the little bronze dancing Shiva that Jake had recently given him.

Rudi continued chanting his phrase: *"...bargo devasya dhimahi dhyiyo yo nah pracodayāt."*

Rudi was chanting the *gāyatrī-mantra*, perhaps the most famous mantra in the yoga tradition. "Let us contemplate the beautiful splendor of God, that he may inspire our vision."[2] The *gāyatrī-mantra* has been recited in exactly the same fashion for thousands of years.

I studied Rudi for a moment. He was such an unlikely-looking yogi. He was heavyset, with a big frame—punctuated by an undomesticated gray beard and a wild shock of salt-and-pepper hair. His features were big, but well-proportioned. (One friend said he looked like an aging Herman Melville—a Berkshire eccentric from an earlier age.)

Rudi lived as a kind of hermit at Acorn Cottage, and functioned as a caretaker for the new owners of the estate. Most people in Lenox thought of him as the kindly and generous local gardener. He was that, of course. But he was also a remarkable yogi. Rudi had lived in an ashram in India for fifteen years, and now he occupied himself quietly doing yard work and gardening for the great estates in the area—but also practicing, reading, and meditating. He had become a friend and mentor to me and now to my friends as well.

I looked at his face closely. Rudi looked younger than his sixty-two years. His skin was darkened by decades of wandering (sometimes more than half-naked) in the Berkshire Hills. Though furrowed, one could see the boy in the man's face: open to awe, sensitive, alert to life—an unusual combination of ruggedness and sweetness.

I was aware, too, of Maggie next to me. I found her physical presence reassuring. Maggie had drawn her prayer beads from their little velvet pouch, and had begun to finger them, eyes closed, silently intoning her prayer. Recently, Maggie had revealed to me that she never used the ancient yogic *mantra* Rudi had taught her—but, rather, a prayer from her Episcopal upbringing: "Hail Mary full of grace, the Lord is with thee..." When Maggie joined us a year earlier, she was surprised to find this old *mantra* from childhood still alive in her imagination. Rudi suggested that she stay with it.

I closed my eyes and began to intone the words of my own *mantra*, the one that Swami Kripalu, the founder of the contemporary Kripalu lineage, had taught the community many years earlier: *"Om namo bhagavate vasudevaya."* (Within the community, this *mantra* has often been loosely translated to mean, "Thy will, O Lord, not mine, be done." Its more precise meaning is, "I bow to you, O Lord, who are the very essence of divinity.")

Rudi, Maggie, and I had been practicing *mantra* together every Friday night for the past year. We had developed a kind of group rhythm: Rudi set up the altar, Maggie prepared the incense, and I said a ritual prayer from an ancient text. Practice and concentration deepened almost as soon as we took our accustomed places. Maggie sat in a chair by the window, next to me, and Rudi and I faced each other on meditation mats in front of the altar.

I began to move the coarse *rudraksha* seeds of my *mālā* through my fingers. This particular set of beads was auspicious. It had been blessed many years ago by Swami Kripalu at a ceremony at the Temple of Kayavarohan, his spiritual seat in India. I fancied that it was still infused with incense from the temple. I kept it with me always. On those frequent nights when I fell asleep saying *mantra*, I slept with it around my wrist.

Incense wafted up from the small altar now, and a deep stillness began to overtake us.

Mantra japa (literally, "recitation") is one of the oldest forms of meditation. The practice most likely grew out of the ritual recitation of the sacred Vedic texts in ancient India (well prior to 1500 BCE). The ritual repetition of these texts required the utmost concentration, since, as yoga scholar Georg Feuerstein tells us, "Each holy word had to be perfectly pronounced lest it should adversely influence the outcome of the sacrificial ritual."[3]

Rudi, Maggie, and I had discovered that we were all devotees of *mantra japa*—but each in our own fashion. Though Rudi's *mantra* was an ancient Vedic chant, its function was identical to my somewhat more recent yogic *mantra* and to Maggie's Christian prayer. We would each begin by voicing our *mantra* out loud. After a while, as our minds became still and absorbed in the vibration of the phrases, the sound spontaneously became more subtle and quiet. Eventually, the words became altogether inaudible. Our minds were then absorbed in the inner vibrations, to the exclusion of all other thoughts, and consciousness would often descend into a compelling stillness.

This movement from verbal recitation to mental recitation probably reenacts the history of the science of meditation itself. Yogis discovered that the *mantra* could be either voiced fully, or whispered. According to the *Yoga-Yājnavalkya* (a second century CE text on yoga), says Feuerstein, "Whispered recitation is a thousand times better than voiced *japa*; whereas mental recitation is a thousand times better than whispered *japa*."[4] *Sramanas* experimenting with meditation discovered a principle that appears over and over again in yogic science: The more subtle the object of awareness, the more one-pointed the mind has to become in order to apprehend it. (Whispered sound is more subtle than spoken sound. Silently repeated words are more subtle yet.) These subtle objects "draw the mind down," as Rudi would say.

These Friday evening sessions brought me routinely into delightful altered states: I would sense every cell in my body vibrating with the subtle *mantra*; I would often have the experience of bright light vibrating in my body; I could feel energy pulsing from the bodies of my friends in the room—and even inanimate objects. Sometimes I sensed that my body was shrinking to the size of a grain of sand, or expanding to the size of a Macy's Thanksgiving Day Parade balloon. At others, I would feel that I was all head and no body. After a while, time boundaries collapsed, and at any given moment it was difficult to know whether we had been practicing for three minutes or for an hour.

Rudi's little Zen alarm clock began to gong softly at eight fifteen. We had been immersed in our practice for almost an hour and fifteen minutes.

After the gong, Rudi, Maggie, and I sat for a while in silence. The pine boughs in the corner wafted a sweet scent through the room. I could feel the softness of Maggie's breath next to me, and the warmth of her body.

Finally, Rudi smiled, and, gesturing to the new bronze Shiva on his altar, said, "Thanks to Jake, we have a new guest. He's added extra voltage to my practice."

A famous yogic scripture encourages mantra recitation in the presence of Shiva. The *Linga-Pūrana* says (charmingly) that "recitation in one's home is good, but recitation in a cow pen is a hundred times better and on a riverbank a thousand times better yet." Furthermore, the text notes, "in the presence of Shiva, recitation is infinitely efficacious!"[5]

Maggie's face was set in a question, which she soon addressed to both of us: "Is your *mantra* kind of saying itself all the time in the background of your mind?"

She went on to observe that in the week since our last practice, she had found her *mantra* spontaneously intoning itself throughout the day. Rudi said that, yes, his, too, came and went.

Rudi explained: This spontaneous inner repetition of *mantra* is quite normal for practitioners. The more one says the *mantra*, the more it gets grooved into the synapses, neurons, dendrites of the nervous system. It becomes a kind of background "hum" in the brain, so that when we need its power—the power of a concentrated, equanimous mind—all we need do is to say one or two rounds, and the whole altered state can be automatically cued. We can always dip into the stream of *mantra* which is continuously being chanted in the deepest parts of the mind.

Maggie nodded her head and pondered his answer. She wondered out loud: "Do you think *mantras* have magical powers?"

Rudi laughed. "That's probably a myth. *Mantras* have power, sure. But it's just the power of concentrated mind."

Rudi spoke the view accepted by most yogis: *mantras* do not themselves have magical powers. This is not to say that they cannot be the doorway to supernormal powers. But any supernormal powers which arise through use of a *mantra*, arise simply because of its use as an object to focus the already existing powers of the mind.

And, as Rudi, Maggie, and I would soon discover, concentrated mind has surprising possibilities indeed.

DHĀRANĀ: TYING THE PUPPY TO A POST

In their exploration of *mantra* and ritual recitation, yogis stumbled onto the secret antidote to Puppy Mind: when the mind is focused repeatedly on one object, it naturally settles. Here, then, is a possible solution to the restlessness of ordinary mind! Tie the wild animal of the mind to an object. Tie the puppy to a post.

In *mantra* recitation, yogis were simply binding the mind to the object of sound, letting awareness come back again and again to this object of concentration. This was a momentous, though probably accidental, discovery.

When the puppy is tied to the post, he may at first object, and pull against the restraint. But eventually he will calm down, quiet, and settle. And so, too, the mind. Initially the mind wanders, adopting its characteristic discursive quality, but eventually it settles into the object.

As we have seen, early meditation experiences bring an almost immediate revelation of Puppy Mind. But persistent investigation inevitably brings an encounter with this first strategy for stilling the mind: find any stable, neutral, immovable object and lash the mind to it. Tie the mind to a *mantra*. Or an icon. Or tie the mind to the breath. Tie the mind to any ritual repetition—the *gāyatrī-mantra*, the Hail Mary, or any external or internal object. Bring attention back over and over again to this one object.

om namo bhagavate vasudevaya
om namo bhagavate vasudevaya
om namo bhagavate vasudevaya

When the mind settles into this phrase over and over again, it eventually gives up its battle and surrenders.

Yogis discovered that this capacity to concentrate is already an innate part of the mind. The experience of concentrated mind happens quite naturally in the course of everyday life. Perhaps we are at a symphony concert, and for several moments we are completely rapt by a beautiful melodic line in the violin—in, say, the haunting largo of a Bach violin concerto. Our attention goes out to meet the music, and stays right with it—not missing a single note. The mind is tied to the object.

Or perhaps we're at the beach. As we're lying facedown on our towel, we become fascinated with a small granite stone just in front of us on the sand. We examine it and explore it with our awareness. Our attention is drawn by the object, and, at least for a moment, settles into the object. We're riveted.

As Rudi, Maggie, and I had discovered in our mantra practice, these experiences of concentration bring with them certain very pleasing side effects. As the attention holds the object, it becomes very one-pointed—that is to say, it does not flicker and drift, but stays settled on the object. Distracting thoughts are blocked out by the one-pointedness, and mental restlessness abates. The stream of discursive thought narrows. This produces a slowing of the brain waves, a calming of the nervous system and the breath, and often the sense of bliss, well-being, happiness, and—in more advanced stages—rapture. The body and mind are suffused with a sense of calm abiding.

These commonly occurring experiences can arise either in relationship to an external object like the violin melody and the rock, or an internal object—say, a visualization, or a physical sensation like the breath.

The meditation traditions discovered that this normal capacity to focus attention can be intentionally cultivated, and that these everyday experiences of concentration can be profoundly deepened. Usually, in the *rāja-yoga* tradition, the practice of concentration begins with what is called "concentration in front," learning to focus attention upon an external object *(trātaka)*—like an icon or a candle. Then, the practitioner can move to an "internal object" like the breath.

When the mind settles into an object, we may begin to experience *dhāranā*, the first stage of meditation. *Dhāranā* is taken from the root *dhr*, which means to "hold fast." At this stage, says I. K. Taimni, one of the great modern commentators on the *Yoga-Sūtra*, the mind is "confined within a limited sphere defined by the object which is being concentrated upon. . . . The mind is *interned,* as it were, within a limited mental territory and has to be brought back immediately if it strays out."[6]

Patanjali begins the third chapter of his *Yoga-Sūtra* with his simple description of *dhāranā*.

Concentration locks consciousness on a single area. (3.1)

Patanjali tells us early on in the first part of the *Yoga-Sūtra* (1.39) that the distractions of mind are "subdued" through "meditative absorption in any desired object."

Yogis discovered a remarkable by-product of this absorption.

When the mind is highly concentrated or absorbed in an object, it becomes capable of "knowing" that object in a special way. This characteristic of concentrated mind also sometimes manifests itself in everyday life. One of the most powerful common experiences of this "knowing" happens during lovemaking. When making love, our attention often becomes rapt and one-pointed; the stream of attention narrows, and the rest of the world is obliterated; nothing exists but the beloved.

In these moments, something else may happen: our perceptual acuity may be enormously heightened. We're aware of every cell in this beloved body. We "know" the love object with all of our senses—smell, touch, taste. We may have a sense of direct connectedness to the essence of this person. Indeed, at a certain point we may feel One with the object of our love. We may experience a state of bliss, of intense happiness in conjunction with this sense of union with the beloved.

So sweet is this experience of union with a beloved that many of us at some point will organize our lives around it. We throw caution to the wind in order to have it. The bliss and rapture of this experience is the engine that drives much of our art and literature, and it is an endless source of human inquiry. For this reason, the image of the beloved is often used in yogic teaching to evoke our longing for these states. For some of us, it is the closest we get in ordinary experience to the experience of "yoga," or "union" with another object.

Profoundly unitive experience is not confined, of course, to lovemaking: we may experience variations of the state of *dhāranā* whenever our attention is drawn fully into any task—playing the flute, swimming laps, building a stone wall, making soup. When all of our mental faculties become involved in the task at hand, action and awareness are drawn together. The mind becomes one-pointed. Distractions fade away. The pressure of time fades. We feel profoundly absorbed.

In these normal experiences of highly focused attention, we have a taste of the fruits of attentional training at which all contemplative practice aims—a rudimentary introduction to the experience of "union." But even the deepest experiences of everyday concentration are only a small taste of the concentrated states yogis experience in meditation. Patanjali's teachings will show us that deep states of mental absorption differ from our everyday one-pointedness even more than those seemingly concentrated states differ from ordinary states of sheer inattention.

SECLUSION!

After our session of *mantra japa*, Maggie and I walked home together from Acorn Cottage—a two-mile trek through the woods. We stopped for a while at the cemetery across the street from our houses.

The night had turned cool, and we could see our breath in the distant light of the moon as we walked among the two-hundred-year-old gravestones. Orange and yellow leaves had begun to pile up around the base of the granite monuments. We stopped at the Winslow plot, and Maggie sat down on the edge of the enormous family obelisk, facing the Berkshire Hills. I sat in a pile of crunchy leaves and leaned against the gray stone base. Neither of us was in a hurry for this night to end.

Maggie took a deep breath of the crisp air. "Everything is more alive after these sessions, you know? Colors look brighter. Everything is so vivid."

Maggie's declaration was a sign that her concentration had indeed progressed into the state of *dhāranā*. As meditation practice progresses, we will experience seemingly miraculous moments, however brief, when our attention really does move toward the object in a steady stream. It is well-aimed, alert, and unwavering. At first, we experience these truly concentrated states for only seconds at a time.

But these seconds are powerful indeed. They permanently change the mind.

There is a simple reason for this. In those moments of unwavering concentration, the mind is free of craving and aversion. In those moments of *dhāranā*, we are conflict-free. The mind, at these times, is said to be "secluded" from the *kleshas*—detached from the pull of the afflictions.

Sramanas discovered that in these states, the very roots of suffering are subdued.

> **In their gross form, as patterns of consciousness, they [these causes of suffering] are subdued through meditative absorption.** (2.11)

The great Thai meditation teacher Mahasi Sayadaw explains precisely how this works:

> When the mind is concentrated on the object of meditation, it does not attach itself to other thoughts, nor does it desire pleasant sights and sounds. Pleasurable objects lose their power over the mind. Dispersion and dissipation cannot occur.... As concentration takes the mind to more subtle levels, deep interest arises. Rapture and joy fill one's being. This development frees the mind... for anger and aversion cannot coexist with joy.[7]

We respond powerfully to this experience. The self, accustomed to internal states of fragmentation, alienation, self-estrangement, and anxiety, will inevitably find a deep quality of refreshment in these experiences of seclusion—a reliable sense that everything really is OK.

Something fascinating is happening here—something not yet accounted for in our Western psychologies of transformation. In these highly concentrated moments, we experience precisely the kind of fulfillment for which we have been longing. I have said that the ego ideal organizes our longing to be held in the state of perfection which we have once known (however fleetingly). Well, here it is. Here is the state of perfection for which we have longed. Here is the state toward which the ego ideal has been driving us. In the Buddhist tradition, these states of seclusion are often called "the experiences of delight" for they reliably bring with them feelings of "bliss, rapture, contentment, harmony, and expansiveness."[8]

There is, in these secluded states, all the sweetness we could want. There is nowhere to go. Nothing more to do. For a few precious moments we can let go of the search for the Yellow-Crested Firebird. There is no more reaching. Why bother looking elsewhere? Paradise is right here.

These conflict-free moments temporarily suspend the forward motion into which the ego ideal perpetually drives us. We are home. From this settled state, it will be possible, later on, to investigate the more difficult and imperious inner representations of the ideal ego. Concentration practices like this lay the foundation for all the further work necessary to free us from the delusional aspects of the quest for the Firebird. For this reason, some form of concentrative practice is found in every spiritual tradition. This practice systematically promotes the development of equanimity, steadiness, and nonreactivity. Later on, as we shall see, these qualities become the all-important foundation for investigation of the very ways in which the illusory aspects of the self are constructed.

Patanjali and his colleagues and students explored all of this internal territory directly—using only the tools of their own highly developed minds and bodies. In recent years, however, human beings have brought new tools to bear on the same problems and questions that preoccupied Patanjali. We have brought the contemporary tools of neuroscience, which include things like EEGs and sophisticated functional MRIs. Careful research into the physiological effects of meditation and yoga have begun to confirm the discoveries of the yogis in contemporary, scientific terms—lending an interesting new layer of knowledge and experience to Patanjali's text.

We now know, for example, that as we enter highly concentrated states of meditation, the fundamental physiological components of stress and anxiety are profoundly altered. We know that "seclusion" promotes states of equanimity in several ways: The levels of stress hormones—epinephrine, norepinephrine, and cortisol—are ratcheted down, calming the nervous system. Heart rate and blood pressure drop and the breathing rate slows as the body's need for oxygen is reduced. Metabolism slows. Muscle tension is relaxed significantly. Brain wave activity begins to shift from the "beta waves" of regular wakefulness to somewhat longer, slower "alpha waves." We feel what it's like to inhabit a truly calm body.

New research shows, too, that meditation produces identifiable changes in the brain. Studies by a team of researchers including Richard Davidson and Jon Kabat-Zinn have shown (through EEG readings) that meditation increases activity in the areas of the brain associated with positive feelings, reduction in anxiety, and faster recovery after negative provocation.[9] Another study suggests that meditation not only changes the way the brain works in the short term, but very likely creates permanent changes that enhance equanimity.[10]

One of the first fruits of this physiological experience of equanimity is an enhanced sense of realness, and a heightened perception of the body. We can often have the experience during meditation, as Maggie did, of being more real than ever, more present.

The experience of "landing" in the present moment can be a powerful one. In ordinary states of consciousness, this is not available, because the mind is so constantly churned by its identification with the past and the future—and these thoughts of past and future are often associated with guilt, remorse, longing, anxiety, or fear. (These afflicted states then inevitably bring with them a surge of stress hormones, and an increase in heart rate, blood pressure, and breathing rate.)

When the mind is not afflicted with grasping or aversion, it does not lean forward or backward. For the moment, awareness is just here, just now. During our practice of *mantra*, for example, Maggie discovered that she had absolutely no negative self-talk—no lingering doubts about the meaning and purpose of her life.

But now we must confront an even more curious by-product of meditative absorption. We discover, as Maggie will, that as the mind becomes truly concentrated, it reveals wholly new powers. Concentration training brings us access to altogether new mental possibilities.

In concentrated states, the boundaries of the conscious mind are relaxed, and feelings, memories, and thoughts which had been just out of awareness become available to consciousness. There is an enhanced sense of receptivity to our own intuition and to the intelligence of our unconscious. We may come out of these concentrated states noticing that a thorny problem or question in our life has been solved—that we "know" how to proceed, even though we have not been thinking about it at all.

Contemporary science has shown that these concentrated states give us greater access to the right hemisphere of the brain, which is the sphere of symbols, dreams, and archetypes—where a special quality of nonrational, nonlinear wisdom resides. The discovery of this repository of wisdom can leave us with a deeper sense of trust in inner wisdom.

When the right hemisphere of the brain becomes dominant, we experience a loss of a linear sense of time. We may also experience distortions in the proprioceptive sense of the body, as I had during *mantra* practice. At these times, the body may seem to get very large, or very small, or parts of it disappear altogether.

William James, one of America's first psychologists, and a pioneer in the investigation of altered states of consciousness, said it over a hundred years ago: Our normal waking consciousness is separated only by the flimsiest of veils from vast, and unexplored worlds of consciousness.[11] In early states of meditation such as Maggie was experiencing, we step through the veil. We can be captivated by what we experience on the other side. There may be a sense of heightened spirituality and enchantment that accompanies the inevitable perceptual and time distortions that arise. We come back from meditative states knowing that we are somehow not separate from the realms of mind and matter that ordinarily seem to lie just out of reach.

Chapter 5

EXPLORERS OF INNER SPACE

MYSTERIES OF THE MIND

"Sit with me for a moment, can you?" Maggie asked. We had arrived back at her dark porch, and she seemed reluctant to let me go. She gestured to the two old Kennedy rockers on the wide front porch.

We sat for a while, rocking and looking at the moon, as Maggie told me what was on her mind. Some of it I had already guessed. Some of it astonished me.

Over the past year, Maggie had noticed a shift in both her yoga practice and her meditation practice. Although she had been a yoga student for well over a decade, Maggie had begun, just a year earlier, to take four or five classes a week instead of her usual one or two. She began to notice new wellsprings of stamina and energy. After years of half-hearted and intermittent practice, Maggie's daily practice had begun to gain momentum. She felt, I think correctly, that our Friday evening *mantra*/meditation sessions had contributed to this acceleration.

There were subtle changes in her body which she thought were a result of her increased practice, and she recounted these to me. But the changes that most puzzled her were the mental changes.

"About six months ago, I began entering deep states of concentration in yoga class," she said. "Almost like a trance. They were something new for me."

Maggie described the "trance" in detail: Her mind became quiet and focused. External distractions melted away. She was relaxed, even in difficult postures. She felt a sense of inner warmth and light. At times, the external world itself disappeared, and she was aware only of bare sensation, movement, and inner stillness. Time evaporated.

Her face changed as she spoke. Even in the moonlight, there was an intensity to the glow in her skin.

"The most astonishing thing is that this very same trance has started coming into my writing."

Maggie continued, with a skeptical sense of wonder in her voice: "I sit down at my desk. Close my eyes. I breathe—slowly and deeply. Almost like in postures. I may meditate, or hear my inner *mantra* chanting away. Then at a certain point—who knows how long—my eyes open and the writing begins. I don't even know where it comes from."

Maggie described how she found her writing in these times to be effortless. She had no sense of time as she sat at the computer. She felt a distinct sense of guidance—guidance from what she described as intuition, hunches, inner cues. "There is an inner knowing that is almost like a voice but not quite a voice.

"It was about nine months ago when I began to write the new novel. Remember? Well, from the beginning this novel came out in an entirely new voice. It wasn't really 'my' voice. I've never written like this before. I don't know *how* to write like this."

Maggie described how this experience of writing was different from all of her earlier experiences. "When I started writing, over twelve years ago," she said, "what I really needed was to hear my own voice." Her first novels helped her to define herself, she said. But this was different. It wasn't so much Her Voice now, as The Voice. It was no longer about self-expression, exactly, but about getting out of her own way enough to let this bigger, more mysterious voice come through.

Maggie described the difficulties of letting this voice emerge. It required patience, trust, and (she smiled) "ridiculous amounts of time." Sometimes her efforts were rewarded with unusual energy and creativity.

She leaned forward in the dark. "It scared me at first. It was so powerful. As if I were being taken over."

Maggie explained that in her earlier novels she had been "trying too hard—trying to control." This time, perhaps out of desperation, she had let go. And the floodgates of her mind opened.

Now Maggie told me something that stunned me. She had been secretive about the content of her book all along. I just assumed that it was how she preferred to work. Actually, she was nervous about telling me the whole truth.

It spilled out: Maggie was writing this book in the first person, in the voice, in fact, of a real person. Well, a real dead person. His name had been Duncan Gregor. I knew of him, just by chance, through a former writing teacher of mine: He had been a little appreciated but gifted English novelist in the 1930s and 1940s. His novels had long been out of print—indeed, were not even that well-known in his time.

I was stunned. How on earth, I wondered to myself, did Maggie find this particular voice? What was the attraction?

"It's as if I accidentally tuned in to a special frequency on a radio," Maggie continued. "And there he was. Duncan Gregor. God. Of all people. His voice. His personality. His whole drama.

"The writing begins as images in my mind sometimes—images that are almost like memories. Like something that actually happened to *me*."

The process, she said, was leading her into a novel that was more complex than anything she had written—way beyond what she imagined her skills to be. But she was just going with it. The characters that emerged were compelling, unsettling.

"At any rate, I just can't stop. I'm drawn on. I know I'm becoming even more peculiar than before. Which is saying quite a bit."

Then Maggie told me something she had shared with no one—indeed, something that she believed no one else on earth knew:

Georgiana Winslow might have had a brief affair with Duncan Gregor. Maggie had only pieced this together in the last year or so. About a year earlier, she found a collection of Gregor's novels, and two slim volumes of his poetry, in her grandmother's library. The books had been read repeatedly. Many of them had notes in the margins, in Georgiana's hand—as though Georgie had not only read them, but pored over them. In studying these volumes, and the marginal notes, Maggie had found a small section of love poetry that she convinced herself was dedicated to Georgiana. She believed the affair had happened in the summer of 1921, when Gregor visited Lenox.

Since the novel had begun to write itself, Maggie told me, she had been ransacking her attic for her grandmother's diaries. She hoped she might find some hints in them of the story that was unfolding in her own mind. Was it real? Was it imagination? Was it memory?

"I'm sure of one thing," she said. "This whole book process is somehow connected to yoga. The more I practice, the deeper it all goes."

We sat in silence together, enchanted momentarily by the moon, and the ripple of a breeze fluttering through the leaves strewn about the front lawn.

Maggie added a postscript. "I need your help. This voice. Is it inside me? Outside me? An angel? A muse? My own imagination?"

A final concern tumbled out. "I wonder," mused Maggie, as much to herself as to me, "if this preoccupation with inner worlds isn't separating me from real life."

She turned to me. "Do you think I'm OK?"

KOSHA: THE SUBTLE STRUCTURE
OF THE INTERIOR WORLD

Maggie's discovery parallels one of the central findings of the *sramanic* tradition: the mind has many layers. What we most often experience as "mind" is merely the surface of the mind (Puppy Mind), where the currents and eddies of discursive thought keep us persistently stirred up. Beneath this choppy surface, however, lie vast depths. In these depths, the mind lies still and transparent, with possibilities and powers which we in the West have imagined mostly in science fiction.

These possibilities of mind emerge hand in hand with the deeper stages of concentration and seclusion. As meditative skills develop, we will inevitably penetrate what the twentieth century Indian philosopher Aurobindo called Illumined Mind.[1] Some of the hallmarks of this Illumined Mind were already there in Maggie's new writing practice: the experience of mental absorption; the capacity to attend to a task with complete absence of self-consciousness; the evaporation of a sense of time; supernormal powers of perception; the experience of "knowing" an object of concentration without "thinking about it"; an ineffable sense of higher guidance.

Yogi *sramanas* found that when the mind is not afflicted, it manifests some surprising new powers. Sri Aurobindo and many other yoga philosophers have mapped these powers in detail. It is commonly acknowledged, among yoga adepts, for example, that Illumined Mind:

~ Transcends the ordinary space-time continuum
~ Can directly know the subtle interior life of all objects
~ Can directly know the mind itself
~ Perceives the interconnectedness of all created things
~ Perceives all the *potential* events in the universe in each aspect of the universe
~ Sees the identity of microcosm and macrocosm (This feature of Illumined Mind is called complementarity.)
~ Thoroughly knows the universal through the particular
~ Sees the whole field of mind and matter to be made of "the same stuff" (This feature of Illumined Mind is called coalescence.)

In chapter three of the *Yoga-Sūtra,* Patanjali describes many of these vast powers of Illumined Mind. His descriptions are much more colorful than the somewhat sanitized list above. He says, for example:

Focusing with perfect discipline on the powers of an elephant or other entities, one acquires those powers. (3.25)

The powers of an elephant!

Many of the *sūtras* of chapter three—from 3.16 through 3.56—are equally intriguing.

Being absorbed in the play of the mind's luminosity yields insight about the subtle, hidden, and distant.

Focusing with perfect discipline on the sun yields insight about the universe.

Focusing with perfect discipline on the moon yields insight about the stars' positions. (3.26–28)

Most of these powers make Maggie's connection to the mind of Duncan Gregor seem mundane by comparison. But we are once again getting ahead of our story. Later on I will examine in more detail precisely how—and why—these supernormal powers emerge and what Patanjali means by "perfect discipline."

All traditions that cultivate mental stillness inevitably discover the deeper reaches of the mind explored by Patanjali and his peers. Carlos Castaneda's teacher, Don Juan, discovers them when he "stops the world"—and his description of them is strikingly similar to Patanjali's. Thomas Merton discovers them when he empties himself for God.

Aurobindo's use of the term Illumined Mind is apt, because in all contemplative traditions its characteristics are associated with light, luminosity, and radiance. As Emerson said, "To the illumined mind, the whole world burns and sparkles with light." In the yoga tradition, Patanjali, when describing this mind, is moved to the use of uncharacteristically poetic language, referring to the mind as a highly polished "gemstone."

The Quakers describe in great detail their common experience of "the light within"; Kabalah, the mystical tradition of Judaism, describes "the divine light"; Shaker writings are full of references to the light generated through concentrated work and worship—and the Shakers' elegant artwork overflows with images of both inner and outer light.

The compelling luminosity of "deep mind" draws the seeker's awareness increasingly inward. In the yoga tradition, this increasing interiority is seen as a developmental imperative. All adult development moves from the external to the internal. That is to say, our experience of each stage of our "waking up" process is inevitably one of deepening interiority. We experience each newly developing level of consciousness as *interior* to the preceding level (not literally inside it, as the mind is not inside the brain, but interior to it, in an ineffable fashion).[2] Each new discovery of the interior light cultivates a strengthened capacity for what yogis called "introversion"—the drawing down of consciousness toward its source and origin. And who is not compelled to follow? Introversion draws us into an exploration of the compelling inner structures of the mind.

Yogis found that virtually everything that exists, seen and unseen, physical and mental, has a subtle inner structure. The *Yoga-Sūtra* is threaded with references to this subtle inner world. Patanjali frequently uses the Sanskrit word *sūkshma* to describe this subtlety.[3] In the yogic view, even subtle structures have subtle structures—layer upon layer of increasing subtlety which may at times seem to regress infinitely. Again, this view, so central to yoga, is common to many esoteric spiritual paths. A fourth century Jewish mystical text describes in great detail the seven layers of heaven leading to the rebuilt temple, and the final layer (composed of "wings") above which was "the Holy One."[4]

The best-known model of this view in the yoga traditions is the

Vedantic description of the *koshas,* or "sheaths." This model, developed in the early Upanishads, found the human self to be composed of increasingly subtle sheaths of matter, energy, intelligence, and consciousness. The physical body, which we normally think of as the substance of the self, is only the most gross and obvious layer of this reality. Beneath this gross sheath (or *anna-maya-kosha*—literally, the "sheath of food"), lie four increasingly subtle layers of reality. For practicing yogis, these "sheaths" were not a theory, but a reality they routinely experienced.

The *prāna-maya-kosha,* or "sheath of energy," lies interior to the physical body, as it were. This sheath of energy is the link between the physical body and the mind. The next subtle layer, or *mano-maya-kosha,* manifests the basic functions of mind. The next sheath, *vijnāna-maya-kosha,* is the subtle mind—the mind which includes higher, discriminating activities, such as discernment and wisdom. And underlying it all is the *ānanda-maya-kosha,* or sheath of bliss— the subtle, interior blueprint upon which all human psycho-mental structures are built.

The idea of sheaths first appeared over three thousand years ago, in the ancient *Taittiriya Upanishad,* and reappears in differing forms in almost every subsequent generation of yogis. Yogis' model-making has for the most part been driven not by the desire to create complicated metaphysical theories, but simply to map the actual experiences yogis had in meditation—the direct experience of increasingly subtle realms beneath the gross surface of everyday reality. *Sramanas* struggled to name and describe the multidimensional structure of the universe that they routinely discovered in their internal investigations. The maps they drew made it easier for those who followed them to orient themselves on their inward odysseys. On the whole, their maps are remarkably similar to one another, though some are much more detailed and elaborate than others.

Although Patanjali does not specify in the *Yoga-Sūtra,* it appears likely that he was influenced by the view of the ancient *Sāmkhya* philosophy, whose map of the subtle realms enumerated twenty-five categories of existence. Patanjali's interior map, in a significant modification from the ancient view, had twenty-six categories (or *tattvas*) since he includes in the *Yoga-Sūtra* a category called *īshvara,* or "the Lord." As we will see, his inclusion of "the Lord" will have a central and fateful impact on the way he sees practice and development unfolding in the process of yoga.

Yogis often described these subtle inner structures as "seeds," and found that there were seeds within seeds within seeds—regressing almost infinitely, like nested Russian dolls. Patanjali and his colleagues believed that freedom and the end of suffering come inevitably as the result of opening and knowing these seeds, systematically, carefully, one at a time. As each seed is opened and explored, our view of reality is profoundly altered, and we're drawn deeper, into the next seed. We cannot help ourselves. We want to know this subtle interior structure. We're drawn to it, as Maggie is in her writing practice, and feel it to be somehow more real than anything else. Paradoxically, in the view of the yogis, what seems *less* real (less gross, more subtle) is actually *more* real. Patanjali's map offers one of the world's most sophisticated tools for the navigation of this unknown inner territory.

The whole of life, in the view of the yogis, is a great journey in which we trace our way back through this territory, step-by-step— like following a magnificent river all the way back to its source. The source of this river is small, quiet, and subtle, but when we find it, we know we are home. When, after months of struggle and quest, Lewis and Clark discovered the source of the great Missouri, they stood awestruck in the face of this small eruption of water from the earth. They knew incontrovertibly that they had found it: home. The source. They wept. This journey of human life, too, is about tracing everything back to its source. And near the source of this great river, as we shall see, is *īshvara,* "the Lord."

Introversion is simply the process of knowing these increasingly subtle aspects of experience—and this knowing proceeds automatically as the mind quiets. As I have said earlier, the path of meditation is sometimes described as *marga,* the hunter's path. Since the dawn of time, human beings have been hunters—sitting, watching, waiting, and sometimes following the tracks of animals back to their nests. In Patanjali's view, through the practice of yoga we follow our own tracks—retracing our steps backward toward stillness *(nirodha),* cessation, and freedom.

As this natural process of introversion proceeds, it is quite common to experience the minds of other beings, just as Maggie had apparently begun to experience the mind of Duncan Gregor. From the perspective of yoga, this is not at all strange. Yogis' close investigations of "deep mind," yielded insights remarkably similar to those of contemporary physics. They found that objects that appear utterly separate and discrete are actually woven together in the fabric of space and time—and are in some ways profoundly entangled with one another. This entanglement includes even what we think of as "our minds."[5] They found, indeed, that the entire universe is more like an interwoven whole than like a collection of discrete objects—more like an enormous sweater. Tug on any corner of this sweater, and the whole of it is moved.

The nineteenth century English poet Francis Thompson said it eloquently:

> *All things by immortal power,*
> *Near and Far*
> *Hiddenly*
> *To each other linked are,*
> *That thou canst not stir a flower*
> *Without troubling of a star.*[6]

Through practice, we will discover that all minds are one—connected at the source. Just as whales communicate across vast distances of ocean, so, too, our minds—also connected as family—communicate across vast distances of time and space.

Maggie's great fear, when learning of the process of introversion, was that it would separate her from others in some way—that it would separate her from the world. In fact, the outcome of introversion is just the reverse. As we proceed to know our own minds and our own deeper reaches, we begin to know the subtle world of all so-called external objects as well, and we will finally discover that (as Patanjali will instruct us) "we are all made of the same stuff."

Part Three

KARMA
AND
CHARACTER:
THE BONDAGE
TO
PATTERN

CHARACTER traits are the etchings carved into the mind by one's thoughts and actions. The mind is a veritable museum of character traits, from this life as well as countless previous lifetimes. It can be said that one's personality is the sum total of his character traits, and that one's actions tend in a direction prompted by his mental store of character traits. That is why [yoga] places such importance on character-building principles. We can try to straighten out the tail of a dog, but the moment we let it go, it snaps back into its original shape.

—Swami Kripalu

Character is fate.

—Heraclitus

SUSAN

Filling the Hungry Heart

I FIRST met Susan Goldstein at the opening party for a new art exhibition in Lenox. I already knew her by reputation as a much sought after interior decorator, and I had often seen her picture on the society page of the local newspaper. In person, though, I found that she was not at all as I had imagined her. Susan was a short woman, now in her early forties, with a beautiful almond-shaped face, a full figure, and a curly shock of chestnut hair. Her big brown eyes were alert and happy (though I later discovered that they could take on a slightly hysterical look under stress). At the party, I found Susan to be outgoing, friendly, and very funny at times. I so enjoyed her company that I offhandedly invited her to come to one of my yoga classes at Kripalu.

Much to my surprise, she showed up. There she was, one sunny spring day, in the front row of my 4:15 yoga class, all smiles, wide-eyed and eager to please. (And also impossible not to notice: her stylish aquamarine leotard was arresting, and made her look, amidst the sea of modest brown and black outfits, as if she had dropped in from some wild Caribbean isle.)

At the beginning of class that day, I asked the students, as I often do, to close their eyes, and "investigate inside" for a few moments. "Notice the most prominent sensations in your body right now. How is it in there?"

The class quickly became quiet and introspective. Susan, however, sat with her eyes wide open, apparently investigating the ceiling, the artwork in the room, and the carpet. Susan couldn't seem to find "inside." It was, apparently, a world that did not yet quite exist for her—or, perhaps, a world that was too painful for her to enter.

After class, Susan and I chatted briefly. She told me that she had discovered yoga through her personal trainer at the gym, and said she sensed there was something important in it for her. In that moment she had no idea just how prescient this thought was.

Soon, Susan and her seemingly endless collection of designer leotards became a fixture in class, and within a few months, she and I had adopted each other. Susan was warmhearted and guileless—completely without pretense. I found her to be a very generous friend.

In the first year of our friendship, however, I thought Susan would drive me crazy in yoga classes. She had a mind-boggling lack of body awareness. The combination of her hunger to learn and her world-class awkwardness challenged me at every turn. Because Susan had so little sense of her own body, she relied on her notion that yoga postures were about taking something from the outside in. If she could only get the perfect posture *inside* her body—transpose it from the book, or from me, or from that woman next to her in the front row of the class. If she could just get *that*. Replicate that. Be that. She would be OK. She would have it.

Of course, yoga doesn't work that way. In really effective *hatha-yoga* practice, the postures need to grow from the inside out. So, the harder Susan tried, the more the authentic experience of postures eluded her. Several months into our joint project to teach her yoga, Susan seemed stuck in a kind of hell-realm. She was frustrated. Hungrier than ever. Defeated. As I got to know her better, I would come to discover that this was precisely the same hell-realm that Susan quietly created in almost every aspect of her life.

The yoga tradition developed an apt name for Susan's form of *duhkha*. They called it the realm of the Hungry Ghost.[1] The Hungry

Ghost has a large mouth and belly, but a very, very skinny neck. While her belly constantly cries out for food, she is destined to remain empty because only a limited amount of food can pass through that teeny little neck. This character is bound to a painful fate— everlasting and irremediable hunger.

The Hungry Ghost is a character style also recognized in the Western psychological tradition. In psychoanalytic circles it is sometimes referred to as the Oral Incorporative Character (a wonderfully evocative phrase). Those of us afflicted with this malady (and I say "us" because many of us have at least a touch of it) exhibit symptoms of a gnawing and secret hunger. Unlike ordinary hunger, however, this hunger is so desperate that we cannot actually bear to feel it. Rather than feel it, we "act it out"—that is to say, we unconsciously organize our life around trying to fill the belly that cannot be filled. Any object will do to fill the hole: Food. Shopping. Money. Love. Sex. Like Susan, we try to devour the objects of our longing, and thus to incorporate them.

It is sometimes said that the Oral Incorporative is a character who will swallow anything. In classic psychoanalytic literature, he is often seen as "over-indulged, optimistic, gullible, and passive" (egad), or "affable, chubby, and loquacious" (aacckk).[2] This character is said to be in conflict around "establishing healthy dependency needs." This is, perhaps, an understatement. The condition of Oral Incorporativity lends itself to high clinical drama, and so, when describing it, professors of psychiatry find dramatic images understandably irresistible. It is so much fun to bring up extreme cases like Spanish painter Goya's famous rendering of Saturn eating his babies, or the infamous cannibal-shrink of the American film world, Dr. Lecter—the psychopathic killer who eats his victims.

In comparison, Susan had only a mild case. And there it was— exhibiting itself right in the middle of my 4:15 yoga classes. Susan would stand wide-eyed, watching me demonstrate a posture, and then would keep her gaze fixed on me as she contorted her body into some surprising facsimile thereof. She would smile broadly at me, drinking me in with her eyes. This scared me. The Oral Incorporative patient in psychotherapy is famous for wanting to eat the therapist, absorb him, get him inside. The same, apparently, for the Oral Incorporative yoga student.

Early on in our work, Susan was simply not able to reference her own body's intelligence. At times it seemed, maddeningly, that there was no There there. What was not there, of course, (and what is by definition not there in this particular character style) was the Witness. I should say, rather, that the Witness was there only in seed form.

American writer and teacher Geneen Roth says that awareness (the seed of Witness) is "the process of joining yourself, of keeping yourself company while you live."[3] Exactly. The Hungry Ghost has not yet learned to keep herself company. At the core of the Oral Incorporative Character is a profound sense of aloneness—a kind of aloneness that seemingly cannot be assuaged. The Buddhist image of "ghost" is exactly right. The internal experience of this condition is one of emptiness and unrealness—a ghostly sense of existence. No There there. This alarming emptiness (that bottomless pit of a belly) drives us always to try to get someone or something inside to relieve it.

As Susan began to share with me the details of her story, it became clear that she had grown up in an entire household of Hungry Ghosts. Life at the Goldsteins was organized as a competition for scarce goods. And, of course, everything important was believed to be scarce: Food. Love. Money. Susan told me how her mother withheld food and love from her when she was a child. A telling example: Susan was not allowed to snack, even when she came home hungry after school. So she would routinely sneak into the kitchen under cover of night, stealthily open the refrigerator, then wolf down some purloined goods. "It's a wonder my parents didn't put a padlock on the damned fridge," Susan said.

Susan's family did not know how to be at ease with their own longings. And so longing itself became the enemy. The Goldsteins came to believe (unconsciously) that longing—if fully experienced—would annihilate them. Paradoxically, they did not actually feel their hunger or the longing that drove it. Their various "acting out" behaviors kept the feelings of longing split off and disavowed.

There was another painful side effect of the Goldsteins' problem: hungry and empty as they felt, no one in Susan's family believed they could be OK on their own. Not having come to terms with their own desperation, they could not develop appropriate feelings of autonomy. As a result, they were constantly involved in one another's business. And continue to be to this day. Cell phone technology turns out to be perfect for their condition, providing them with a network of intrusion that just never stops. At any hour of the day or night, Susan's mother might call: "Hi, Susan. What're you *doing*?" When I first met her, Susan felt powerless to stop this intrusion. It would soon become obvious to me why this was so.

As I came to know Susan better, I discovered an even darker side to the Hungry Ghost phenomenon. Susan and her whole family lived with a quiet self-loathing. They worked hard to cover up the extent of their hunger, to control it. But unconsciously they felt themselves to be monsters. They feared that, like Saturn, their hunger would destroy its own objects. They feared that if they let their hungers rip, they would destroy their own love objects. This fear led to a heightened objectification of people, places, and things, making these objects at one and the same time more attractive and more impossible to possess—the classic trap of the Oral Incorporative.

Because of these many unconscious and disavowed fears (and especially because of the conflicted relationship with autonomy), the Oral Incorporative Character has to modulate distance in relationships. If he cannot, then others will surely do it for him. Susan's husband, Phillip, for example, seemed to create this needed distance through the scheduling of endless business trips. Monica, their daughter, was in every extracurricular activity known to mankind. They liked being close to Susan—but not too close.

In the first year of our friendship, I myself experienced some fear in the face of Susan's hunger. At times, I felt compelled to keep her at a distance. Sometimes I would intentionally plan to include others in our get-togethers, in order to take some of the heat of her neediness off myself. This was her worst fear, of course, and paradoxically it was the reaction which her behavior was guaranteed to produce.

Happily, Susan's healthier instincts had brought her to the doorstep of several techniques that would help her to examine both her emptiness and her fullness. The first of these was Overeaters Anonymous, which she had discovered two years before I met her. Susan had already been quite successful in her OA program—and had been mostly free of compulsive eating for the past two years. And now, Susan was ready to add yoga to her repertoire. I knew through personal experience that the practices of yoga would help her. And the first step in this process would be an increasing awareness of the dynamics of her own hunger, and its relationship to her deeper, and perfectly healthy, longings.

THE ROOTS OF SUFFERING

HIJACKED!

"Steve?"

The phone had rung just as I was getting ready for my early morning walk to the cemetery to meet Jake. It was Susan. She sounded out of control.

"Can you come to the house?"

I was not prepared for the scene I found at Susan's house. Phillip, Susan's husband, had taken their daughter, Monica, to Belize on a birding trip, and had left Susan at home. The place was a mess—and this was utterly out of character for Susan, whose interior worlds were so well-ordered. I wondered: was Susan eating compulsively again?

I found Susan on the sunporch in her oversized terrycloth bathrobe. She was sitting in fetal position on a corner of the porch swing in a pool of sunshine with Boots the cat curled up next to her.

She lifted her head and looked at me, then covered her head with her arms. "Oh God. I cannot believe you're seeing me like this. Such a pretty picture."

I sat next to her, picked up Boots and put him in my lap.

"The hair. The bathrobe," said Susan, wincing.

"OK, Susan. Forget about that. I've seen it before."

"Oh, it's just so pathetic," she said, drawing a deep breath.

95

"I was in the parking lot of the Stop & Shop with a goddamned cart full of pastries. Last night. About eleven." Susan looked up. "Tried to call you on my cell. Tried to call my OA sponsor. Nobody home. Finally I just sat in my car and prayed."

After praying, Susan had found the strength to start the car and drive away. She had slept poorly. She'd just spoken with her OA sponsor when I arrived.

"I left the goddamned cart full of food right in the middle of the parking lot."

We looked at each other for a moment, and something between a grimace and a smile began to flicker across her face. The image was irresistible: A lonely shopping cart filled with Sara Lee cheesecakes and chocolate truffles. Fully paid for. Adrift in a sea of empty parking spaces.

Susan got up and walked to the window, looking out on her manicured garden.

"Just before I got into the car to drive to the Stop & Shop, I was standing right here. It was like standing on a bridge deciding whether or not to jump."

She turned back to me. "You know what I wanted? I just wanted complete oblivion. I wanted to get totally lost. In chocolate cake. To bury my face in it. To devour about ten of the fucking things."

Susan had been shaky for weeks. I had seen it. She had been distracted. Uncharacteristically irritable, and barely present. We had all noticed it at yoga the previous Saturday morning, when she had snapped angrily at Jake, and then at Maggie.

Susan was pacing now, rolling up the wide terrycloth collar to cradle her face. "There's something going on here that I just can't bear. Just can't bear."

Slowly the story spilled out. Susan had been home to spend some time with her parents in New York City. "I had another huge scene with them.

"I swear to God, Steve," she began, shaking her head. "We went out to eat. First of all, my mother showed up looking like Astor's pet horse. Ridiculously overdressed. Then it started. They're in my food. She's got her fork in my Cornish hen. He's got his fork in her profiteroles. She's criticizing my weight. They're all over Monica for not visiting them." Shaking her head now, as if in astonishment, she says, "I got up and stormed out.

"Shit. And I said some very nasty things."

She picked up Boots. "Steve, this is pathetic. They're old people now. But I just cannot bear who they are. Jesus, they're completely enmeshed."

Susan gave me a slightly desperate look and walked back to the window.

I understood *exactly* how Susan felt standing on that imaginary bridge: The aversion to being present with the moment. The craving for a different moment, a different mind-state.

Susan's voice began to shake. "I thought I was beginning to set better boundaries. To take better care of myself. All that yoga. Oh, Steve, I just feel so discouraged. I'm so fucked up."

She sat back down on the swing. "I hate my life. This is hell.

"And now I'm a middle-aged fat person. Just like them."

She flung herself back on the porch swing dramatically. "Shit. They won."

Susan was having a "multiple affliction attack": craving, aversion, and delusion all at the same time. Talk about the War With Reality. Susan was at war with everything. Her parents. Her career. (She confessed that she'd been refusing to return phone calls from clients for weeks.) She was at war with her own moment-to-moment experience of life. With pain. With sensation. She couldn't get comfortable in her own body.

THE CHAINING OF THOUGHTS, FEELINGS, IMPULSES, AND ACTIONS

Each of us has had an experience like Susan's—hijacked by a state of craving or aversion that we did not understand. These experiences can be bewildering. Susan felt captive—bound to an invisible chain of events which she could not fathom, much less control. She could see the pattern in this chain of events. She had lived it out over and over again. But she felt powerless over it. Alas, a good deal of human life is characterized by this sense of loss of control to patterns driven by inscrutable motivations. All systems of human transformation are compelled to notice this problem. St. Paul noticed it in his own life: "The good I would do, I do not; the evil I would not do, I do." Freud spent his life studying it, and postulated an unconscious, which is the repository of these hidden motivations.

How do yogis understand these unseen forces at work in the human experience? I had a personal reason for wanting to know. Not long before Susan's meltdown, I had had a food hijacking myself. It came with the same feelings of powerlessness as Susan's had. Since that event, I had begun to study precisely how these unconscious reactive dramas unfold—and particularly how Patanjali might work with such a situation. How would his view differ, say, from St. Paul's or Freud's—or Susan's OA sponsor?

I had been teaching a morning seminar in the Sunset Room at Kripalu—which is located just adjacent to the bakery. Almost every day the Kripalu bakery produces fresh bread, along with a steady stream of scones, muffins, and cookies. I was teaching a seminar on yoga philosophy when I became mildly aware of the scent of freshly baked banana muffins, wafting through the open windows of the room. "Banana muffins," I thought vaguely when I smelled them.

At the mid-morning break, I found myself in the bakery eating banana muffins. As we all stood around the bakery table and noshed on muffins, I said to myself, "How did I get here?" How did I end up in the bakery eating a muffin at ten thirty AM? For the previous three months, as an experiment, I had been observing a diet with no wheat or sweeteners. These muffins were loaded with both. At what point did I decide to ditch my diet? When was the moment of choice? Or was I choiceless in the matter? Am I powerless over muffins? Am I powerless over these dense states of craving and aversion? Do we have free will, or don't we?

It turns out that yogis adopted these hijackings—and the allied questions about will, power, and choice—as a central object of their intensive meditative scrutiny. They were compelled to. After all, these dense experiences of craving and aversion seem to be a universal part of human experience. The good I would do, I do not. The evil I would not do, I do. These moments of hijacking by afflictive forces seem to be central stumbling blocks to happiness.

The first response of the yogis was, as always, Stop the world! Stop the world. Quiet down. Investigate. Look closely. How, precisely, have we created this particular knot in our experience? This theme of self-investigation, self-scrutiny, self-study is perhaps the central theme in the great symphony of yoga. Patanjali and his peers were interested in investigating these states closely in their meditation laboratories—using themselves as the objects of their scrutiny. Quite by accident, they found that investigation itself is the first part of a highly effective strategy to attenuate these densely afflicted states. As we shall see, the power of investigation to expose and end suffering will become another major theme in Patanjali's work.

In the *Yoga-Sūtra,* Patanjali recommends the strategy of observing these afflicted states so closely that the hidden volitions that drive them are fully exposed.

> **In their subtle form, these causes of suffering are subdued by**
> **seeing where they come from. (2.10)**

When foiled by afflictive patterns, says Patanjali, trace them back to their source. Expose their roots!

So, yogis investigated. They looked carefully at the chain of events that leads to these dense states of craving and aversion. They saw precisely how craving and aversion first emerge in the stream of consciousness, and how they influence behavior. And finally, as Patanjali suggests, they were successful in tracing these tendencies in the mind back to their origins. While we may find this kind of scrutiny of motivation and behavior tedious, an understanding of it is an essential building block in Patanjali's eventual solution. Here's what the yogis discovered:

1. First of all, when they looked closely at our moment-by-moment experience, yogis discovered that "consciousness" (or *citta*) is constantly being bombarded by input from the so-called six sense doors. Whatever can this mean?

Let's begin with Patanjali's word *citta,* or consciousness. Patanjali's meaning of consciousness is rather different from ours. We tend to separate mind and body and think of "consciousness" as more akin to mind, or awareness. Patanjali did not do this. *Sramanic* investigations had found that consciousness includes both the mind and the body. So, for Patanjali (and in the language of our last chapter) consciousness, or *citta,* includes all the sheaths of human experience, all *koshas*—the physical body, the energy body, the mental bodies, even the most subtle bliss body.

And what did he mean by "six sense doors"? The six sense doors include the five senses that we all recognize, of course—taste, touch, smell, sight, and sound. Consciousness is constantly being bombarded by sensations from these senses—bombarded by smell of the muffin; by beautiful sights; by difficult sounds; by painful touch; by delightful tastes. We can see that. But what we may not immediately see is that these "inputs" also include a sixth class of inputs called "thoughts"—which include thoughts, memories, and feelings. Every one of us has over sixty thousand thoughts a day,[1] and it turns out that consciousness treats each one of these just like it does a bit of sensory input. Consciousness treats a thought just the same way it treats a smell. So in the meditation traditions these thoughts are referred to as "sixth sense doors."

In any moment, then, consciousness is being zapped by multiple sensations, thoughts, feelings, and memories. Each one of these zaps (when an input—which is sometimes called an "object"—comes in contact with a sense door) involves a complicated chain of events in the mind-body.

2. The yogi's next discovery is astonishing—and completely supported by contemporary neuroscience. Consciousness is constantly bombarded by input, as I have said. Then, in a rapid-fire sequence, consciousness *evaluates* each of these sensory inputs—each one of these zaps. Each input is first "recognized," and then it is "appraised" as pleasant, unpleasant, or neutral. Every single one!

This is a mind-altering discovery. Consciousness, simply doing its job, recognizes and evaluates each and every input—determining it to be pleasant, unpleasant, or neutral. So, as we sit hunched over the computer: Ah! Sensation in my right hip! Unpleasant. Or as we drive down a country road, and come upon an outlook onto a lovely distant lake. Oh! Vision of beauty. Pleasant! Each of the sixty thousand thoughts is appraised. Cowabunga. All input from the six sense doors is appraised: Pleasant. Unpleasant. Neutral.

3. Now another critical function of consciousness comes into play: after "recognition" and "appraisal," consciousness reacts. Yogis found that consciousness *reacts* to each appraisal with attraction or aversion (or neutrality). To a stimulus it appraises as pleasant, consciousness reacts with attraction. To a stimulus it appraises as unpleasant, consciousness reacts with aversion. And to each stimulus it appraises as neutral, with neutrality. Ah! This sensation in my hip is most unpleasant. I hate it. Aversion arises. Or, Gee, that lake scene is lovely. I like it very much. Craving arises.

4. So, first appraisal: pleasant, unpleasant, neutral. Then impulse: craving, aversion, neutrality. Now, inevitably, comes the final link on this chain: action. In the case of aversion, we push away the object: I unconsciously shift my body in the office chair, and readjust my posture, attempting to alleviate the sensation (unpleasant!) to which I have now become averse. Or, in the case of craving, we reach for the object. I slow down the car, and pull into the outlook (pleasant!) so

that I can drink in the lake scene to which I have become so immediately attracted.

Appraisal. Impulse. Action. This same process happens a gazillion times a day. As it turns out, of course, we are mostly oblivious of it. We have highly patterned and conditioned ways of handling all of this activity. Indeed, if we did not, it would overwhelm our capacity to function. However, as we shall see, the practice of meditation sharpens our awareness of this ordinarily subthreshold process. As mind becomes more concentrated, subtle internal events that were previously out of our perceptual range now become identifiable. We begin to notice that living in a human body is like living in an ongoing light, sound, smell, touch, taste show—with thousands of complicated reactions going on at every moment. No wonder we have Puppy Mind.

Cognitive psychologists, using sophisticated brain-mapping techniques, have observed the same sequence of events noticed by yogis. Just after the stimulation of one of the six sense doors, say psychologists, there comes a rapid-fire "appraisal" of that stimulus in terms of "affective tone" (whether it feels good, bad, or indifferent). Psychologists call this "hedonic appraisal." It is not yet a "feeling," but just an immediate evaluation of a perceptual stimulus. Immediately following hedonic appraisal, another discrete process happens—the so-called hedonic impulse. This is the impulse to approach the pleasant, or to avoid the unpleasant. This entire sequence takes place in nanoseconds—so quickly that it is entirely out of our ordinary perceptual range. As a result, these subthreshold reactions may imperiously drive us to actions we do not understand—an unconscious chaining of events of which we see only the last link in the chain: action. These contemporary discoveries support the ancient yogic views of the process with remarkable precision.

My muffin moment, of course, followed precisely the chain of events described by yogis: Appraisal. Impulse. Action. An object came into contact with my sense door: smell of muffin. I recognized the object. Muffin! I immediately had a pleasurable sensation in my consciousness. A simple biochemical event. And on the heels of this sensation, I had a reaction to it: I like it! This reaction (pleasurable!) was immediately converted into an impulse for action, as my energy was impelled toward the object. A thought formed out of the re-action, "I want the muffin." And finally, of course—the action. Suddenly, I'm in the bakery, eating. Yum.

Yes, yum. But what of the consequences? Did I really want the muffin? Need the muffin? Was it a discerning choice? Yogis found that this chain of events—appraisal, impulse, action—runs our lives more than we would like to believe. They found, too, that it often leads to suffering, because we make poor choices while caught up un-consciously in its thrall. Or rather, we make no choices at all.

Yogis studied this chaining intensely. Was there a strategy that could successfully interrupt this chaining of thought, reaction, action? Could suffering be *systematically ended*? They kept returning again and again to their meditation laboratories—looking for the key.

In fact, they discovered a remarkably simple strategy for breaking the chain. Here it is: Even though we tend to collapse the steps in the sequence—appraisal, impulse, action—yogis discovered that there really are three discrete "mind-moments" here. Three completely dif-ferent, and separate, events. A highly trained awareness can perceive them each in sequence, and thus can intervene, so that action does not tumble inexorably out of reaction, like the falling of so many dominoes.

This discovery is important: while "appraisal" is an inevitable re-sponse to sense-door stimulation, the impulse to approach or avoid is not inevitable. It is highly influenced by our habits and patterns. It is conditioned by our experience. It can, therefore, be de-conditioned. Impulse can thereby be de-linked from appraisal.

Action, too, then, can likewise be de-linked from impulse.

To the discerning and highly trained awareness, the chain can be broken either between appraisal and impulse, or between impulse and action. Of course, this breaking of the chain requires tremendous familiarity with the process of chaining, and moment-by-moment presence with the process—something most of us have not developed. Instead, we have the Stop & Shop moment, and the banana muffin moment.

Naturally, beginners focus more on de-linking action from impulse. The task here is to acknowledge, experience, and bear the experience of the impulse without taking it into action. Feeling the hunger for the muffin, but not eating the muffin. More advanced meditators, however, can actually de-link impulse from appraisal— becoming aware earlier and earlier of the impulse as it arises and muting the intensity of the impulse itself.

It is important to understand what a radical discovery this is: *it is possible to experience pain and pleasure without being unconsciously driven to act upon them.* Desire itself is not the problem. Attraction is not the problem. Aversion is not the problem.

When awareness is brought to bear on the visceral, biochemical experience of attraction and aversion, the chain can be broken, and a driven, unconscious reaction can be avoided. Here's the brilliant strategy discovered by yogis: freedom comes through familiarizing ourselves with this chain of events—and eventually recognizing it as it is happening. This, obviously, requires a careful training of attention. And this training is precisely the role of meditation.

So, Patanjali's advice? Pay close attention. Learn to be present for experience.

Close examination of the chaining of thoughts, reactions, and actions led yogis to another important discovery that concerns our relationship to the object world—a quite remarkable discovery I will introduce here briefly, and then expand upon once our understanding of Patanjali's method is fleshed out a bit more. Again, we can experience this discovery in the muffin moment. After we devour the muffin, we discover something puzzling. The muffin (the object) doesn't really completely satisfy me. I want more. Even though I'm not really hungry (I had plenty of breakfast just an hour and a half ago) nonetheless I want, want, crave, crave. Where's the muffin? It's gone! Now I experience devouring the muffin as *the loss of the muffin.* It's not as though I now *have* it, possess it, *am* it. I've lost it. This pain on the loss of the object, this craving for more all creates another, and more subtle, loop of *duhkha*.

At some point in our own personal investigation of *duhkha*, we will begin to suspect that the relationship between objects (having them or not having them) and happiness is much more complex than we thought. The delusion that it is objects—people, places, things—that are the source of happiness is a subtle distortion in perception with which we will eventually have to grapple. As we shall see in future chapters, yogis found that it is precisely this confusion around objects that is an "erroneous belief" that keeps us at right angles to life.

PAIN OR SUFFERING?

Several days after her near slip, Susan and I were investigating her experience together, looking at each moment in the chain of events that had led to the parking lot.

"Go back to the moment just before you left for Stop & Shop," I suggested. "You were standing by the window in your sunroom. You wanted to jump off the bridge. What were you feeling?"

"I wanted oblivion. I just wanted to get lost."

She looked up for a moment and studied my face. "And, actually, I still do. Right this minute."

There was a moment of quiet. It had begun to rain, and the only sound now was a steady plinking of drops on the metal roof of Susan's sunporch.

Susan was breathing fast, almost panting. For a moment she seemed overwhelmed by feelings. But she was staying with them—not moving away from the feelings, but toward them. Into them. Investigating them. The chain was breaking apart.

Finally, Susan took a deep breath and settled back into her chair. She sat staring out at the birdfeeder. "You know," she said finally, "no matter how painful it is, it's a relief just to feel it."

Yogis discovered that the possibility of freedom from impulsive, driven behavior exists in every single mind moment—but only through the practice of being present for experience. This requires that we familiarize ourselves with precisely how thoughts, feelings, and impulses arise in the stream of experience. This is, indeed, precisely what meditation is for. In fact, one word for meditation in Tibetan means familiarization. Meditation is a process of getting to know the mind. It turns out, as we shall see, that this "knowing" itself interrupts these chains of reactive thoughts and feelings.

We are freed from the prison of reactivity only when we can begin to be present for the sensations in the body that result from the stimulus of thoughts or senses. And in order to know the sensation before the whole chain of reaction and action has started, we must hone a subtle awareness at the level of the body.

Mere presence interrupts the "chaining" of thoughts and feelings as they tumble toward action. If, for example, as I was teaching my class that morning, I had noticed, "Ah, pleasurable sensation in the body—muffin," and felt that sensation fully, observed, allowed it to be present—the attraction would have passed away eventually. The chain would have been broken right there. And I could have chosen more consciously. The stage would have been set for me to explore my reality. How is it, really, right now, in my body? What are these sensations like? What does this craving feel like? I could then have asked the all-important question: Do I want to choose the muffin? Or not?

In their subtle form, these causes of suffering are subdued by tracing them back to their inception," says Patanjali. Here, then, is the winning strategy discovered by strivers:

~ Train awareness to familiarize itself with the internal chain of events leading to the arising of craving and clinging, aversion and hatred.
~ Let awareness penetrate the experience of craving and aversion in its visceral fullness.
~ In the light of awareness, the experience of attraction or aversion is revealed to be permeable—not dense and solid as we first experience it, but fleeting, impermanent, like the weather.
~ Finally, exposed to the light of the Witness, craving and aversion evaporate.

In her experience with her near slip, Susan had come to understand a central discovery of the yoga tradition: pain that is not resisted begins to soften. "No matter how painful it is," said Susan, "it's a relief just to feel it." As our reactivity softens, we see a subtle distinction between pain and suffering. We each have pain. It comes with the territory of being a human being. And, pain that is fully experienced is, of course, painful. But suffering—*duhkha*—is something different. *Duhkha* is the *resistance* to that pain. *Duhkha* is the reactivity to that pain. *Duhkha* is what Chögyam Trungpa Rinpoche called "the pain of pain." As the Buddhist teacher Sylvia Boorstein says, "Pain is inevitable. Suffering is optional."[2] For now, Susan was just learning to be with "bare pain." It was hard. But it was OK. "A relief to feel it," even. She had broken the chain between impulse and action.

This was a wonderful moment. Suffering is created by wanting things to be other than they are. It's that simple. As soon as we relax into how they are—as soon as we stop the War With Reality—happiness and sweetness begin to subtly arise, dusting our insides not with craving and aversion, but with equanimity. This miracle can happen even in the midst of the most difficult of human vicissitudes.

Repeated exploration of reality reveals the incontrovertible fact that it is the attempt to hold on, or to push away the flow of life that creates *duhkha. The reactive mind is itself the source of suffering*. Pleasure can be fully experienced, but must be allowed its impermanent nature. It will pass away. "Kiss the joy as it flies," said William Blake. Pain can be fully experienced. But when we resist it, react to it, push it away, we simply get an intensified version of pain. We get both the pain, and the "pain of pain." The reaction to the pain.

Putting this discovery into practice will require us not to tune out our experience of attraction and aversion, but to tune it in even more deeply. As the Tibetan meditation tradition exhorts us, we will have to "stare into" the bare experience of the discomfort. If we could learn to train our awareness enough to acknowledge sensations as they arise, to experience them fully and to bear them, we would no longer be bound by our conditioned responses.

Susan and I, in the hours after her near slip, had a lesson in understanding Patanjali's view of hidden motivation, volition, and action. But we had only begun to scratch the surface of his surprising teaching. There would be more lessons to come.

Chapter 7

THE LAWS OF CAUSE AND EFFECT

THE POWER OF DISAVOWED PATTERNS

"I don't know, it's like I get overtaken by an alien force or something," said Jake.

I looked at Susan and she lifted her eyebrows in response (thinking, perhaps, of her own alien forces). Jake was describing his latest relationship disaster—and truly one did not know whether to laugh or cry. This pattern was so predictable. And though he could see it to some extent, he seemed powerless to change it.

Maggie was hosting Rudi, Susan, Jake, Kate, and me for lunch several weeks after Susan's near meltdown. We had just finished a meal of vegetable lasagna, Caesar salad, and warm garlic bread, and were still sitting at the table.

It was a stormy afternoon in early November. The yards and walks were tossed with leaves and small branches—which were now being blown about by gusts of chill wind. Jake had started two fires—one in Maggie's ornate Tudor dining room, and one in the big front parlor. From the leaded-glass windows of Maggie's dining room, I could see the winds whip yellow leaves around the yard of my own white cottage next door.

As we settled in, the storm began to grow in ferocity. It felt cozy being together in Maggie's damask-draped rooms—like being se-creted in a time warp. The fires were roaring.

Jake continued, chuckling to himself at the absurdity of his rela-tionship pattern. "At times like this my mom used to say, 'The Devil is on you, Jake O'Brien.' I guess she was right."

"I'm curious, Jake," said Rudi, rubbing his head with his big hand. "You've mentioned this before—that sometimes you feel taken over by this alien force."

Jake cocked his head. "Yeah."

"What happens?" Rudi queried.

Susan and I exchanged glances again. Jake was toast. Once Rudi got hold of any line of thinking with even a whiff of delusion, he was like a dog with a bone. He couldn't help himself. He would hunt it down, expose it. Rudi taught not by giving answers, but by asking questions (just as he had been taught by his teacher in India). Rudi was a master in the yogic art of investigation.

Jake thought for a moment, then gave more detail. "When I'm be-ginning to get close to a woman, it's always the same damned thing. It starts out with this bonfire of great sex. And closeness. Staring into each other's eyes. Taking baths together. Maybe we're together three, four months. Then one morning, out of the blue, I wake up curled on the far side of the bed. Wham. It's over. Suddenly she doesn't look so good anymore. I wanna just run like hell."

"Then what?" countered Rudi.

Jake brushed his hand through his thick hair, uttered a sigh, and said, "I figure out a way to piss her off. She leaves. I feel relieved no end. A month later, two months later I start to feel lonely again. I start to prowl.

"Caroline suffered through it longer than anyone," Jake said, now leaning forward on the table, head hung, and supporting himself on his elbows. "Of course, I did spend most of this past summer sleeping up in the woods, and not with her," he said pensively.

And then, almost absentmindedly, "She came up with a name for me. 'Desperado.'"

He lifted his head to look at Maggie, afraid she might not get the reference. "You know that song. 'Desperado, come down from your fences.'"

Maggie nodded. We all knew "Desperado."

"So, Jake. Is this Desperado thing accurate? Is Desperado *you*? I mean, is he the real you?" Rudi asked, looking intently at Jake.

"You missed the point, Rudi," said Jake, dropping his head in exasperation. "He's not me at all. I don't *want* him to show up. I'm taken over. Like I said, I feel hijacked. No different from Susan and her damned Sara Lee."

"But Jake," said Susan, now piling on, "it seems like your girlfriends think Desperado *is* the real you. I mean, it's the one they leave, isn't it?"

Jake got up now, and started pacing. "No." His voice had an edge. "The *real* me wants a relationship. Right up to that point. And Desperado comes in and takes over, and that's that. I'm, like, powerless when it begins to happen."

Susan was shaking her head in sympathy with Jake's dilemma. So was I. For the next forty-five minutes, we talked about the oh-so-common human experience of being taken over by these alien sub-personalities—parts of ourselves that we think of as Not Me.

It took little effort for any of us to discover these alien, intrusive parts. And it was, for a while, very entertaining to name them:

"The Inner Pulitzer Prize Winner," said Maggie. "She won't let me relax, drives me relentlessly to dig deeper, do better. A kind of perfectionist, I guess. The damned woman gives me no peace. I'd like to get rid of her, frankly."

"The Food Pig," said Susan. "The part of myself that wants to find oblivion in food. Dive into chocolate cake. Whipped cream, sour cream frosting. She comes out of the blue, and when she invades, most evenings around nine, there is no peace in my mind."

"Miss Phony," said Kate. (I couldn't believe she was admitting to this.) "Sometimes I hear myself making up the most outrageous things to make myself look better. To live up to the family image, I guess. Sometimes I just lie. I see myself, and I mean I'm embarrassed, but I continue to do it anyway."

"Mr. Boring-Ass Scholar," I said. "This guy is so serious and strait-laced that he's got to be some kind of Calvinist hangover from my Presbyterian background. He's all fear. I can tell when he's out because people roll their eyes and try to change whatever subject I might be holding forth on. He's an embarrassing windbag."

"The Wanderer," said Rudi. "Off and on through the years he'll come on and drag me away. He wants to get up and go. Like Clint Eastwood on a horse, just heading out over the hills. Like James Dean on a road trip. Those times all I can do is spend as much time as possible in the woods."

"The Devil," said Jake. "Like the one my mom invented for me. But I started making it come true. The Devil comes on me and I want to be *so so* bad. Actually, I love it. I really get into being bad. Surrender to the Devil can be very cool."

"Ms. Catastrophe," said Susan. "This is another one I have where it just invades. I go totally into catastrophizing. Everything's going to hell. I'm going to be a bag lady before the week is out. Sometimes I can't shake her at all. My analyst says I'm a hysteric—whatever that is."

"The Big Hurt," said Kate. "My sister coined that phrase. She says I get taken over by this victim thing. I feel hurt. So hurt. When it comes on, I can't let it go. I feel like such a baby. Like I should be sucking my thumb. It's mortifying."

"But now I have another question," said Rudi. "Are we sure these personalities are *not us*? I mean, come on. If these are tunes, then we know them by heart, don't we?"

Once again, Rudi got Jake in his sights. "Jake, can you identify the pattern of Desperado from the very first moment when it's triggered? For example, when you first see the object of your next bonfire of love. Then what happens? See if you can trace this, step-by-step from the trigger all the way through to that inevitable final scene. Diagram it for us, draw it like stage instructions for a character."

"Huh?" said Jake.

"Well," said Rudi, thinking. "Visualize, perhaps, Tweetie Bird, goading Sylvester the Cat. For the gazillionth time, Sylvester takes the bait and ends up flattened by a big iron skillet. An entirely predictable pattern."

Jake just looked back at Rudi with a vacant stare. I thought I saw Jake's anger beginning to ignite.

Susan understood where Rudi was going, and saving Jake, shared "Food Pig." She began with the trigger of a television commercial for strawberry cheesecake coming right after a disastrous telephone call with her father. And she followed it step-by-step all the way through a period of recovery in her twelve-step program. Susan was able to spell out the steps in sequence with astonishing detail and precision, just as she had with me after her slip. In fact, today she did it with some glee. (I noticed the change in her tone about recovery—from the suffering she felt after her slip, to her sense of confidence in helping to teach Jake. This was a small sign of liberation.)

The conclusion was obvious: each pattern is composed of a complicated skein of stimulus, trigger, reaction, action, repetition, pattern.

We sat in silence for a while as the fires crackled in the background. It was clear that for each of us, this chain of events, however complex, was remarkably predictable.

Are we run by these patterns? Are they us?

What we were trying to unpack was a central and radical component of the yogic view, and we would spend the next hour investigating it.

Just as the deep roots of craving and aversion normally lie beyond our awareness, yet deeply shape our behavior, so too do these more complex skeins of stimulus, trigger, reaction, action. In fact, we live most of our lives in thrall to this chain of events.

Yogis discovered that consciousness is dominated by highly conditioned patterns of reactivity—patterns that are deeply grooved, and very difficult to change once established. And as Freud also discovered, the power of these patterns is mostly denied in daily life.

Understanding the power of these patterns brings a new wrinkle into our strategy. The practice of being present for experience which we examined in the previous chapter is perhaps more challenging than we thought—*because, as yogis discovered, this moment does not stand alone. This moment is highly conditioned by previous moments.*

Yogis realized that in order to train awareness to remain present, we would have to deconstruct these unconscious patterns. And to do that, we would have to understand *precisely* how they are created, how they are built piece by piece. In the language of our last chapter, we would have to *familiarize* ourselves with them. Yogis studied these patterns carefully, and through this study came up with a highly nuanced understanding of the laws of cause and effect—known as the laws of *karma*, or, literally, the laws of action.

These laws of cause and effect are the keystone of Patanjali's understanding of suffering. Every action (and this includes every thought) conditions the mind. Every action motivated by craving or aversion conditions the mind to more of the same. And we cannot fully understand the challenge of being present with experience, of cutting the chain of affliction, without understanding how this works.

SAMSKĀRA: SUBLIMINAL ACTIVATOR

Every action based on craving or aversion leaves a subliminal impression on the mind. These impressions are called *samskāras*, or, literally, "subliminal activators." Yogis sometimes think of these subliminal activators as being pressed into the "hot wax of the mind." So, for example, my craving for the muffin was deeply pressed into the subtle parts of my mind and body.

Samskāras are like little tracks, little vectors, little ruts in the muddy road. The next time the car travels that road, these muddy ruts will have hardened into permanent fixtures, and the car wheels will want to slide into them. Indeed, it's easier to steer right into them than to try to avoid them.

Yogis, not having cars, have used a different metaphor. *Samskāras* are traditionally described as "seeds." When *samskāric* seeds ripen, they release a subtle new volitional impulse into the mind-stream. These seeds are powerful unconscious motivators of action which lead to an unconscious repetition of old actions. In this way, the self is bound by its previous actions. Or, as the Buddha said it, "We are heirs of our actions."[1]

Samskāras remain latent in the mind until they are triggered by some life circumstance into releasing their "fruit." My first banana muffin planted a seed which ripened when the next batch of muffins arrived. After a year or so, that one small seed had grown into a very sizeable tree, with hundreds of new seeds of its own. This process of ripening and multiplication of seeds is sometimes called "proliferation."

The moment of freedom that we examined in the last section (the muffin moment) now becomes more complex. The reactivity of the mind to any stimulus is highly conditioned by past experience. We have to add a new vector, a new variable, into our diagram—the vector of conditioning.

115

Over time certain objects and experiences in our lives become charged with memories and associations—both negative and positive. Many of these are entirely unconscious. In my relationship with muffins, what had initially been a conscious act of choice, soon became highly conditioned. This unconscious conditioning can trigger chain reactions in the body which detonate an intense series of actions and reactions—either positive or negative. Reactions to reactions may go on intensifying long before they are detected by the unattuned mind. And that series of reactions becomes part of our perception of the external object.

Patanjali comments on this process:

People perceive the same object differently, as each person's perception follows a separate path from another's. (4.15)

Our conditioned awareness begins to interact with external reality—modifying what we think of as "objective reality" through the complicated history we have with it.

Susan's reaction to chocolate cake is not really so much about the chocolate cake itself, as about her own history with it—the patterning of her own brain chemistry. Each of us has complex histories of attraction and aversion that ignite the chaining of appraisal, impulse, action in ways that seem beyond our control—and that appear to give the object itself enormous power over us. We each have certain sexual histories that result in powerful repetitive sexual fantasies; we have aversions to certain kinds of people or behaviors—even the brief appearance of which can drive us wild with antipathy; we have inexplicable attractions to objects whose roots lie deeply buried in our past.

In fact, as we will come to discover, our own perception of the so-called object world is not objective at all. It is deeply distorted by our history with it. We will also discover that in the fast pace of our lives, the line between object and subject becomes blurred, because much of what we think of as our relationship with an object is really about our relationship with our own neuro-biochemical patterning.

"We own our actions," said the Buddha. "We inherit our actions, we are our actions."

The yogic view of *karma* is not even remotely like our popular, Westernized concepts of it. Influenced by our mainstream views of karma, we may make it up, for example (only half jokingly) that if we tease our vulnerable younger sister we'll spend our next lifetime as a guinea pig kept in a cage by a sadistic ten-year-old boy. No. The laws of cause and effect so clearly enunciated by Patanjali have more in common with the laws of contemporary physics—which portray the way in which all effects have a cause and all causes have an effect. At the heart of Patanjali's view is a radical insight: all actions in the world are interrelated and interdependent. We create our world through our actions. Every act has the power to change the entire field of mind and matter. The universe is like one big sweater, and each one of us is knit into it. When you tug on any part of it the whole sweater moves.

The laws of *karma* account, too, for the fact that our actions are based on our perceptions—and our perceptions have been shaped by our earlier actions. It's all a great loop. We own, inherit, and are shaped by our actions. And our actions profoundly influence our perceptions of the world in which we live. We create our minds, and then our minds create us. It's as simple—and as complicated—as that.

WE SEE THE WORLD NOT AS IT IS, BUT AS WE ARE

Our collective inquiry had now brought the group squarely to the central problem with which yogis concerned themselves: *the direct connection between* duhkha *and the inability to perceive reality accurately.* As we sat around the fire, I could feel everyone bearing down on this thorny set of issues—in order to understand them.

Our reactions to many stimuli are programmed in—"hard-wired" through the processes of development, and further programmed through ongoing conditioning. The result is that *we perceive not what is there, but what we expect to perceive.* The very instruments of perception are programmed to see reality in one highly patterned fashion—and it cannot see any other. We see over and over again in our experience only *what we already believe to be true.*

Contemporary brain researchers have demonstrated the many concrete ways in which this is true. Nobel Prize–winning researchers David Hubel and Torsten Wiesel devised a study involving newborn kittens.[2] The kittens were divided into three groups, each placed in a different environment during the critical few days when they were opening their eyes, and when sight was developing. The first group was placed in a white box painted with horizontal black stripes, the second in a white box painted with vertical black stripes, and the third in a pure white box.

The imprinting of those critical first days stayed with the kittens for life. The kittens raised in a world with only horizontal stripes could not properly see anything vertical. They routinely ran into chair legs, or other vertical realities which they literally could not perceive. The kittens raised in a vertical world could not see horizontal lines. The kittens raised in an all-white world were even more disoriented, and had difficulty relating to any object correctly.

"We see the world not as it is," says the Talmud, "but as we are."

Cognitive psychologists have discovered that most of what we *perceive* is a function of the perceptive apparatus—that is to say, in yogic terms, *the cumulation of samskāras.* It is not just that the mind cannot see certain aspects of reality. The infrastructure of the brain and nervous system, shaped by the forces of development and conditioning, is actually not capable of perceiving the way it is—only the way it was, and the way we expect it to be again.

Our inter-neuronal connections develop as a result of our initial sensory experiences, and along the way we develop our own consistent interpretations of these experiences. Psychologists have found that the nervous system and the brain continue to reinforce these interpretations over and over again—as if the only reason for the nervous system were simply to reinforce the picture of reality that we already have. This process involves not just visual perception—as in the case of the kittens—but all kinds of patterning of experience.

Though this process sounds complex, it's actually quite simple: the synaptic connections that are used become reinforced. One of my first yoga teachers had an elegant way of saying this: what you practice gets stronger! What we didn't know until recently, of course, was that the patterned use of synaptic connections physically changes the brain. These patterns become structured into the brain itself. (The brain is more "plastic" than we used to think. We'll look at this in more detail in chapter ten.) Our nervous system then simply serves to project the internal architecture of the brain onto external experience. The shape of this world, the look of it, the feel of it is actually a function of our own nervous system.

"There is a crack in everything," says Emerson. Is this the crack in the design of the human being?

Let's go back to our model of stimulation at the six sense doors in chapter six. In order to manage the sheer volume of this input (sixty thousand thoughts daily!) the human mind must organize experience into predictable patterns. Our minds are then cued by small parts of a pattern into perceiving the entire thing.

Yogis were perfectly aware of this. It spawned one of the great overused teaching stories of all time: the elephant and the five blind men. Most of us know the story: The blind man feeling only the leg of the elephant thinks the unidentified object in front of him is a post. The blind man feeling only the tail thinks the heretofore unidentified object is a switch, and so on. From one small piece of experience, our brains and nervous systems cue an entire pattern—based on past experience and conditioning. None of the blind men perceived the object accurately. We're all blind.

It gets even more convoluted. *Samskāras*, as they actually show up in our lives, are not just single impressions, but complexes of linked activators which when combined into groups are called *vāsanās*.

In the yogic description, these *vāsanās*, these groupings of subliminal patterns, are much like Carl Jung's notion of the "complex"— with an original "wound" at the center. Jung believed that certain early experiences (often difficult experiences) organize our view of reality so profoundly that they became unconscious "hubs" of our internal organization—providing a kind of hidden center around which thoughts, feelings, and behaviors rotate. In his view, much of psychotherapy involves a kind of unpacking of these complexes. Yogis saw the development of psycho-mental structure in much the same way. They, too, found that these highly-charged patterns (*samskāras*) over time draw in layers of more and more complex reactions—or clusters of habits (*vāsanās*).

Early on in the second part of the *Yoga-Sūtra,* Patanjali states the classical yogic view of *karma, samskāra,* and the root of suffering.

> *The causes of suffering are the root source of actions; each action deposits latent impressions deep in the mind, to be activated and experienced later in this birth or lie hidden awaiting a future one.*
>
> *So long as this root source exists, its contents will ripen into a birth, a life, and experience.*
>
> *This life will be marked by delight or anguish, in proportion to those good or bad actions that created its store of latent impressions.* (2.12–14)

Each *vāsanā* can be thought of as a kind of *karmic* blueprint which emerges full-blown at the proper trigger. In the case of Desperado, for example, this trigger could be Jake's rising fear of being overwhelmed by his latest intimate attachment. For Food Pig, the trigger could be Susan's unbearable feelings of powerlessness with her parents. These initial triggers set off a chain of linked detonations. Boom, boom, boom, boom, *kabaam!* (Sylvester the Cat flattened by a cast-iron skillet for the millionth time.)

Why do we enjoy watching Tweetie Bird and Sylvester play out the same entirely predictable patterns over and over again? Because we do it day in and day out ourselves. It is so very human. The distance between the cartoon and the reality of our own lives is shorter than we'd like to think.

Scientists have now begun to unearth biochemical data for precisely the kind of relentless *samskāric* patterning that ancient yogis described. Psychologist and teacher Richard Schwartz, in his groundbreaking work on internal patterns, says:

> Neuroscientists speak of "states of mind" or "modules" as discrete clusters of related mental processes that are linked into cohesive submind-like states. [T]he brain is designed to form these clusters—connections among certain memories, emotions, ways of perceiving the world, and behaviors—so that they stay together as internal units that can be activated when needed.[3]
>
> For example, neuropsychiatrist Daniel Siegel writes that a fearful state of mind [Ms. Catastrophe, for example] clusters together a state of heightened caution, focal attention, behavioral hypervigilance, memories of past experiences of threat, models of the self as victim in need of protection, and emotional arousal alerting the body and mind to prepare for harm.[4]

On the night of his enlightenment, the Buddha said, "I have seen the builder of the house." It was precisely this subtle construction of pattern that he saw. The Witness had become so powerful that he now saw the way in which character and personality are actually designed, and built, one *samskāra* at a time, into a house of complex and intractable patterns. But that night, the Buddha discovered that when we see through these patterns, we can devise a strategy to dismantle them.

Chapter 8

THE WEB OF "I"

ASMITĀ: THE ILLUSORY "I" AND THE DEEPER ROOTS OF AFFLICTED MIND

"And now, the Sixty-Four Thousand Dollar Question," said Rudi.

"Who's the Real One?" I said.

"Yes!!"

We were now settled into Maggie's parlor. Susan had made a batch of spiced tea. The storm had abated and Jake opened the leaded-glass doors to the back terrace, scenting the room with the smell of rain-soaked leaves. The late afternoon sun sent shafts of golden light along the aging oak floor.

We were already several hours into our afternoon's explorations of pattern with Rudi. In our exploration, we had discovered that each of us at any given time is running many, many patterns. There are dozens of characters inside us whose roles we know. Dozens of voices on endless loop tapes. Dozens of Tweetie Bird and Sylvester the Cat moments. And the kicker is this: oftentimes they don't really fit together that well. This web of patterns is full of paradox and contradiction.

"Jake," said Rudi, "you say that Desperado is not you?"

"Of course not."

"Then who is the Real You?" Rudi shot back.

Jake made a stab at describing the Real Jake. It came out something like this: The Steady and Earnest but Wronged and Misunderstood Boy Who's Just Looking for Love and Working as Hard as He Possibly Can Against All Odds to Get It.

Maggie rolled her eyes.

Kate took a stab at it: "Well, I have one who kind of manages the others. Like I manage the household. I would call her Boss Lady. Would that be the Real Me?"

"I have one of those, too," said Maggie. "I might call this one Mother. The Mother part seems like it must be the Real Me. But somehow it doesn't feel that way."

"I have one that makes lists," I said. "Huge numbers of lists with things to do. Mine is a relentless organizer."

We shared more about Real Me for a few moments, and as we described our "Real Me's," they sounded much like Kate's and Maggie's and mine: managers. Real Me as a kind of manager of all the crazy internal drama. Some were the intellectual part. Others, the organized, steady part. Others, the caretaker.

Rudi's point began to make itself: Even Real Me began to sound more and more like a pattern. It just happened to be the pattern that was in the foreground (Ms. Manager, The Intellect, The Director). The pattern with which we happen to most identify.

Who is the Real Me, then? This is an unsettling question, to be sure. The fantasy that we're just one synchronous person is something we work hard to convey—to ourselves and to others. Much of Western history since the Renaissance is tied up in an attempt to make a unitary "I"—to make a Real Me. This is a highly charged endeavor. But when we investigate our own experience more deeply, it turns out to be a shell game. Where is "I"?

Yogis discovered that the belief in a central "I" is driven by equal parts wish and fear. Actually, what yogis observed (as we'd been discovering all afternoon) is that we're composed of many patterns, and, indeed, many patterns that do not even fit so well together—like a puzzle that has both too many and too few pieces. And none of the pieces it *does* have seem to have exclusive title to "I." It is partly the driven attempt to make all of the pieces fit nicely together that keeps us so often at right angles to life.

It is true, of course, that we need an integrator—a symphony conductor of sorts. But what is the nature of this integrator? And how well does she function in her role—even in the best of times? Much of the time, the orchestra just plays on in spite of her—going its own highly programmed direction.

Yogis' investigations led them to see that the self as we want to think of it, as we hope to think of it, as we long to know it, does not exist. This "self" is more circumscribed than we want it to be—and replete with paradox. When we examine "ourselves," all we can find is a grouping of functions, all arising as a result of the laws of cause and effect.

Furthermore, the clinging to our ideas of self—to the particular set of *vāsanās* that we choose to call "me"—causes suffering. Patanjali sees this as an extremely problematic affliction, and he gives it the name *asmitā*. *Asmitā* is the phenomenon of "self-feeling," the sense that "I am a self." It involves the deepest and most intractable kind of *klesha*—the clinging to a nonexistent entity. It involves the reification of an "I," of a "me," and a "mine" which don't really exist.

Patanjali describes how the vast array of patterns and perceptions masquerade as an individual self:

> *Feeling like a self is the frame that orients consciousness toward individuation.*
> *A succession of consciousnesses, generating a vast array of distinctive perceptions, appears to consolidate into one individual consciousness.* (4.4–5)

One of the central discoveries of yoga is that we are not the self we think we are. This "self" masquerading as a single entity under its own power is really only a confederation of interacting *samskāric* patterns. The "self," like all aspects of the created world, is compound in nature, not singular. It is determined by antecedent causes and conditions, and is not in any way "under its own power."

Says Buddhist scholar Mu Soeng: "It is through delusion or distorted perception that we project a permanent and substantialized self in a separated and autonomous relationship with the world. The task of practice is to see that."[1]

The fire crackled. The room was still, as we all sat with this classic understanding of *asmitā*. Kate looked seriously unsettled, her brow furrowed. Jake was closely examining the tassel on the arm of Maggie's tattered damask sofa. I couldn't tell what he was thinking— but I sensed that he had taken himself away to an inner world.

Susan, however, was right there with me. "Well, in a way it makes sense," she said. "I mean for years I've been feeling like Sybil anyway. I thought I was a multiple personality disorder." She smiled wanly.

Secretly, of course, we all think we're multiple personalities at times. And why wouldn't we? There are those unsettling parts of us that don't really seem to fit. Those mysterious urges. Those intrusive thoughts and behaviors we try to hide from ourselves and from others (like Crazy Uncle Fred who we keep locked up in the basement). And then there are those infernal hijackings.

Since the birth of modern Western psychology, a number of its leading thinkers have come to the same conclusion as yogis: we are more like multiple selves than unitary selves. But this view has always been marginalized in Western psychological thinking. Roberto Assagioli, the Italian founder of psychosynthesis, described a multiplicity of selves and the idea of sub-personalities, but his work never gained wide acceptance.[2]

Jung also recognized this multiplicity, and used a process called active imagination to gain access to the inner world of the "parts." But even though Jung has made a profound impact on our understanding of the psyche, this particular aspect of his teaching has usually been ignored.

There is undeniable genius, though, in seeing human personality as the sum of multiple interacting patterns. In fact, we are just beginning to have some neurobiological data to show that this may be precisely how the mind works. Richard Schwartz notes that "neurobiologists and computer scientists have recognized the multiplicity of the normal mind and come up with their own explanations and models. Computer scientists find that parallel processing computers, which consist of many small processors all working independently on a problem, operate more similarly to the human mind than the older, serial processing computers."[3]

So, who is the Real Me?" asked Kate with a sense of urgency. "We still haven't answered Susan's question."

"None of them is the Real You," said Rudi. "The self is a process, not an entity. And a very complex and paradoxical process at that."

Yogis found that the entire human bio-psycho-mental complex is composed of patterns created by causes and conditions, and triggered by any number of random stimuli. These patterns are *impersonal.* This is their central feature. Once we grasp this central characteristic, we have already begun to free ourselves of their capacity to drive us.

In the view of yoga, the only Real Self is the Witness—the mind that sees and knows it all without judgment. The eternal Seer that does not choose for or against any part. Says Patanjali:

> *Patterns of consciousness are always known by pure aware-ness, their ultimate, unchanging witness.* (4.18)

The Witness is clear-seeing, nonreactive, and free of pattern. The Witness is the only real force for integration (for making it One)—the only real Ground in the picture. This seeing, knowing experience is the only place of rest.

Knowing this, we can stop the war with all of the fantastic parts of our experience. We can soften our clinging and craving for "I," "me," and "mine." We can soften our aversion to difficult parts. We can stop trying to make them all fit together nicely.

Jake, where are you?" I asked. He had been somewhere else for virtually the entire conversation.

"Huh?" he answered.

Something about this conversation had so challenged him, that we were getting to see Desperado right there in the room, in the moment. He had left. Gone wandering.

"It's all bullshit," said Jake, now slightly irritated to have been brought back. "What does it have to do with me, anyway?"

"Well," said Rudi, "it means that you don't have to choose between The Earnest Boy and Mr. Desperado. You don't have to choose one side and disavow the other. You can allow yourself to see both, and to accept that they are both patterns you play out."

Susan had understood this in a visceral way. "It has everything to do with you, Jake," she said. "Seeing in this way gives you a lot of freedom that I would think you might want."

THE UNHAPPINESS OF THE ISOLATED "I"

"This doesn't make any sense," said Kate, now frustrated. "I have to have a self, don't I?" she said to no one in particular. "Otherwise I'd be psychotic!"

Jake gave a vague nod to Kate's frustration. Maggie looked puzzled, but was not going to commit herself one way or the other. Only Rudi, Susan, and I seemed to have any sympathy at all for this facet of the yogic view.

Kate's question was important—and her skepticism completely understandable. She needed an answer, and I was pretty sure the classical answer would not satisfy her. In the view of the yoga tradition, it's just more complex than Kate would like it to be. The belief in a unitary "I" is a useful organizing device and a necessary stage in our development as adults. Our belief in a solid, unitary self under its own power serves as a stepping stone, or a way of remaining internally organized, until we can know the paradox and complexity of living as simple presence.

This interim "I" is for a time, a kind of sustaining fantasy. Without it we can never proceed to a more nuanced view of self. (Indeed, for those of us with shaky childhood foundations, much of adult life can be a quest to simply establish this important sustaining fantasy.) But if, in the process of development, we get stuck here, if we continue to confuse this illusory "I" with the Witness (with pure seeing and knowing), then we begin to deepen our *duhkha*—as Jake did in the years just before his summer at Kripalu. When we continue to identify exclusively with this "I" well into middle age, we begin to live more and more at right angles to life—struggling to get from life something it cannot give. Belief in this nonexistent subject is inherently deluded, and therefore inherently afflicted.

Again the Buddhist teacher Mu Soeng says it well:

> Through ownership of something that's going on exclusively inside our heads, we are constantly and unconsciously defining ourselves, and creating self-serving feedback loops of immense complexity. We create layers of selfhood that become their own trap. In all these feedback loops, the contents of the internal chatter present themselves as compellingly real and valid. Rarely do we realize that they are nothing more than mere views and opinions, created by a specific set of feedback loops. Such is our investment in our views that we are always willing to defend them over the views of others, implicitly believing that our views are real while others' views are mere opinions.[4]

Yogis in their cave-laboratories found that grasping for this "I" is one of the deepest roots of unhappiness. Why?

First of all, in order to create this "I," we must create a "not-I." So we draw a boundary around "I," and everything outside that boundary is experienced as alien to it. In order to create the boundary, we must choose *for* some aspects of our process (our patterns and behaviors) and *against* others. Jake had to choose *against* some part of his experience: so Desperado was disavowed. Susan chooses against Food Pig. Maggie against Pulitzer Prize winner. This is how we create "I." To bolster an inherently tenuous position, we cling to "me" and "mine" and push away "not me" or "not mine." We are constantly forced to shore up our position.

This device, this category of "I," can occasionally give us a qualified sense of mastery over a circumscribed sphere, but it comes with a large price tag: it automatically creates an "other" which is *outside* our control. And this split becomes another source of affliction.

Says psychologist, author, and yoga scholar Swami Ajaya about this problem:

> The very power and control that is acquired by drawing a boundary around oneself is gained through the creation of its complement: an overwhelming sense of helplessness and weakness. By defining itself in a very circumscribed and narrow way, the ego gains the leverage to master that small sphere called I. But at the same time the other side of the polarity manifests; one becomes very small and relatively weak and helpless before the vast world that exists outside of those narrow boundaries, outside of oneself as one thinks himself to be.... This I is like a country surrounded by foreign powers: it may be overrun by any quality that it has defined as being outside its boundary. As a consequence of its extremely insecure ground, the ego devotes a great deal of its energy to bolstering its position.[5]

The act of creating a subject automatically creates the rest of the world as object. And now we are separate from it. This is precisely what Carl Jung saw: "All ego consciousness is isolated: because it separates and discriminates, it knows only particulars.... Its essence is limitation."[6]

So, we are stranded on an island of our own making. An imposter Bali Hai. We experience intense loneliness, isolation, and longing for what is outside the boundary. We seek to *complete* ourselves. We seek out those objects and conditions we have separated off. But these objects, as long as they are objects, remain incapable of truly creating wholeness. By definition we remain distinct and separate from the object. We have already seen that objects remain empty of the capacity to satisfy us. Now we have a further explanation of why this is so: There is no happiness in *having* (possessing) a self. There is happiness only in *knowing* the experience of being.

The illusory "I" brings in its wake the same three characteristics of suffering as the more gross afflictions of craving and aversion. Clinging to "I" creates disturbance, obscuration, and separation.

Disturbance The "I" introduces a subtle and ineffable new object of grasping and aversion. We cling to I, Me, and Mine, and we experience aversion to all that threatens them. In the Western psychological view, these subtle and often invisible forms of craving and aversion are treated as if they were built into the structure of the mind itself. Yogis found, however, that—as with all afflictions—they do not exist in the deepest parts of the mind.

Obscuration The clinging to I, Me, and Mine, leads to the overvaluation of a nonexistent entity, which is the deepest source of delusion. This self can either be overvalued or undervalued—seen as all good or all bad. Either way, these evaluations are delusive since they are a reaction to habits and patterns which are artifacts of causes and conditions—impersonal in nature and not under their own power.

Separation Finally, this "I" separates us from an experience of bare reality—of being itself. Just as clinging and grasping to possess any object paradoxically separates us from truly knowing the object, our delusion of self separates us from knowing life in its real fullness. We recognize this separation during the occasional moments of its temporary dissolution—on the yoga mat, the meditation cushion, while communing with nature, or in any spontaneous moment when the veil drops away. At these times, we know our profound oneness with the world.

Yogis found that all objects in the created world, including our illusory "I," are compound in nature, arise because of causes and conditions, and have no inherent self. But having named them, and clung to them, we give them a power they don't really possess. The world that is splendidly composed of patterns and processes—a river of energy and intelligence—is then seen in categories that make it appear more solid, more boundaried, more stuck in Time and Space than it actually is. We have become trapped in what yogis call "the world of name and form."

SELF-OBSERVATION WITHOUT JUDGMENT

"I'm not sure what to do with all of this," said Kate. "I mean, really. So what?"

The storm had abated now, and the sky was clear. The terrace doors were open to a cool breeze, and occasionally a yellow leaf blew in. We would soon have to leave for our hike to the ridge if we were to make it up and back by sunset.

"I guess I just don't understand the implications for my life," she finished, somewhat defeated.

"OK," said Rudi, leaning forward. "Here's what you might try, Kate. See if this makes any sense at all." I knew what was coming, because Rudi had once given me the same instructions in response to a similar question.

"Start noticing the most unacceptable parts of yourself. I mean the ones that you can barely stand to let out of the basement where you also keep your crazy aunt Sally. I mean the ones that are surrounded by shame and dread. The ones you wouldn't dream of telling us about."

"OK," said Kate, tentatively.

"Find those parts, and make them OK. Make room for them. Let go of judgments. Just watch them. Befriend them."

Kate was perfectly still.

"Name them, like we've been doing today. Learn all you can about them. As if you were Maggie, writing a character in a novel. What triggers the pattern? How does it develop?

"Then, notice that just knowing the pattern automatically begins to interrupt it. Takes the air out of it.

"Most important, remember: none of these patterns is *you*. You are the part that *knows* the patterns. The Witness. The Seer of it all. And you are absolutely OK in spite of the fact that you're running these old blueprints."

"But that's exactly what I can't do, Rudi. And besides. Why should I? These parts of me are no good."

Kate was reacting—flustered. This conversation had hit her central defensive structure: denial and delusion. Kate painted pictures on reality. We all knew it. Rudi was pushing her to be with bare reality.

"OK," said Rudi, now scooting his chair closer to Kate's. "Just stop. Notice how you're feeling right now. Notice your reactivity to this conversation. To me. Just see if you can be with it for a minute. Can you make this OK, too?"

Kate sat back in her chair.

Rudi was teaching the central view of yoga: the antidote to *duhkha* is simple (but not easy): stop the War With Reality. The rest of the path tumbles out from there:

~ Interrupt the chain of reactivity at the earliest possible "link."

~ If necessary, begin by interrupting the reactivity to the reactivity!

~ Then, as soon as the War With Reality is interrupted, consciousness begins to settle.

~ As consciousness settles, patterns come more clearly into the light of awareness and are exposed for what they are.

~ Now, slightly freed up from the war, we can begin to observe and interrupt the chain of reactivity at even earlier and earlier points.

~ Eventually, we can trace *samskāra* and *vāsanā* back to their roots.

~ In this way, *samskāras* are attenuated and "burned up."

~ As *samskāras* are attenuated through exposure, consciousness becomes still.

~ In the stillness, Illumined Mind shines through, and catches a glimpse of itself in the mirror of Pure Awareness.

This sounds magical and mysterious. And it is, I think. But in practice, it is important not to have unrealistic expectations of the process. Our patterns continue to spin themselves out, even as we become more and more conscious—although their intensity is gradually abated. No matter how much investigation we do, the shadows of *samskāra* and *vāsanā* remain.

A classic yogic text called the *Sāmkhya-Kārikā*—written in the centuries just before the *Yoga-Sūtra*—describes it this way, using an analogy to a potter's wheel: The potter is turning the wheel, working on a pot. Eventually, the pot is finished, and the potter stops turning the wheel. But even after the potter has stopped cranking the treadle with her foot, the wheel continues to spin—out of sheer momentum.

Even after we've stopped putting energy into our patterns, they continue to play themselves out. The good news, though, is that the practice of witnessing also continues: just watch. See that the patterns are not "me." See that these patterns are now only ghosts—shadows of their former selves.

Yogis discovered that through practicing in this way, something subtle but astonishing begins to happen: we stop taking these patterns personally. We stop naming them "I." We stop identifying with them. We see that they are impersonal.

American writer Phillip Moffitt tells it in an essay about his practice of yoga and meditation:

> The most profound change I'm aware of just now is a growing realization that life is not personal. This may seem a surprising or even strange view to those unfamiliar with Eastern spirituality, but it has powerful implications. It's very freeing to see that events in my life are arising because of circumstances in which I'm involved, but that I'm not at the center of them in any particular way. They're impersonal. They're arising because of causes and conditions. They are not "me." There is a profound freedom in this. It makes life much more peaceful and harmonious because I'm not in reaction to events all the time.[7]

Yogis suggest that we are too caught up in our own personal stories, and that these stories are, after all, just that—stories. Like the ongoing saga of Tweetie Bird and Sylvester.

When Swami Kripalu came to visit America in 1981, he went directly to Kripalu Ashram—then located in eastern Pennsylvania. Early on in his stay in this spiritual center, he had an introduction to our Western proclivity for overidentifying with our stories and dramas. Swami Kripalu overheard wailing, crying, and screaming coming from a nearby program room. "What is that?" he asked, alarmed.

He was told that it was an Intensive, an opportunity for students to "cathart out" their pain—to scream, to cry, to vent anger on a pillow or other inanimate object.

He shook his head in disbelief, and thought a lot about this while he was in America. Later, he suggested that what American students need most is what he called the practice of "self-observation without judgment." "The major principle in self-observation is that the observer remains neutral and objective. To whatever extent you are able to be objective in your self-observation, to *that* extent you will receive the light.... Do not wrestle with a fault that you want to remove. Wrestling increases the disturbance of the mind and allows the excited fault to lift you up and slam you to the ground."[8]

The genius of the yogic strategy is the understanding that resistance and reactivity to patterns just create more problems: the Tar Baby Effect. The more we push and pull and resist, the more deeply we become enmeshed in grasping, aversion, and afflicted mind. And afflicted mind can only take us deeper into suffering.

All wisdom traditions eventually discover the practice of self-observation without judgment. As Swami Kripalu noted, effective observation cannot take place in the context of reactivity. So radical acceptance is required. Accept everything, said the swami—those things we label good and those things we label bad. All *sramanic* traditions lead beyond these so-called pairs of opposites—beyond pleasure and pain, gain and loss, praise and blame, wish and fear. This is where psychoanalysis leads, as well. It is where science leads. It is where mystical Christianity leads (the Christianity of William Blake and Meister Eckhart and St. John of the Cross).

One of Carl Jung's longtime patients wrote to Jung describing this same relationship between radical self-acceptance and self-knowledge:

> By keeping quiet, repressing nothing, remaining attentive, and by accepting reality—taking things as they are, and not as I wanted them to be—by doing all this, unusual knowledge has come to me,

and unusual powers as well, such as I could never have imagined before. I always thought that when we accepted things, they over-powered us in some way or other. This turns out not to be true at all, and it is only by accepting them that one can assume an attitude to-wards them. So now I intend to play the game of life, being recep-tive to whatever comes to me, good and bad, sun and shadow forever alternating, and in this way, also accepting my own nature with its positive and negative sides. Thus everything becomes more alive to me. What a fool I was! How I tried to force everything to go according to the way I thought it ought to.[9]

AWAKENING THE WITNESS: THE EIGHT-LIMBED PATH

"I have one small argument with all this," said Susan, with some hesi-tation, furrowing her brow. "In fact, maybe it's not so small.

"My twelve-step program taught me that I'm powerless over these patterns. And I really think it's true. I have no power over them what-soever. Acknowledging this was the first step in my recovery from compulsive eating."

Jake rolled his eyes.

"Jake, stop it. I know what I'm talking about here. As soon as you try to control the patterns, you're screwed. You're Brer Rabbit, as Steve would say."

There was wisdom in Susan's declaration. In fact, yogi-*sramanas* came to an identical conclusion: ordinary mind cannot transcend pat-tern. Even the mind that is occasionally capable of seeing, "Oh, I'm stuck in pattern," is *not* capable of transcending that pattern. As we have seen, ordinary mind is inherently afflicted, disturbed, obscured, separate.

Of course, we have momentary freedom from striving, and these moments are tremendously powerful: Jake in the shower, Maggie at her writing desk, Rudi, Maggie, and me in *mantra* practice. They give us a taste of a new way of Being: Happiness with Being Itself. And they bring glimpses of Illumined Mind. But these awakenings are fragile. They collapse under the tremendous power of the self-representation—I, Me, and Mine—and the chain of longing, clinging, craving, and *duhkha* begins all over again. Even the mind that *seems to break free* does not and cannot finally break free of *samskāra* and *vāsanā*.

The power of affliction, of *rāga* and *dvesha*, is so great that when combined with *asmitā, samskāra,* and *vāsanā*, it simply cannot be deconstructed by the unaided human will.

We're caught. We're Brer Rabbit, hopelessly stuck to Tar Baby. Is real freedom a possibility?

The answer is, happily, a qualified yes. Freedom is a possibility. *Sramanas* discovered an escape from the bind of *karma*. A narrow door. They discovered that, indeed, all actions are motivated by latent impressions, and most of these actions lead to further bondage. These actions are called *klishta,* or "actions resulting in bondage." Brer Rabbit actions. There are, however, certain kinds of actions which lead to the *attenuation of affliction,* and to the resurgence of true self, subtle mind, Illumined Mind. These actions are called *aklishta*—"actions not resulting in bondage." Actions which are *aklishta* are those actions which quiet the crazy puppy; actions which help us familiarize ourselves with pattern; actions which help us attune to the wisdom of Illumined Mind; actions which promote self-observation without judgment.

Here's an interesting twist: these actions still create patterns—because the human psycho-mental structure is built on *samskāra* and *vāsanā*. But actions which are *aklishta* create patterns which finally set us free from pattern—which have no Tar Baby Effect.

This is a remarkable discovery, and one that Patanjali, had he been a more colorful writer, might have accompanied with bells, whistles, and trombones. *The causes of affliction contain within themselves the possible vehicles of their own destruction.* We can enlist the very tendency to habit and pattern as an aid to end habit and pattern. These techniques (*aklishta!*) seize the vehicles of affliction and subtly redirect them—like a mill which begins by grinding the coarse grain, but eventually grinds even itself into dust.

These kinds of actions are what Patanjali calls *yoga kriyā*—yogic actions, or actions that yoke us to the process of interiorization and introversion. *Yoga-kriyā* move us gradually toward a heightened attunement to Illumined Mind. They awaken the Witness.

Patanjali says simply:

> *When the components of yoga are practiced, impurities dwindle; then the light of understanding can shine forth, illuminating the way to discriminative awareness.* (2.28)

Now, perhaps, we're getting somewhere. And what, precisely, are these actions? Patanjali will go on to describe them in detail. In the next *sūtra*, he gives us the classic Eight-Limbed Path of yoga, or *ashta-anga-yoga,* literally "eight-limbed yoking."

> *The eight components of yoga are external discipline, internal discipline, posture, breath regulation, withdrawal of the senses, concentration, meditative absorption, and integration.* (2.29)

In this pivotal *sūtra,* Patanjali offers what is certainly one of the most simple and elegant plans for optimal living ever devised by the human mind—a non–Tar Baby plan for unwinding the patterns that keep us snared in *duhkha.* Eight-Limbed Yoga is not, of course, Patanjali's own invention, but rather a stunningly concise summation of centuries of *sramanic* wisdom. It begins with what will be for us a radical reframe of ethical practice, moves through a careful description of attitudes about living, introduces a methodical program of concentration and meditation, and ends with a complete deconstruction of the architecture of ordinary mind. Who is not intrigued by a program that begins by challenging the most basic mischief of everyday life (lying, stealing) and takes us all the way to ecstasy?

From the moment I first met these Eight Limbs early on in my yoga career, I have remained fascinated by this developmental scheme. So simple—yet so psychologically sophisticated. It was my fascination with this practical psychology of liberation that kept me glued to those dusty old texts all those years. How does this program actually work? I wondered. And what kind of human beings does it create?

Most intriguing, I think, is the way Patanjali's model of human development remains as relevant today as it was two thousand years ago. It seems to uncover some archetypal inner structure—and keeps a finger on both the roots of suffering and the possibilities of happiness and fulfillment.

Patanjali's exposition is at one and the same time a *description* of optimal human living, and a *path to attain* optimal human living. It succinctly describes both the path and the goal of yoga. All the practices of the Eight Limbs are potentially *yoga-kriyā*—aids to freedom. They lead to a gradual disidentification with afflicted mind, to attenuation of the *kleshas* and to the gradual revelation of Illumined Mind.

Here is the Eight-Limbed Yoga described by Patanjali:

> *yama:* external disciplines and ethical practice
> *niyama:* internal disciplines
> *āsana:* posture for meditation
> *prānāyāma:* breath regulation
> *pratyāhāra:* withdrawal of the senses
> *dhāranā:* concentration
> *dhyāna:* meditative absorption
> *samādhi:* oneness

The remainder of this book is organized around a systematic inquiry into these Eight Limbs.

Our afternoon at Maggie's house ended with a hike up into the now-yellowed and denuded woods behind the cemetery. As we hiked single file through the cool forest, I thought back on the preceding months. It was now early November. Maggie, Jake, Susan, Kate, Rudi, and I had been together as an informal group since early May. It had been six months since Jake arrived from Boston—and a little more than two months since our picnic on the ridge.

This November afternoon marked the beginning of a new phase in our life together as a group. From this point on, over the course of the next two years, our work would take on a new intentionality—as the complexities of our lives prompted us to try on the various practices of yoga. We tried these practices not because we believed in them as one might believe in a religion, but because they were the tools we had, the tools that were in front of us.

Over the course of the next two years, our group would experiment with Patanjali's aids to freedom. Each in our own way, we would conduct what Gandhi called "experiments in Truth," both with ourselves, and with one another. In particular, we would each wrestle with some developmental task that was made easier by yoga practice. We would find that these practices required a new kind of effort. They stood aspects of Western psychological thinking on its head. And they led to surprising changes in every one of us.

Part Four

THE FREEDOM
IN
SKILLFUL ACTION

You must assume responsibility for being here. You must make every act count, since you are going to be here for only a short while. Treat every act as if it were your last act on earth.

—Don Juan to his student, Carlos Castaneda
Journey to Ixtlan: The Lessons of Don Juan

Precise acts and feelings and decisions were infinitely more effective than the blundering idiocy I called my life.

—Carlos Castaneda
Journey to Ixtlan: The Lessons of Don Juan

KATE

The Invisible Suffering of Delusion

I HAD known Kate since she was a child. Our families lived near each other in small-town Ohio, and I had watched her grow up. When Kate decided to become a dancer, I supported her in every way I could. I felt a thrill in watching her proceed skillfully up the career ladder of the dance world.

Kate was now a beautiful woman of thirty-six. She had a delicate face—perfectly proportioned, with fine features and blue eyes. Her hair, which she wore long, was naturally blonde, and her figure was lean.

As adults, our friendship deepened when Kate spent a summer at the Jacob's Pillow Dance Festival, just a few miles from Kripalu. Kate was the star of the scholarship class at "the Pillow" that summer. She had an ideal dancer's body—long legs and arms, and beautiful feet. She could jump. She could turn. She had a compelling presence on stage.

Kate glided through life on talent and good looks. Even as a child, she'd been a gifted athlete. Every team wanted her. Doors had opened. There had been few hard edges for Kate—or so it appeared to those who didn't know her. She told me (with some bewilderment) that some of the other dancers at the dance festival resented her.

Kate's easy success had made her somewhat entitled, it was true, but also in a strange way confident and fearless. She was mischievous, fun, and something of a daredevil. Kate was devoted to cycling—as I was—and during the summer of her residency at the Pillow, we often spent her day off exploring the Berkshire Hills together on our bikes, stopping in fields and on mountaintops to talk, and then cycling to Lake Mahkeenac for a swim.

For Kate, life was enchanted. There was a downside to this enchantment, though—at least in my view. I noticed that it seemed to be supported by a good deal of delusive thinking. For example: Kate once told me with a flip of her blonde hair that she believed she had had the most ideal childhood. I almost choked. I knew better. As a result of her wishful thinking about life, Kate seemed vulnerable to every scam. It irritated me that she was taken in by every fantastic new hoax, every New Age ploy, and every self-help guru.

When her bicycle was stolen that summer, I confronted her. "Kate, I reminded you to lock your bike. I even loaned you my spare lock."

She flipped her hair and smiled. "It will come back to me, I know it will."

"Come back to you?" I said, exasperated.

It didn't come back to her. And I wondered—what was this view she had of the world, and where did it come from? It worried me. There was something willful about it—as if she could will the world to be the way she wanted it to be. She assumed, too, that because I was involved in the world of yoga, I would naturally share her view of the world. I did not. She accused me of a lack of "trust in Life."

In the ten years since her stay at Jacob's Pillow, Kate and I had remained in touch, and occasionally visited each other. She had become the star of a regional ballet company in the Midwest—until she had a serious foot injury at thirty-four, just two years before she came to Kripalu. The injury forced her retirement. It had come (maddeningly to me) as a result of her willfully ignoring her trainer's caution not to dance a program with a pulled muscle in her back. In compensating for the back injury, she had injured her foot. Seriously. And perhaps irreparably.

I helped Kate—by phone—through a yearlong depression. During that period, I suggested she try yoga. I explained that yoga might give her a lot of the same wonderful feelings as dance—and that, besides, it was a great antidote for depression. Kate tried it, and became an enthusiastic practitioner. It did help her with her depression. However, Kate was never able to dance again professionally. This loss left her with a deep sadness. After this, her face changed. She looked tired, older.

Kate's marriage to Ward, a prominent cardiologist, began—as everything in her life did, I suppose—as a fairy-tale romance. I rolled my eyes when, years earlier during their whirlwind courtship, she described him to me in the most glowing phrases. I thought to myself: this is too good to be true.

Kate was devastated when she learned, at thirty-six, that Ward had been regularly cheating on her for years. Everyone in town knew, of course, but Kate had not seen any of the signs. When she discovered the truth, she was bewildered, furious, confused, and depressed. She simply had no way to fathom betrayal. She asked Ward to leave the house, and they entered into a trial separation.

Soon afterward, Ward left the Midwest for a yearlong fellowship in New York City. Astonishingly, Kate had not yet had enough of Ward, and she hatched a scheme to come to Kripalu for the year—in part because she wanted to be closer to him, hoping to work things out. But also, she said, so she could get more deeply into yoga.

When Kate decamped to Kripalu, her friends back home had been skeptical. One of them said, "Great, Kate. From one unreal world to another." Nonetheless, they hoped that the program would enable her to look at how she had gotten herself into this crippled marriage. Could yoga, perhaps, help her to be a little less clueless in life?

During her first summer at Kripalu, I noticed right away that there was something new in Kate's approach to life: humility. Kate had a new willingness to look more deeply into things. She saw that she'd been skating on the surface of life. To me, this was a much more interesting Kate.

Kate had become aware, too, of her delusive style, and it scared her. She could see, at least at times, that this style had not gained her any ground in life. She was coasting toward middle age with her brilliant dance career behind her, and nothing new on the horizon. And, now, her painful marital woes.

Unlike the Kate of earlier years, she was looking more honestly at her early family life as well. In our long talks together at Kripalu during her first summer, we uncovered some painful truths—a darker side to her fairy-tale childhood. Her parents were not all sweetness and goodness. There was a hard, cold side to them that I had always seen. Her mother could be controlling, willful, and irritatingly phony—and was the world's most transparent social climber. Her father was distant, haughty, and judgmental. Together, her parents insisted on making the world over into their own image. And more than anything else, they were committed to the social triumph of their little girl, Kate.

In our first year together at Kripalu, I discovered something else about Kate—something I hadn't remembered, or perhaps hadn't noticed, when she was a kid. Kate lied. She lied without even knowing it. She would say something and I would look at her and say, "Kate, that's not true. I know that's not true." She would look back blankly. I could begin to see how her fairy-tale world was sustained, one fabrication at a time.

I confronted Kate with these lies. She was amazed. She began to see them, too. Surprisingly, she was not at all defensive about this. She was troubled at the cavalier way in which she made up truth. She was beginning to see the underpinnings of her fairy-tale world. (That November afternoon at Maggie's—six months into her stay at Kripalu—she had amazed me by identifying a sub-personality called Miss Phony.) As Kate began to see the depth of her pattern of delusive thinking, she wondered out loud to me if she could really trust herself with any major decisions.

I liked this new depth to Kate. In our friendship now, I felt needed and trusted. We spent more time together. The Kripalu community took her in, and after some intensive study, Kate became a popular yoga teacher. As it turned out, she stayed with us for a little more than two years. Through her difficult first year with us, she had to look honestly at her relationship with Ward. And as she did, she found it empty of everything she really wanted and needed in a marriage.

In the months to come, Kate would find in the yoga tradition a particularly effective set of practices that allowed her to work skillfully with her delusional style. Delusion is one of the most difficult of the afflictive styles. The ideal ego can profoundly disrupt our capacity for "reality-testing," and leave us at War With Reality all the time—but a particularly shadowy, slippery, and elusive kind of war. Kate would have to work systematically in order to uncover the sources of her delusive style, and to cultivate a habit of honesty with herself and others.

Chapter 9

THE HIDDEN POWER
OF RESTRAINT

YAMA: RESTRAINT

"We were in New York City, at the restaurant, before the show," said Kate. She shook her head slowly, and squinted—evincing what seemed to be sadness tinged with disgust.

It was a sunny Saturday morning in mid-January, and Kate, Susan, and I were sitting on Susan's sunporch after yoga. The snow was melting fast in the heat of the midday sun, and though holiday decorations were still up, it smelled like spring. Kate was describing her recent trip with Ward to New York City (a part of their ongoing attempts to reconcile).

"It was all very elegant and beautiful, as it usually is with Ward. He's got his world so well-ordered. There's no room for slipups."

Kate brushed her long blonde hair off to one side. "He's gazing into my eyes like a lovesick teenager. And I know he's doing it just because it's his *idea* of how this particular scene should go."

Kate stopped, and then slowly got up and moved toward the window—visibly upset. She turned back to face Susan and me: "It's empty, you guys. It's all staged. For whom, I don't know. For his family? All I know for sure is that I'm just a prop.

"I'm just playing the role with him." She shook her head in disbelief. "I've convinced everyone. Even myself.

"I always remember something my mom said to me when I was learning to dance: 'If you believe it's real, it's real. If you believe you're a princess, you're a princess.' Then she would shove me out onto the stage." And Kate exaggeratedly mimed her mother's sadistic push.

"You have no idea how far that way of thinking went into my head. 'If you believe you love him, you'll love him.'"

For a long moment, we all watched a lone starling grousing for food at the birdfeeder.

Kate looked up again and continued the story: "He's looking into my eyes. I know he's got a new emerald ring for me. He says, 'Do you love me, Boo?'

"I looked right at him and said without any hesitation at all, 'You know I do.'

"And right there, *in that very moment,* I saw myself," Kate said directly to me. "Suddenly that little piece of ground that you talk about opened up, Steve, and I was standing on solid ground. I was seeing the whole picture."

Kate was now shaking her head. "It wasn't true. Of course I don't love him. I have never loved him, really. I've been using him, just as much as he's been using me.

"But what shocked me is that I saw *how easily I lie.* Not even realizing it. So smooth. And I just watched myself, as you might during an automobile accident or something. In slow motion."

After her epiphany in the restaurant, Kate had excused herself and gone to the ladies' room—where she had looked long at herself in the mirror. She had said out loud, "Who are you?" Staring back, she saw a beautiful woman. An elegant black dress from Saks. A new emerald ring. But inside she felt terrified. As if she were going crazy. Everything was cracking.

"And I told myself, right there in the mirror, 'Kate, that is the *very last lie. The very last one.* These lies are killing you.'"

This moment would prove to be the beginning of the end for Kate's marriage. The decision to acknowledge her lying would lead inevitably to a clearer perception of Ward—who had never been good husband material, and who had no interest whatsoever in changing.

I think she's hit bottom with this delusion stuff," Susan said to me when Kate went to the kitchen to get a drink of water.

Susan's "hitting bottom" analogy was exactly right. Patterns—like Kate's chronic and unconscious lying—function exactly like addictions. Hitting bottom is jargon for the moment when the *suffering* of pattern reveals itself. When we see the direct connection between *vāsanā* (pattern) and *duhkha* for the first time.

Every addict who has recovered will describe a similar experience that marked the beginning of recovery. Suddenly, for just one brain-altering moment, they *saw*. The Witness awoke. For a brief moment, they had one foot on that small patch of ground.

This moment is life-changing. Almost everyone who has had it claims that this moment of clarity came from God.

Most of us have had moments like this with our sub-personalities—with Desperado and Inner Nazi, and Food Pig. At least once. At least one time, we've stopped right in the middle of the behavior, with chocolate cake smeared all over our faces, and said, Oh my God, what am I doing? How did I get here? The light has gone on.

Kate had now caught The Liar in action. And she saw that this self-defeating behavior was one of the major strategies she used to conduct her life. Kate always had a rationale for lying: It kept her safe. It greased the gears of life. But now she had seen how the lies create suffering—each one a little betrayal. She was now living with a mountain of small betrayals, and she was no longer even sure who she was.

Kate had seen her bondage to pattern. And it scared her. It mortified her, too. She realized that everyone knew about this pattern.

There she was, standing for just a moment with her foot on the island of land at the corner of the picture. She didn't dare take her foot off that island of sanity until she had a plan.

"When I said that was the last lie, I meant it, Susan," said Kate when she returned from the kitchen. "I realize what my work is. It's just telling the truth. Telling the truth. Like Jake said. It's life or death."

The Eight-Limbed Path of yoga begins with a list of ethical practices, called *yama*—the "restraints," or the five external disciplines—which constitute the "great vow" of yoga.

> *The five external disciplines are not harming, truthfulness, not stealing, celibacy, and not being acquisitive.*
> *These universals, transcending birth, place, era, or circumstance constitute the great vow of yoga.* (2.30–31)

There are many lists in yogic writings of the particular kinds of behaviors which must be restrained in order for the true self to emerge. Swami Kripalu lists eleven. Others list thirteen. But, typically, Patanjali has created the most concise organization of them. The five restraints which comprise the "great vow" (*maha-vrata*) in classical yoga are identical to the first five training precepts in Buddhism. They are as follows:

ahimsā: not harming
satya: truthfulness
asteyā: not stealing
bramacharya: celibacy
aparigraha: not being acquisitive

These five restraints, according to the *sūtras*, should be practiced continuously—"irrespective of place, time, circumstance, or social status." (In Patanjali's time it was revolutionary to prescribe a code of ethical behavior that cut across all classes and castes and circumstances.)

"Don't harm other beings, lie, steal, commit sexual indiscretions, or cling."

Virtually all expositions on yoga since Patanjali begin with lists of ethical practices and warnings about bad behavior. The implication is that these behaviors here, on the left side of the column (lying, stealing, cheating on your income tax, gossiping, being mean to your little sister), are the unwholesome ones. Don't do them. These other behaviors here, on the right side of the column are skillful (being nice to babies and old folks, volunteering at the soup kitchen, giving to the United Fund). Do them.

Immediately we're faced with a conundrum. How? We've been doing those things in that left-hand column all our lives (lying, being mean to our little sister). At least in small ways. How do we stop?

Do this. Don't do that. This is the Nancy Reagan approach to ethics. "Just say no to bad behavior." This is so much pissing in the wind. Because saying no is precisely what we cannot do!! St. Paul, again: "The good I would do I do not; the evil I would not do, I do."

Susan was exactly right: patterns—like lying, stealing, cheating—function exactly like addictions. They are complicated chains of reactivity, driven by highly conditioned brain chemistry and personality structure. They begin with attraction and aversion, of course. Then they're driven by habit, *samskāra* and *vāsanā*. And finally they're characterized by powerlessness and loss of control.

Surely we've learned one thing by the time we've become adults: New Year's resolutions last until February fifteenth if we're lucky. Diets, self-improvement schemes of all kinds, including this ideal list of ethical behaviors, are the imprecations of Sunday school teachers. Willpower is nothing when facing the beasts of greed, hatred, and delusion.

Patterns emerge from a murky world of hidden motivations, incomprehensible volitions, and an internal river of greed all mixed up with brain chemistry. They are characterized by:

Denial. For the most part, we cannot see these behaviors. They are the water in which we swim.

Identification. We think these behaviors *are* us.

A *sense of drivenness and loss of control.* Motivations for these
behaviors remain out of our awareness, in the dark waters of the
unconscious. It usually feels as though they drive us, rather than
the other way around.

Tolerance. We need more and more extreme forms of the behavior
in order to feel satisfied.

Withdrawal when we try to stop them. A sense of panic, fear,
agitation, or restlessness will emerge when we try to stop the
pattern.

Trying to interrupt *samskāric* patterns with willpower is like trying
to fix a computer by pounding it with a plumber's wrench. It is the
caveman approach. Without the right tool, we will never successfully
interrupt pattern.

Kate had her work cut out for her. But she now had the one thing
she most needed: Motivation. Vehemence. *Samvega!!* She wanted to
live fully. Luckily, she also had the brilliance of the yogic solution for
working with *samskāra* and *vāsanā*.

TAPAS: THE GENIUS OF THE *VIA NEGATIVA*

One of the first things we notice about the *yamas* is that they are often stated in the negative: non-harming, non-stealing, and so forth.
Yama is *restraint* from harming other living creatures, from false-
hood, from theft, from sexual incontinence, and from greed.

As Swami Kripalu often pointed out, Eight-Limbed Yoga begins
not necessarily with the admonition to tell the truth, to be generous,
chaste, and so forth, but, rather, to *be a little less greedy, a little less
untruthful, a little less unchaste.*

With regard to non-lying, Swami Kripalu said: "Our condition is
such that we need not worry about practicing truth in speech, but
merely need to delete a little untruth from the mass of untruth we

usually speak. Therefore, to practice truth, we should decrease our practice of untruth."[1]

Yama does not attempt to challenge so-called unwholesome behaviors head-on (for just the reasons Kate had discovered), but rather sneaks in around behind them in a brilliant psychological maneuver.

Here is the brilliance of the yogic technique: Acknowledge the pattern. Study it. Observe it. Respect its power. And, if possible, make an intention to interrupt it just at its very endpoint. For most of us, as we've already seen, that endpoint is the *reaction to the reaction:* Self-hatred. Negative self-talk. Moralizing. Guilt. Let's begin by deleting a little of that, and then a little more.

Kate found that her reactions to her lying—her shame, her guilt— had actually helped to keep the behavior in place for many years. These difficult feelings had forced her to deny the troubling behavior. Now, practicing non-reactivity and non-judgment, she could bear to lift her head and look. In order to untie this mother-of-all-knots in the shoelace of her psyche, she had to begin by inspecting it without reactivity. How, precisely, did this get tangled? How to reverse the tangle?

When we pare away judgment, something remarkable happens. We're free, for the first time, to observe how the pattern really works. Once some of the painful shame and guilt are cleared away, the pattern becomes clearer. Its edges are sharper. "Oh, I see how this works. First this arises, and then that, and then that. And that is how I got here."

Now, we can begin to see clearly. Observe the pattern like a surgeon with a scalpel. Bring your capacity for observation right to that last little segment of the pattern. That little white lie, that little gossipy riff. Right there. Whack. Lay it bare to the light. Expose it, and then just for the merest moment, don't act on it. Just a small, tolerable moment of restraint. Not a huge power-saw taken to the root. No need to cut out your tongue. Just that little moment of restraint will do.

Twelve-step programs use an identical approach: breaking down the difficult behaviors (drugs, sex, booze, food, gambling) into the *smallest possible piece.* All of the "slogans" of twelve-step work support this strategy: Just for Today. A Day at a Time. Just Don't Pick Up That First Drink. They target the precise behavior. Like a laser. And they work skillfully with the fact that *little behaviors trigger bigger ones.* One small moment of effort, with a dash of strong determination, well placed. Zaaaappp!

Yogis discovered that this small, unprepossessing moment is a moment of freedom. It has all the power of discerning action: action that watches and then skillfully cuts into pattern without reactivity; action not based on greed or hatred.

It's a great moment. A small, but heroic moment.

For Kate it would mean interrupting her lies at the very easiest spot: Notice the temptation to gossip. To confabulate. To embroider the truth. Just notice when it's happening, and see what it's like to restrain that one dishy comment. Even this can hurt, of course. Forget about Truth with a capital *T.* As Swami Kripalu taught, just try non-lying.

I have said that *samskāras* are like ruts in a road, and that as the ruts deepen through repetition, it becomes inevitable that the car will slide into them unawares. Any intentional effort to restrain the car from slipping into the rut is called *tapas.*

Tapas is the energy of restraint. It is one of the most ancient of yogic practices—and it saturates many aspects of yogic discipline. (Patanjali includes it in his list of "internal disciplines," as we will see in the next chapter.) *Tapas* requires a particular kind of attention—precisely the kind required when driving on a rutted road. We need to be awake. We need to be concentrated in order to avoid the edges of the ruts. And sometimes we need to pull the car wheels—with considerable effort—out of the ridges in the road.

Virtually all spiritual paths have some form of *tapas.* In the West, these forms are often called "the negative way" *(la via negativa)* because they work through elimination, through restraining behaviors that create more suffering.

Tapas involves a delicate interplay between will and surrender that is more heavily weighted in terms of will. But not will as the caveman uses it. Not the club! It turns out that small amounts of effort intelligently directed yield big results. Just restrain one dishy comment at a time. Just restrain one verbal "embroidery" at a time.

The surrender part of this practice is this: We don't have to worry about Truth because Truth is what emerges when we are not lying. Truth is impervious to any form of will whatsoever.

At the core of the negative way is the belief that *once you expose so-called gross unwholesome behavior, the luminous, clear, and compassionate true nature of the self will shine through, and wholesome acts will naturally arise.* As we attenuate the impulse to harmful speech, truth begins to arise naturally—and effortlessly. As the English psychoanalyst D. W. Winnicott recognized (and I paraphrase him), we don't really need a description of the True Self. All we need to do is expose the false self, and the True Self will manifest itself, in its own idiosyncratic way.

Yogis came to understand the power of restraint. They saw the moment of restraint—of pulling back from the impulse to harm, to lie, to act out sexually, or to take something that has not been freely offered—as a moment of power and profound devotion to life. Each one of these moments of discriminating restraint, no matter how simple or invisible to the eye, creates the fruit of happiness both now and for the future. With each moment of restraint, the mind becomes a little more transparent. A little more reflective. A little more still. A little less reactive.

We are back, as always, to stillness. *Nirodha.* The moment of restraint leaves the mind at the deepest levels just a little cooler, clearer, more equanimous—free from the heat of remorse. As the first step on the Eight-Limbed Path, the *yamas* methodically create a resting place, a safe haven from the insanity of clinging and grasping, of hatred and aversion—a place of quiet and safety that at the very least does not create more suffering.

RESTRAINT AND THE TRANSMUTATION OF ENERGY

In late January, Kate asked Rudi to help her structure a guided retreat in which she could practice non-lying. She met with him once a week at Acorn Cottage for coaching. Her informal retreat lasted three months, though her work with non-lying continued well into our second year together.

In helping me to reconstruct an account of her inquiry into non-lying during this period, Kate lent me her journal—a navy blue, leather-bound journal that she bought in the Kripalu bookstore, and filled almost entirely with notes written during those first three months. In selecting short quotes from her journal, I will attempt to faithfully communicate some of her insights.

At their first meeting, Rudi asked Kate to write a statement of intent. ("It's impossible to overestimate the power of a clear intention in these things," he often said.) She wrote her intention in the front of her journal, and put a copy on her mirror at home:

> FEBRUARY 1: *I commit to right speech for the next three months. My practice will be this: before speaking (or writing) I will ask myself two questions, "Is it true?" and "Is it useful?" I will conduct this practice with compassion for myself. I will not beat myself up when I goof up, but just watch and see how it all unfolds.*

In exploring the details of the practice of non-lying, Kate had discovered (with Rudi's help) that there are several tests that help to determine "right speech"—not only the obvious "Is it true?" But also, "Is it useful?" *Speech which is true but which nonetheless violates one of the other yamas is not right speech. If something is true but causes harm, then it must be restrained.* This, of course, eliminates gossip, which Kate discovered had been one of her major non-truth genres. With this simple intention, she launched into her experiment.

———

The first several days of Kate's practice were a revelation. She wrote in her journal almost constantly throughout the day. The writing is hurried, urgent. She seems hungry to get it down.

> FEBRUARY 2: *As I begin to try to totally stop lying, suddenly I see how much I actually do lie. Yikes! As I begin to stop what Rudi calls "the gross apparent lies" on the surface, the mountain of little white lies I tell every day begins to surface. So many lies I didn't even know I was telling are suddenly so obvious! Oh my God.*

Just as our first attempts to meditate reveal the craziness of ordinary mind, so, too, our first attempts at restraint of speech immediately reveal another problem: our minds are deeply conditioned to untruth. The big, dramatic lies which we occasionally see on the surface of our lives are only the tip of the iceberg. They are relatively easy to spot. It's the little, unconscious, chronic lies that really undermine us: So sorry to have missed the party. I had a family emergency (not). Yes, that new dress is really gorgeous (not). Gee, I sent that payment in last week (not). Every time we lie—which most of us do in small ways quite unawares—we deepen the groove of our capacity for untruth. We become less uncomfortable with it.

Kate noticed early on in her practice that it was not so hard to give up the big, obvious lies. It was the little lies that hung under the surface of her awareness that were most difficult. Almost immediately, she began to feel her resistance to giving these up.

> FEBRUARY 6: *Wow! Telling the truth every time? No matter what? This is terrifying. Where will it lead? Once I start telling the truth to myself, I'm afraid it's going to change my life. I don't know if I want my life changed that much. There is part of me that already wants out of this commitment.*

FEBRUARY 8: *The thing I'm noticing now is the shocking amount of my speech which is just plain old gossip. This is kind of embarrassing. When I can actually remember to stop it, I discover something amazing. Gossip turns out to be a way of discharging painful feelings—like anger, envy, sadness, or loneliness. Rather than feeling these, Rudi says that in gossiping I'm acting them out unconsciously through my speech. Who knew?*

Part of the genius of restraint in speech is that when the acting-out behavior (gossip, lying, malicious talk) is removed, the underlying tension that is driving these behaviors can become conscious.

We all know the feelings that accompany this kind of acting out: the momentary high of that quick addictive hit—a discharge of energy that we may find in small binges of eating, sexualizing, or gossiping. Actually, though, if we look under the surface in those moments, we will see that the body and mind have become hotter, more restless, more agitated. We are heirs of our actions in the very instant of gossiping. We have increased our unhappiness.

Acting out the feeling does make us momentarily more comfortable, but it ultimately reduces the amount of energy that is available to us for creating a new internal psychological organization. There is a recognition in yoga that the very tension and discomfort that we experience when energy builds in the system (as conditioned discharge patterns are blocked) can itself be transmuted into seeds of happiness rather than suffering.

FEBRUARY 12: *Today I'm feeling overwhelmed. With feelings. With just, I don't know, energy. Also discouraged. I'm amazed at how much of my speech is not all that wholesome. Even worse, I find how deep my habits of speech are. I don't know if I can change them. I've been doing quite a bit of reading about this in the yogic literature that Rudi gave me, and discovered that for most yogis some period of silence is required. I think it may be necessary for me, too. I may have to just stop talking. How radical is that? I can't talk without lying in some way?*

If our minds and bodies are so conditioned to untruth how do we de-condition them? Yogis have taken this problem seriously. Most have come, eventually, to the same solution as Swami Kripalu finally did: the only way to really get underneath untruth is to begin with some practice of intentional silence. Said Swami Kripalu:

> We can only begin to curb our speech and conduct by grasping their vital points with the forceps of silence. . . . Silence is the first step toward obtaining truth since it helps us to curb untruth, which we generally express by talking excessively all day. This incessant flood of speech makes us prone to the bad habit of speaking untruth. Now, this habit might be tolerable if it died with our bodies, but it goes on affecting us life after life. Speaking untruth is, consequently, a major cause of our downfall.[2]

Yogis, of course, are not the only ones to have discovered this principle. In the Native American tradition, when a young man set out to find the vision that would direct and give meaning to his life, he would leave his people to fast in solitude and silence. In silence the Spirit would come and speak to him. He would return home full of the Spirit—quieter on the outside, more full of life on the inside. "Guard your tongue in youth," advised the Lakota chief Wabashaw, "and in age you may mature a thought that will be of service to your people."[3]

Kate made the decision about two weeks into her practice: *I've decided to practice social silence for the next week. Only talking when absolutely necessary for life needs!*

Kate's journal shifts dramatically at this point. The quality of the writing is less pressured, the writing more organized and relaxed, and her musings more meditative.

FEBRUARY 16: *It's like a whole new inner world has opened up. As I quiet down the external chatter chatter chatter of my mind, the internal world of chatter comes into focus. This afternoon, I found something in Swami Kripalu's writing on* satya *that really rings true. I'm going to paraphrase it here:*

When the gross, unconscious and reactive lying behavior is eliminated, the work has only just begun. Simply stopping speaking is not the answer—it is only the crowbar that helps us to get under the rock of untruth. One cannot restrain his thoughts merely by restraining speech. On the contrary. When one observes silence and seclusion, even more thought flows are generated. The yogi then becomes acutely aware of the types of thoughts that fill his mind. With more practice, he progresses naturally from introspection to self-observation.[4]

This is exactly what happened to me! I've shifted from plain old introspection to this kind of self-observation. It's the Witness. I see how it works now!! Talking is just the final stage of the process. It all begins in thinking. In thoughts. Deep in the mind!!

Anyone who has undertaken some period of silence will understand why it is such a useful intervention in undermining the habit of speaking untruth. In silence, we can get closer to the subtle roots of speech. These roots of untruth are revealed to be deep in our thoughts—and in silence we can pay closer attention to the arising and passing away of these thoughts.

Swami Kripalu was a master of this stage of practice:

Thought, which is the first stage of the speech process, is subtle, covert, and unverbalized speech. That which we call speech is the overt, gross, verbalized thought that is in spoken or written form and is the second stage of the speech process.[5]

The swami's experiments with silence reveal a fundamental principle of yoga: when we penetrate the gross external realities of our lives, we discover their roots to be at more subtle levels. The practice of restraint acts like a knife, cutting away the hard shell of the external to reveal a less apparent internal world of energy.

Kate's anticipated week of silence turned into twenty days. She could not get enough. Her journal is filled with exclamations of delight at the benefits of this practice.

FEBRUARY 22: *I'm beginning to feel like a monk. Or a nun, I guess you would say. I never understood why all those Catholic girls wanted to go off and be nuns, but now I think I do. Really. This is the most amazing period of my life.*

FEBRUARY 28: *I'm feeling so safe. So happy. My mind is calmed down. I sleep well. I can't even believe this. My dreams are so amazing. I've had a couple of weeks of, like, Technicolor dreams, including a couple of nightmares. I just realized that I've been having the kind of clarity I used to get when I was fasting before a big performance— because I am fasting: fasting from lying, from gossip, from acting out through words. Susan helped me to see this in our talk last night at Kripalu. The principle is just the same as with a food fast. In my fasting, I'm discovering insights into my intentions, motivations, and what Rudi calls those deep roots of my speech.*

What may appear to us as simply a voluntary self-denial of speech is described by yogis as an experience rich in deepening interiority— an experience in which not just gross speech, but the very nature of thought itself (the subtle and constant chatter of the mind) is revealed for observation and study, creating a new level of witness consciousness. Swami Kripalu's reverence for this practice colors his language at every turn.

Silence with discrimination is like a wish-fulfilling tree or a touchstone; it has the power to transform an ordinary seeker into an accomplished master.... Although I have not noted specifically what silence has given me, it has brought me everything worth having without my asking for it. Silence has enabled me to practice *yoga-sadhana* steadily.[6]

MARCH 9: *After practicing for thirty-seven days now, I really know why Swami Kripalu called silence a "wish-fulfilling tree." I've discovered the hidden power of the restraints. My energy is clear. It's powerful. It's focused, and quiet all at the same time. I seem to get tons of direct guidance—from God? I know what to do and what not to do. I can feel that a whole life lived like this would be remarkable. Would I be brave enough to live this way all the time? Mostly, I think, I notice the clarity of my mind, my thoughts, and also my sense of connection to the world. To every tree. To the clouds. To my friends. I'm so, so lucky. I feel so grateful.*

The *yamas* are based on a fundamental yogic law of bio-psycho-spiritual energy that runs deeply throughout the architecture of the *sūtras*. It is the Law of Transmutation of Energy: *wherever human energy is discerningly restrained, that energy is transmuted into some more subtle physical or mental power.*

In *Yoga: Immortality and Freedom*, Mircea Eliade comments on this law of energy extensively, and though his language is tinged with a moralism that is not in the original scriptures, nonetheless, he grasps the important point:

To renounce a temptation is not only to "purify" oneself in the negative sense of the word; it is also to realize a true and positive gain; the yogin thereby extends his power over that which he had begun by renouncing. Even more: he reaches the point of mastering not only the objects that he had renounced, but also a magical force infinitely more precious than all objects as such. For example, he who realizes the restraint *asteyā* (non-stealing), "sees all jewels come to him"... The concept of this almost physical equilibrium between renunciation and the magical fruit of renunciation is remarkable.[7]

Yogis discovered that as we restrain our energy from flowing into unskillful acts of body, speech, and mind, the restrained energy is gradually transmuted into supernormal powers *(siddhis)*. Patanjali is specific about the results of restraint. In his text, he lists the *yamas* in conjunction with their "companion" states—the supernormal fruits that naturally arise when energy is transmuted through restraint.

> *Being firmly grounded in nonviolence creates an atmosphere in which others can let go of their hostility.*
> *For those grounded in truthfulness, every action and its consequences are imbued with truth.*
> *For those who have no inclination to steal, the truly precious is at hand.*
> *The chaste acquire vitality.*
> *Freedom from wanting unlocks the real purpose of existence.*
> (2.35–39)

Some of the ancient commentators on the *Yoga-Sūtra* are even more colorful than Patanjali in their description of the fruits of restraint. When a yogi has fully mastered the skill of non-harming, according to one commentary, "he begins to experience an aura of peace around himself that neutralizes all feelings of enmity in his presence, even the natural hostility between animal species like the cat and the mouse," or as another commentator charmingly puts it, "the snake and the mongoose."[8]

When established in "perfect truthfulness," says Taimni, "whatever such a person says will come true; whatever he attempts to accomplish will be accomplished."[9] And when "firmly established in honesty," he says, "people around us offer their wealth at our feet, we become mysteriously aware of all kinds of hidden treasures and mines of precious stones hidden within the bowels of the earth."[10]

The Law of Transmutation of Energy is not unique to yoga. It is a subtle undercurrent in many other mystical spiritual traditions. Contemporary yoga scholar Georg Feuerstein reminds us that the notion that "moral perfection should yield a certain power is not surprising to the reader of the New Testament."[11] The miracles of raising the dead (Lazarus), the spontaneous multiplication of the loaves and fishes, and walking on water are all connected with Jesus's faith and purity, and most of all with his surrender of his own will (restraint of willfulness) to that of the Father.

What is dealt with as miraculous in the Christian tradition is seen in yoga as an aspect of the lawful, orderly, and predictable ecology of human energy. As we shall see, the claims of transmutation of energy which are made so methodically in the *Yoga-Sūtra* are not far-fetched. Through practice we can all experience some aspect of this ourselves.

In her final entry from the retreat, Kate sums up what she's learned about the practice of restraint.

> MARCH 15: *I've discovered through this time that what at first just seems like absence and emptiness, actually opens the door to grace. When I'm willing to keep the cup of my life empty, God fills it with a richness of gifts I could never even make up. The moment of letting go of clinging—even to my lies and gossip—is such a holy one. Like incense in a temple, that moment of restraint radiates a divine scent—connecting me to the holiness of others. Restraint does involve a willful death, and God, it is sometimes painful. But I do find that when I die like this in a moment, I'm reborn in some small way to new life. Right in that moment!*
>
> *Every moment of practicing restraint is really a moment of devotion, not just to myself, but to all people in my life—and I see now that I can practice this not out of fear or self-hatred but out of compassion. The most amazing thing of all is that the practice of restraint is not deadening. It's a source of new life. I find that in these*

moments of restraint I touch something so deep inside me, I'm opened to myself in a mysterious new way. And as I experience this deeper connection to my self, I experience, too, a kind of oneness with the whole world.

POSTSCRIPT: RESTRAINT REVEALS THE HIDDEN ROOT

"I guess it's like they say in AA, 'Just don't drink, and everything gets better.' In my case, it's 'just don't lie and everything gets better.'"

Susan, Kate, and I were sitting together on Susan's porch several months after Kate's retreat. Kate was sharing some of the fruits of her practice of non-lying.

"How do you mean?" asked Susan.

"Because it's only in *stopping it* that I can see what's driving it in the first place," said Kate.

Kate was stating an important principle. Restraint reveals the hidden motivations which drive the behavior itself. In the stillness and silence of restraint, the subtle roots of the behavior are revealed, and having been exposed, slowly die. It is simply exposure to the light of awareness that burns them up. This is the genius of *tapas*.

"I understand now why therapy didn't work that well for me," said Kate. "It was because no matter how much insight I got in therapy, I never actually *stopped* telling lies. I talked on and on about the behavior, and spent a fortune of Ward's money on a fancy Midwestern shrink. But I still did it. And, of course, plenty of the times I even lied to the shrink."

Susan was nodding her head vigorously. "Just like addiction," she said. "Exactly the same with me and food. I was in psychoanalysis with old Brenner for ages. Oh, I understood it. But I hadn't stopped it. It wasn't till I *stopped* compulsive eating that I began to really get better."

―――

Kate and Susan had been caught in one of the traps of Western psychotherapy. Most Western psychotherapeutic models scrupulously avoid prescribing any kind of direct and willful cultivation of so-called wholesome behavior. Psychodynamic psychotherapists hold that patients will learn to act in more wholesome ways once they understand the historical and unconscious sources of their problems, and once they have experienced the healing of their capacity to love and be loved in the development and resolution of the therapeutic relationship.

There are serious problems with the strategy. First of all, it is often not true. There are patients for whom a mountain of insight never matures into a molehill of behavior change—or happiness and freedom. We all know them, and some of us know quite a few of them.

In the later years of my practice of psychotherapy, I had to wonder about the limits to the usefulness of insight, because I was confronted weekly with the inevitable patient who seemed to be developing insight into the historical roots and unconscious conflicts motivating her behavior without really changing the behavior at all.

My experience leads me to believe that there is a "glass ceiling" for many psychotherapy patients on how far the process of healing can proceed without the foundational ethical practices described in the contemplative models of transformation. It is no accident that the three-thousand-year-old science of yoga begins with refining and purifying action.

Kate's story provides a real-life model. In the absence of the acting-out behavior, Kate created a clearing in which she could actually experience the "pervasive unsatisfactoriness" behind the symptom. It was in the coolness and asylum of this period that she began to have truly liberating insights into the roots of her behavior.

Kate, what was it that restraint revealed to you?" asked Susan.

"Well, at the beginning, especially in that first period of complete silence, I kept remembering one of my mother's mottos: 'Accentuate

the positive. Eliminate the negative. Don't mess with Mr. In-Between.'
Aacchh."

Kate winced. "Mother always said it in her overly sweet singsong
voice. 'In this family, we always look at the bright side.' That was OK.
Except we could *only* look on the bright side.

"We simply were not allowed to be negative. Anger, sadness, grief,
pain of any kind. We couldn't even acknowledge it."

"What did you think would happen if you did?" asked Susan.

"If we did acknowledge what was going on? It must've felt like it
would have killed us to look. It would have killed Mother, that is. To
see how much pain there really was in our family.

"Somehow," said Kate, "all suffering had to be denied. *Suffering
itself became the enemy.* Then, somehow, all forms of suffering became shameful. Here's what I wrote in my journal: *Suffering itself is
shameful. Must pretend it does not exist.*

"I realized," said Kate, "that my mother had an unwritten motto:
ignorance is bliss."

Kate had unearthed another central principle of yogic wisdom:
ignorance of suffering does not create happiness. The truth is, as
yogis say, "not seeing *duhkha* is *duhkha*." Not seeing suffering is suffering.

Twisting away from the reality of suffering is the deepest pain. No
matter how painful or difficult a family situation, children can survive
if there is someone telling the truth about it. The truth is always a relief. The truth gives us someplace to stand. (That little corner of
ground.) It is when suffering is combined with this willful kind of
delusion that true mental illness can emerge. Delusive family systems
are one of the most virulent creators of suffering.

The word *yama* is not only the word for "restraint," but is also, in yogic lore, the name of the god of death. *Yāma* (the god) and *yama* the
practice are clearly related. Restraint is the beginning of a process in

which a pattern dies—beginning with the outward and visible gross behavior, and culminating with the death of the root of the pattern.

These patterns, of course, take years or even lifetimes to be attenuated. But with each subtle attenuation comes an increasing sense of freedom and energy—precisely the freedom that Kate had experienced.

PRACTICE THE OPPOSITE

KABOOM!

"Jesus, Mother, now you're gonna instruct Maggie in the fine art of Christian doctrine? That's priceless."

Jake's mother, Fiona, looked down her nose at Jake. She was steely-eyed and calm as she turned back to Maggie—addressing her as she might an old confidante.

"Maggie knows very well the problems with today's young people," she said, her head held high. "And she agrees with me I'm sure."

Maggie stood completely still, her eyes moving back and forth from Jake to Fiona. She betrayed no hint of emotion.

Fiona said nothing. She stood straighter.

"Oh, that's just great," said Jake, turning from the conversation. "Christ," he swore in a whisper we could all hear. He downed the glass of sherry he was holding in his hand—then poured himself another.

Jake's mother, Fiona, had come to visit for Easter week, and we had just all participated together in the big Easter Mass at All Saints' Church. Susan, Kate, Maggie, Rudi, and I had come with Jake and his mother as a show of support for Jake. Afterward we were having sherry with the priests and parishioners in the parlor of the old stone church. Fiona had just finished telling Maggie that the central problem with Christianity today was the virtual disappearance of the sacrament of penance (popularly known as confession).

As Jake downed his second sherry, Fiona turned back to him, and fixed him in her sights. "Of course, you don't care about your soul, Jake O'Brien. And never did."

She spoke loud enough for the whole room to hear: "Just like your father. Yoga. Hah! You're doing this just to get back at me." Then she swallowed her own sherry. The fight was on.

Fiona was a slight woman, almost anorexic looking—with virtually no hips and delicate limbs. Her lips were tight and thin, highlighted as they were with too much red lipstick, and her jaw was set. Her helmet of hair, a dull black that did not exist in nature, was too perfectly coiffed. And her eyes, like Jake's, were smoldering. There was intelligence and strength there—and traces of flashing beauty. But she was, as Jake had said, "a hard woman."

"My goodness, she's fiery today," said Rudi to me in a soft aside. Of all our friends, Rudi seemed least put off by Fiona's behavior.

Jake and I had talked about the situation the night before, sitting on the porch at Acorn Cottage—while Maggie took Fiona on a driving tour of Lenox. Jake felt trapped by Fiona's ambition for him, and by her indomitable will and her powerful ideal images of family. She was proud, even regal. She skimped on the food budget so the family could have "proper clothes." It was all about looking the part. And in Jake's case, she felt—perhaps rightly—that some of her efforts had paid off.

"Mother is some kind of weird combination of a Catholic puritan and a social climbing WASP," Jake had said. "Nothing is good enough for her. She's impossible to please." Indeed, this quality was apparent even in her features. A slight sneer of disapproval had shaped her face. She was disapproving of her late husband (who died from complications of alcoholism), condescending to her sons, and easily prone to moral indignation.

Fiona had always been disapproving of Jake's lifestyle. Jake fought her silently by not marrying. The fight between them, it seemed, was so deep that Jake was unconsciously willing to sabotage his life in order to get his revenge. The ongoing struggle between mother and son was more than likely the source of Desperado.

Fiona was also openly furious about Jake's fascination with yoga—an investigation she considered blasphemous. And Jake did enjoy rubbing salt into this wound at every opportunity.

But Jake's relationship with Fiona was more complex than it immediately appeared. Jake hated her, to be sure. But it was not difficult to see, too, that he loved and admired her. Their fights were passionate, hot tempered, and full of feeling—a mother and son squaring off. Indeed, Jake was much like Fiona—a creature of will and considerable discipline. Curiously, though, Jake had disavowed the part of himself that was able to love her, admire her, and acknowledge the gifts she had given him.

Jake spent several years in psychotherapy trying to understand his rage and deny his passion with his mother. But in spite of considerable insight and awareness, his rages only seemed to get more profound with the years. As Jake and I explored the details of "the fight" (as we came to call it) we discovered that rage was a kind of ancient theme in Fiona's family. Fights between sons and mothers went back for generations, and it was considered an inevitable (even exciting) part of the fabric of life. The strongest son survived by fighting.

Sherry hour at All Saints' ended badly, as any of us could have predicted. After seeing Jake take his third or fourth sherry, Maggie foresaw disaster, and just as one final heated exchange seemed to be breaking out, Maggie abruptly offered to take Fiona back to her house for lunch. At which point, Jake stomped off, muttering profanities. Susan stormed off after him, sending visual daggers toward Fiona. The priests and parishioners of the good parish of All Saints' were left in stunned silence.

After a short and animated talk in the parking lot, Susan and Jake ended up at Susan's house, and the rest of us eventually arrived there as well—with the exception of Maggie, who had taken charge of Fiona.

Jake was in shambles—agitated, angry, but also uncharacteristically embarrassed. He knew he had lost it. The Devil had been seen.

We settled into a circle on Susan's sunporch, with Jake occasionally getting up to pace. It was turning into a beautiful spring day—though we'd barely had time to notice. The windows were open onto the sunporch. Everyone began to calm down.

"Can you guys hang out for brunch?" Susan asked.

"Yes" came back unanimously. Susan got to work on omelets and bagels.

Over the next two hours, as the tension (and frank amazement) from the morning's events dissipated, we began to unpack the drama we had just seen. It was, of course, the very drama of reactivity with which we had been working. But there were several pieces of the drama that perfectly illustrated aspects of reactivity with which we'd not yet grappled.

Triggering   In talking over the scene at the church, we began to identify the ways in which subtle mental and emotional cues had detonated a series of linked mental and emotional events. Fiona was triggered by seeing Jake drink. This no doubt ignited a series of thoughts and memories associated with alcoholism at home. She was also triggered by the presence of Jake's yoga group, and perhaps by the challenge she felt to her religious beliefs—challenges which got dangerously close to her sense of Me and Mine. On Jake's side, it was likely that Fiona's hostile disapproval and condescension triggered his chronic feeling of being trapped, and his wish first to lash out and then to flee.

Chaining of Thoughts, Memories, Feelings, Physical States
We examined the chaining of thoughts, memories, feelings, and physical states that occurs once the trigger has been "pulled." We had watched as pattern took over—and as the wheels of the cart dropped

into those well-worn ruts. We saw both Jake and Fiona trapped in a series of highly charged habitual reactions, which at a certain point simply could not be stopped. It all happened in a nanosecond. Thoughts triggered feelings, which triggered brain chemistry, which triggered more feelings and thoughts, and the inevitable fight was on. Tweetie Bird and Sylvester the Cat.

Refractory Period Finally, we took some time to examine the ways in which reality is almost immediately obscured once this chaining of disturbance, obscuration, and separation begins. There is a period of time, which Western psychologists call the "refractory period," during which no new information can enter and the subject is incapable of accurate reality testing. The refractory period may last for a few seconds, or (as in Jake's case) a few hours, or even for days. During the refractory period, the mind is gripped by a particularly dense afflicted state. Any new information that enters during this period is interpreted in ways biased by intractable attraction or aversion. The duration of this refractory period is determined by a number of factors—including the history of the pattern, and its connection to highly charged issues in the subject's life experience, as well as the pattern's connection to any primitive form of anxiety (especially anxiety around being dominated or annihilated).

In the morning's drama, the factors of disturbance, obscuration, and separation were quite apparent. We could feel how dense and intractable they were. We could see the impaired judgment afflicting both Jake and Fiona, and the resulting compulsion to speak, think, and act in biased ways. We had seen how quickly it was all triggered. Boom, boom, boom! And the rapidity with which it spiraled into full-blown warfare.

It's hopeless," said Jake. "She will never change."

"Well, Jake," said Susan, "forget about her. What about *you*? You can change."

"She says she's not depressed," said Jake, brushing off Susan's comment. "Hah! Like Shirley MacLaine's character in the movie *Steel Magnolias:* 'I'm not depressed. I've just been in a bad mood for forty years.' It's her temperament, damn it. It's permanent."

Jake was making a good point: we were dealing here not just with emotions, which last for seconds. Or even with moods, which last for hours. But, rather, with temperament, which is a deeply hardwired pattern. We were also dealing with highly aversive states, which are seen in the yoga tradition to be the deepest kinds of *karma*. (Yogis found that aversion characterizes the most deeply entrenched patterns, greed the second most deeply grooved, and delusion the least.)

We talked together about the strategy of familiarizing oneself with the pattern—identifying it a little earlier. But a general sense of discouragement about this strategy seemed to penetrate our thinking.

"No matter how long we're apart, how much work I do on the yoga mat, or in psychotherapy," Jake said, "it just doesn't matter. This always happens."

Jake completed his thought: "Like Ram Dass said, 'If you think you're enlightened go back and visit your parents.' Ka-boom!! She erupts like fucking Vesuvius."

"Ka-boom," said Susan. "You both erupt like fucking Mount Vesuvius."

We were face-to-face with the immense power of these patterns—and the way in which they mix up thought and emotion.

For now, however, the chain reaction had stopped. Jake's refractory period was over. The group together had become a witness for Jake.

There was in the room a square piece of safe ground upon which we all stood. The sun was shining in. Boots the cat had jumped into my lap. Jake finally settled down in the wicker swing with Susan rubbing his feet. We nibbled on some of Susan's coffee cake, and later chatted together and snoozed in the sun on the porch.

PRACTICE THE OPPOSITE

The *sramanic* traditions developed a multi-pronged strategy for the problem of chaining of thoughts and emotions. The first, as we have seen, is *familiarization*—interrupting the afflictive thought-loops at earlier and earlier points with awareness. Next, again as we have seen, is *restraint*—snipping off afflictive behaviors as early in the chain as possible. But in the yogic view, these two strategies, effective as they are, do not in themselves have the power to fully deconstruct afflictive patterns.

Yoga offers us another altogether different set of skills as an antidote to affliction: the systematic cultivation of the so-called wholesome mind-states. Patanjali states this principle succinctly.

> *Unwholesome thoughts can be neutralized by cultivating wholesome ones.*
> *We ourselves may act upon unwholesome thoughts, such as wanting to harm someone, or we may cause or condone them in others; unwholesome thoughts may arise from greed, anger, or delusion; they may be mild, moderate, or extreme; but they never cease to ripen into ignorance and suffering. This is why one must cultivate wholesome thoughts. (2.33–34)*

Patanjali has here confronted us with a strategy that has almost always taken a backseat in Western psychotherapy, but which has always been central to the contemplative view. The emphasis on this strategy of "cultivating wholesome thoughts and behaviors" is repeated in many of the schools of Buddhism as well as yoga. In the Buddha's various talks on "right effort," for example, he clearly states a two-winged approach that includes both exposing and eliminating afflicted states and "generating wholesome states not yet existing."[1]

Right effort, he says, consists of four practices:

1. To prevent evil, unwholesome states from arising
2. To abandon them if they should arise
3. To generate wholesome states not yet existing
4. To maintain them without lapse, causing them to develop and to reach full growth and perfection.

In the Tibetan tradition, these same practices are sometimes called The Four Great Efforts, and are seen as the key to attenuating afflictive states.

It is the second half of this prescription, of course, which must be so intriguing to the Western mind: Generate wholesome states not yet existing? Cause them to develop and reach full growth and perfection?

At the heart of this strategy is a revolutionary view of human development. The Western born Buddhist monk, Ajahn Sumedho, declares it with passion: "It is not enough to follow the heart. You must train the heart."[2] What is radical here is the very notion that these states can be intentionally and systematically cultivated. We tend to think of love, generosity, compassion, as arising naturally in the flow of experience. We see their value, and their beauty, to be sure, but we tend to believe that unless they arise naturally, and "from the heart," they are not authentic—not real.

Is this true? Not from the contemplative point of view.

Sumedho goes on to teach that all wholesome states can be methodically developed. Where there is greed, we can systematically train the heart toward generosity. Where there is anger, we can train the heart toward loving kindness. Where there is jealousy and envy, we can train the heart toward sympathetic joy. Where there is hatred, train toward compassion—and so forth. In the yoga tradition, each afflictive emotion has its own "opposite" or "antidote" which can be intentionally cultivated.

Training the heart and mind is the central strategy of the second limb of yoga, niyama—or internal discipline. Whereas yama (often stated in the negative) is based on the technique of restraining energy from moving into certain afflictive behaviors, *niyama* (usually stated in the positive) prescribes the active cultivation of non-afflicted actions—particularly loving kindness, compassion, sympathetic joy, gratitude, generosity, patience, humility, and equanimity.

"Practicing the opposite" is another cunning psychological maneuver—once again (as with restraint) sneaking around behind highly conditioned patterns rather than confronting them head-on. It is a strategy not yet well understood in Western psychology, but almost universal in both the Eastern and Western contemplative traditions.

The yoga traditions are specific about which qualities need to be trained. A partial list would be:

Moderation *(mitahar)*
Faith *(āstikya)*
Patience *(dhairya)*
Forbearance *(kshamā)*
Compassion *(daya)*
Straightforwardness *(ārjava)*
Humility *(hrī)*
Steadfastness *(dhriti)*
Loving kindness *(metta)*
Sympathetic joy *(muditā)*
Equanimity *(upeksa)*

Each of the contemplative traditions has lists similar to these. The Buddha, for example, taught the ten *paramis* (or ten perfections): generosity, patience, loving kindness, strong determination, awareness, equanimity, ethical behavior, concentration, insight, and truthfulness. (It was said that the Buddha, before his enlightenment, worked for many lifetimes in the refinement of each one of these qualities of mind and heart. He spent a whole series of lifetimes, for example—as colorfully described in some of the "Jataka tales"—just perfecting strong determination, or patience, or generosity, or compassion.)

In the West, the Christian tradition offers the Seven Heavenly Virtues—faith, hope, charity, fortitude, justice, temperance, and prudence; and the Seven Contrary Virtues—humility, kindness, abstinence, chastity, patience, liberality, and diligence. (The Contrary Virtues are designed specifically to antidote the Seven Deadly Sins.)

The five disciplines (*niyamas*) as codified by Patanjali are:

shauca—purity
samtosha—contentment
tapas—restraint
svādhyāya—self-study
īshvara-pranidhāna—surrender to the Lord

Yogis found that it was useful at times to look away from the difficult, afflictive states, and "dwell" in the wholesome states. Sometimes this is called "soaking"—soaking in love, in compassion, in generosity. In these moments of soaking, suggests Patanjali, don't give attention to the obstacles. Don't struggle with them or remain involved in resisting them. (Remember: what we resist persists—Brer Rabbit's dilemma.) Rather than actively pushing away mind-states characterized by greed, hatred, or delusion, simply give juice to their opposites and the obstacles will naturally fade.

There is fascinating new research that suggests Patanjali knew what he was talking about. One of the most exciting discoveries in neuroscience in the past decade is that the brain is substantially modified through repeated experience. Until recently, scientists believed that adaptive structural and functional changes in the brain were limited to the very young. Now we know that the capacity of the brain to develop new neuronal/synaptic interconnections continues well into adulthood. This means that the adult brain is much more "plastic"— open to reshaping—than we thought. This discovery of "neural plasticity" has led to a fresh understanding of the ways in which experience modifies the brain itself.

Now we suspect something even more dramatic: not only does the brain give rise to mental states, but mental states themselves shape the development of the brain. So repeated experience of states of happiness, loving kindness, or compassion, for example, actually modify the physical structures of the brain, through repeated stimulation.

The brain in all vertebrate species is divided in two, and research shows that in humans the right and left frontal lobes of the brain differ in their functions. Studies have begun to suggest that certain areas in the left frontal cortex play an important role in positive emotions and mental states (happiness, loving kindness, compassion), while the right frontal lobe plays a similar role in the negative states (anger, fear, frustration).

The logic here is obvious—and lines up precisely with the ancient teachings. The more we practice loving kindness, compassion, sympathetic joy, happiness, the stronger they become. The part of the brain that supports these states is strengthened and becomes more robust. As these wholesome states are being practiced, the difficult negative states, involving quite a different set of neural connections, are waning in strength, dominance, and physical development. Again: what we practice gets stronger. And now there is brain science to back up this claim.

These discoveries have other implications, as well—especially for the refractory period. Studies have shown that those who have more developed circuitry for the positive emotions—those who through either good luck or intentional study have practiced happiness and loving kindness—return much more quickly to a calm baseline after being provoked by a negative emotion. They have shorter refractory periods.[3] Interestingly, people with shorter refractory periods also show, in general, a lower level of cortisol—the so-called stress hormone. And these same people also have stronger immune systems.

Because of the way the brain functions, it is difficult to experience both hatred and love at the same time. One set of brain activations will predominate. Studies suggest that through repeated practice of the wholesome states of mind, the afflictive, or negative emotions may be intentionally atrophied. Accentuate the positive! Kate's mother, it turns out, was not entirely wrong.

SOAKING IN LOVING KINDNESS

It was a crystal clear day in mid-June. The sun was warm, the sky deep blue. The delicate fragrance of Queen Anne's lace wafted from the unmowed field behind the old tennis courts near Acorn Cottage, perfuming the mild air. It was quiet, except for a considerable buzzing of bees around the stand of ancient rhododendron next to the fence, just a few yards from my walking spot.

Jake, Susan, and I were doing walking meditation. The clay surface of the old tennis courts was growing warm. Jake was walking barefoot, shirtless, with loose shorts and a tattered Red Sox cap given to him by his father years ago. Susan (who still felt the hint of coolness in the air) was dressed in a black fleece jacket and jeans. And I was in old denim shorts and a T-shirt.

After Easter, Rudi had taught Jake to do walking meditation. Susan had learned it a year earlier on retreat—and I had been doing it for years. In those weeks after Fiona's visit, Jake had been so upset, so regressed, that he simply couldn't sit still. Meditation on the breath had become unbearable for him.

One afternoon at Acorn Cottage, Rudi showed Jake how to focus his awareness in the movement of his feet and legs as he walked. "Lift the right foot. Move it. Slowly place it on the ground in front of you. Feel the pressure as it touches the ground. Good."

Jake loved this practice from the first. The technique had all the benefits of concentration—tying the puppy to the post. And, it brought with it none of the potential difficulties of sitting still.

In addition, of course, Jake loved to be outside. Nature had been the most consistent force for soothing in his life, and it was to the woods he escaped whenever he could. So, from the beginning, he determined to do his walking meditation outside. Jake and I had cleaned up the old clay tennis courts about twenty yards behind Acorn Cottage. (The courts had been hidden in the undergrowth for decades, until we rescued them for their new purpose.) It was a perfect spot for walking meditation—secluded and safe. Since early May, Jake had been walking back and forth, up and down, wearing a path at one end of the green-brown clay.

My concentration in the walking practice this afternoon had gone deep, and at moments I felt a sense of absolute calm and sweetness. Everything was OK. Just walking. Just breathing the clear June air. Feeling my body. And, more even than that, I think, feeling the reassuring presence of my two friends nearby.

Jake was concentrated as well. He was a quick study with anything physical. I could practically see Rudi's instructions in Jake's movements: "Slowly roll the left foot up. Move it. Place. Feel. Lift. Move. Place. Feel." Jake's movements were graceful and deliberate. Like a cat.

The pace of Jake's walking had slowed to a crawl today. I knew from experience that when Jake felt agitated, he walked quickly and aggressively back and forth. We had discovered that this walking technique provided a kind of container for Jake's assertive, aggressive personality. It contained him—made him feel safe. The walking soothed him, and after a spell of more aggressive walking, his pace would eventually slow again, as it had now.

After two months of regular walking meditation practice, Jake created an altar at one end of the court—on the stump of an ancient oak. He added objects regularly: the feather of a hawk, a small quartz crystal, a piece of polished granite from the creek bed behind the cottage.

Jake mastered the walking technique quickly, and within months had begun to cultivate deeper states of concentration. By mid-June, Rudi had resolved to teach him another concentration technique that he could use with his walking practice—one that would deepen his cultivation of equanimity and his sense of well-being. This is a practice called *metta,* or loving kindness meditation.

*M*etta is a classic form of concentration meditation—a technique originally taught by the Buddha to his monks. In those days, the Buddha's monks were living in the woods, surrounded by all the potentially dangerous critters of the Indian subcontinent—snakes and tigers and scorpions. The Buddha saw that they needed a systematic way of subduing fear states, and cultivating equanimity, and so he created *metta* meditation. Seven hundred years later, the technique was adapted by Patanjali, who includes it as part of his strategy for "practicing the opposite."

Patanjali recommends the intentional cultivation of "friendliness toward all beings" as a way of subduing the distractions and "stilling the patterning of consciousness."

> *Consciousness settles as one radiates friendliness, compassion, delight, and equanimity toward all things, whether pleasant or painful, good or bad.* (1.33)

The precise instructions for *metta* meditation, as Rudi taught it, were largely taken from contemporary Buddhist practice. *Metta* involves focusing awareness on a series of repeated phrases of well-wishing, or prayers, such as this:

> *May you feel protected and safe*
> *May you feel contented and pleased*

May your body support you with strength
May your life unfold smoothly and with ease[4]

In the classic teaching, the well-wishing is first aimed toward the self, then toward a "benefactor," then toward a "neutral person," and finally toward the more difficult persons in our lives (or even a so-called "enemy"). In his experiments with this technique, Jake discovered that his mother was both a "benefactor" and a "difficult person," and he soon resolved to dedicate his practice of *metta* to healing his anger with her.

As Jake walked up and down the clay path on the tennis court, he said the *metta* meditation phrases over and over again to himself, aiming the well-wishing toward an internal image of Fiona: "May you feel protected and safe. May you feel contented and pleased. May your body support you with strength. May your life unfold with ease."

Jake discovered that he could conjure up an image of Fiona, and that he could "aim" the phrases toward the image. Eventually the phrases began to emerge spontaneously and effortlessly as he walked up and down the court. He walked on beautiful days. He walked on rainy days. He walked every day. Each session was different. The whole spectrum of feelings arose in his heart—from red rage to compassion. He found, paradoxically, that he could practice saying the *metta* phrases even when another part of his mind was resisting. He just stuck with the phrases. And finally he found that saying the phrases over and over again primed a well of lost or hidden love. These ancient feelings, combined with feelings of rapture and bliss and well-being, automatically emerged from his concentration meditation.

On this particular afternoon, I noticed for the first time that Jake had added a framed picture to his altar: it was a photograph of the young Fiona. She was stunningly beautiful. Black hair. Blazing smile. The resemblance between the youthful mother and son was striking.

For the first time, I saw that they had the same intensity around the eyes. The same potential for ready anger around the mouth. These two shared more than I had ever before understood.

But now there was Fiona, in all her youth and beauty, settled in among the objects of Jake's affection.

Chapter 11

AT THE STILL POINT OF
THE TURNING WORLD

COMING ALIVE IN THE HOUSE OF MEMORY

I awoke with a start. Someone was banging on my back door. I rolled over and squinted at the clock: three AM.

In a haze, I dragged myself out of bed and looked out the window. It was Maggie. She was in housecoat and slippers, carrying a flashlight and looking wild.

I called out the window: "Maggie, what's wrong? Are you OK?"

"Stephen. Get up. You must get up."

"What's happened?"

"Just come with me."

I slipped on some jeans and a fleece jacket. Maggie took me by the arm and we walked across the lawn to her already open door.

I had seen Maggie the previous evening, and I scanned my memory for clues. Maggie had taken my two-hour vigorous yoga class at Kripalu. We had finished with a long *yoga-nidrā* (relaxation). I noticed in the class that Maggie had been particularly concentrated in her postures. Afterward, we sipped jasmine tea in Maggie's garden and played with the animals until the moon came up. I had drifted home around ten PM. All in all it had been a peaceful evening. What ever had happened?

Maggie dragged me into her living room and sat me down. There was a small wooden box open on the coffee table. What appeared to be old letters—yellowed with age, some still in envelopes—were scattered everywhere.

I picked up one of the letters and began to read. The writing was unsteady. It was signed by Georgiana Winslow.

Maggie snatched the letter away from me.

"Not yet." Then she got up and began to walk back toward the kitchen. "I need to make us some tea, first." Maggie looked more than slightly undone.

"Oh for God's sake, Maggie," I said under my breath. She could not do anything important without making tea. A ritual.

While Maggie was in the kitchen, I looked at the portrait of Georgiana on the wall over the fireplace. She was dressed in white satin. The portrait had probably been done for her "coming out" in New York when she was eighteen. She had the most beautiful silky black hair. There was a barely contained wildness in her dark eyes.

Finally, Maggie and I settled into the sofa with cups of jasmine tea, and she began to tell the story.

"After you left last night, I went straight to bed," she said. "It was only ten, but I was exhausted. I fell into a deep sleep right away. Well, I awoke at one AM, drenched in sweat."

Now Maggie hesitated. "At first I thought I'd been having a dream. But, it wasn't exactly a dream. It was more real than that. I'd been drifting in and out of this strange dreamlike state for what seemed like hours."

Maggie stared straight ahead for a moment, as if she had lost the thread.

"So?" I prodded.

"It was a memory of Georgie's death," said Maggie, still staring, as if she were staring right into the memory.

I already knew some of the details of Georgiana Winslow's dramatic death: Georgie had been thrown by a horse at seventy, when Maggie had been just fifteen years old. Lenox society had been scandalized.

Georgiana was reckless and selfish, some said. This was just another confirmation of her unseemly wildness.

Georgiana had died the night after the accident—not of her injuries, apparently, but of a heart attack, brought on by the stress of the fall. All of this had taken place at the old Winslow mansion—near Acorn Cottage where Rudi now lived. Georgie died in her bed, in the room next to Maggie's.

Maggie and I had talked about Georgiana's death several times before, and it was clear that Maggie had only the vaguest memory of the death scene—even though she had been there for the whole drama. It seemed to me that even the memories Maggie did have were constructed from what others had told her about it. Her descriptions never had the ring of emotional truth. They were disconnected, vague, and mechanical. Now, for the first time, Maggie began to remember the scene vividly—moment by moment. As she recounted it to me, I could feel it.

Maggie spoke slowly, telling the story in present tense and still staring into the distance. "Georgie is in her silk bedclothes—trying to put on a good face for me. But she is obviously in pain. The doctors are scurrying around. Charlotte [Georgie's companion] is beside herself. The room is dark."

"I remember, now. Georgie is reaching out to me. 'Oh, darling. What a stupid accident. Please forgive your foolish Gammy.'"

Maggie went on slowly. "Now Charlotte is hurrying me out. I'm crying, and all alone in my bedroom. Lying on my bed."

That was the last Maggie had seen of Georgie. She died, quite unexpectedly, about two hours later. Maggie had never been allowed to see the body. The casket had been closed. Clearly, Maggie had been traumatized by the event—and she had forgotten it altogether.

Now Maggie crumpled onto the sofa, pulling a big comforter around her—perhaps in just the position she'd been in on her own bed the night Georgie died. Maggie didn't cry. (Though later she told me she had cried hard, off and on, during the two hours before she knocked on my door.) I couldn't tell, really, what Maggie was feeling as we sat together, except that she did seem to be in a mild altered state. I offered to hold her. She said no.

"Just stay with me, will you? Just sit here, right here with me."

I sat next to her on the sofa. She curled up in a ball, with her feet just touching my legs. I stretched my legs out on the big ottoman. We both fell asleep.

When I awoke, it was nearly eight AM. I was curled up next to Maggie, with part of her comforter over me. The sun was slanting in through the sheer drapes in the living room. Maggie was still asleep. Her position hadn't changed.

I carefully extracted myself, and shuffled quietly to the kitchen, where I cooked some eggs and made toast for us—laying it all out on the breakfast table with butter and jam, and a pot of Earl Grey tea, Maggie's favorite.

When Maggie finally awoke, she was still in the penumbra of the altered state. I sat next to her on the sofa, rubbing her back, and she responded with a quiet kind of purr.

"I feel in such a haze. It's like I have a hangover. Like I'm still in a kind of dream world." She curled back up in the comforter again, and I rubbed her back and neck. "I don't want to move," she said.

When Maggie did finally stir, we talked for a while. The memories of the night before seemed perfectly intact.

"It's as though I've been living in a house with all these rooms I didn't even know about. It's so strange. Terrifying and comforting at the same time."

We finally padded to the dining room to nibble on breakfast, and Maggie recounted all the new memories to me once again, as she had the night before. With each recounting, however, I noticed that there were new details. It was as though the memory, like a Polaroid picture, was slowly coming into focus.

After we ate, Maggie held my arm firmly and walked me into the living room. There was more.

"Something else very strange happened," she said, now sounding more like herself. "In the 'dream,' I saw Georgie's writing desk. It was scattered with letters as it always was.

"But I noticed something else," she said. "There was a dark wooden letter box on the desk. Her letter box. Her letter box! And in the dream I thought, Of course! I had forgotten all about it!"

Maggie described what had happened next, in the wee hours of the morning. As she awoke from her dream state, she got out of bed and went right to the attic. There she found Georgiana's writing desk, which had been stored among the trunks since the old Winslow mansion had been closed up forty-five years ago. In the desk, she found a cache of letters that had sat in that drawer for at least fifty years. She also found a key, clearly marked, to the bottom drawer of Georgie's writing desk—which, too, had apparently remained un-opened.

In the locked bottom drawer, Maggie found a treasure of information about Georgie's life—a treasure that would begin to unlock the secret of Duncan Gregor.

ĀSANA: FINDING THE IMMOVABLE SPOT

In the weeks that followed, Maggie and I talked about her revelation at length. During this period, her memories deepened and she often seemed to fill with emotion. Occasionally, as she marveled at these spontaneous events, she wondered aloud to me, "Why now? Why should this revelation have come just now in my life?"

Maggie was convinced that the unlocking of her memories was directly related to the fruit of her deepening yoga practice. She believed that there was some magic in the *āsanas*. We had, after all, done deep posture practice and *yoga-nidrā* the evening before her revelation, hadn't we?

"Didn't you notice what was happening to me in class that evening?" asked Maggie once, irritably.

I thought for a minute, furrowing my brow, but produced nothing remarkable.

"You didn't even notice me holding that Triangle Pose?" she queried.

Maggie had held the Triangle for a long time, yes. Much longer than the rest of the class. But this was so common over the past months as to have been a non-event. Maggie often broke away from the class and did her own modifications, and used her own timing in yoga postures.

"Well, tell me," I said. "What was happening?"

Maggie gave me a long description of what had happened to her in her postures the evening before her "dream"—and indeed what often happened to her those days on the yoga mat. Her description was so interesting that later, I asked her if she could write it down for me. This is what she remembered.

We were about halfway through the standing poses when it happened. I had just held an extremely long Warrior II Pose, and Steve asked us to move directly into a Triangle. My body was soaked in sweat, and I could feel it running down my legs, and drenching my sticky mat. In Warrior II, I felt a powerful eruption of energy from my center, and hit one of those places where I knew I could hold that pose forever. Every energy in the universe seemed to be supporting me, and it was effortless in a strange way.

When I moved down into Triangle Pose, I slowly turned my head upward to gaze along my outstretched, reaching left arm. Energy kicked in again, and I felt my body light up like one of those energy charts on the wall at my acupuncturist. I felt all the lines of energy from my left foot up through my spine, and then through the crown of my head, from my sternum up through my left arm and simultaneously down through my right arm which reached toward the ground.

It was the reaching that did it, I think. Reaching up out of the center. Up toward heaven, down toward earth. With my heart and sternum open. And feeling my legs and abdomen so strong. I dropped my left shoulder slightly back, and this opened my sternum and heart even more.

In a flash, I felt energy stream through my arms and legs, pumping blood and heat. The hard shell of my body melted into liquid light, and there was no more posture. Only energy and light and heat and pulsing and oxygen. No me. No effort. No form. Just life. There was no more reaching now—or at least I was not the one doing it. Only a kind of effortless streaming.

I have no idea how long the experience lasted. It was a moment in time out of time. When I awoke from the trance, the rest of the class had moved on to the next posture. For a while I couldn't make out Steve's words. They echoed in my ears like pure sound.

I finished the rest of the class in a state of bliss, and moved in and out of trance. We all lay down for deep relaxation. Steve knelt down next to me and put his right hand lightly on my belly, just above my navel, and his left hand on the crown of my head. I felt an infusion of love such as I had rarely known. A pulsing sensation moved from my heart to my crown. My body was washed with love and healing. I felt waves of relaxation, going deeper and deeper, all the way into my core.

Time disappeared. As I drifted in yoga-nidrā, *I was surprised by a vision of Shiva—and for the first time I got a sense of who that little guy in the statue really was. He was dancing in the ring of fire in the charnel ground—his arms waving, his hair wild like strands of cobras. One of his hands seemed to say to me, "do not be afraid."*

———

After hearing Maggie's account of her posture, I realized that she was probably right. Her dream-revelation may certainly have been connected to her deepening yoga practice—and also, probably, to her continuing practice of meditation and *mantra*.

Āsana awakens the observing part of the self—the witnessing function—and as this becomes stronger and steadier, previously split-off or disavowed aspects of experience become available to awareness. The mind begins to know itself—to know its exiled parts. This observing function is like a powerful searchlight that automatically scans the entire field of experience. As it gets stronger it reaches into the dark corners, exposing memories of experiences that could not be digested at the time they occurred.

Most contemporary practitioners of yoga assume that postures are meant primarily to cultivate some kind of supernormal state of physical training. This is not quite so. In classical yoga, *āsana* was not meant primarily for *physical* training at all. Says Rajneesh, "Postures are concerned not really with any kind of physiological training, but an inner training of being—learning just to be."[1] In the classical tradition, *āsana* is a continuation of the attentional training found in early meditation practice. The single posture with which Patanjali concerned himself was the posture for meditation.

The Sanskrit word *āsana* literally means "seat." In posture practice, we find the seat from which we can witness the play of experience. Joseph Campbell, the great American scholar of myth and comparative religion, called this seat the "immovable spot," or the "still point."[2] *Āsana* cultivates the still point at the center of the dance of experience—the still point at the center of the play of sensation. The immovable spot from which we can witness the chaining of sensations, thoughts, feelings, and actions.

What are the essential ingredients of this "seat"? Patanjali lays it out succinctly.

The postures of meditation should embody steadiness and ease.
This occurs as all effort relaxes and coalescence arises, reveal-ing that the body and the infinite universe are indivisible.
Then one is no longer disturbed by the play of opposites.
   (2.46–48)

In Part Five we will explore the stunning meditative achievement called "coalescence," which Patanjali mentions here but does not ex-plore fully until later in the *Yoga-Sūtra*. Patanjali's first and third *sūtras* on *āsana*, however, lay the groundwork for this fascinating later attainment, and we can now examine them more closely.

In Patanjali's time, as I have said, *āsana* meant "seat for meditation." It did not mean the immensely varied menu of postures with which we're familiar today. This "seat" would have been primarily the Lotus Pose *(padmāsana)*, the first, the primeval posture, and the mother of all postures. *Padmāsana* is the seated pose we often see in pictures of meditation adepts—with a yogi seated upright on the sits-bones, spine straight, legs intertwined, fingers interlaced, and hands—palms up—resting comfortably in his lap, eyes closed. The Lotus Pose con-nects the body directly to the still point—to the immovable spot.

Patanjali investigates the components of this seat. "Steadiness" (or *sthira,* in Sanskrit) is one of the key principles of posture practice. Notice that Patanjali talks about steadiness, ease, and relaxation of ef-fort. The archetypal posture, however, as meditators quickly discover, is not relaxing in the usual sense of the word. In Lotus Pose, and in all postures for meditation, we do not experience the global reduction of random muscle activity that we usually associate with relaxation. The posture is, rather, stabilizing. Rather than "relaxation," what emerges is an increased regularity in the distribution of muscle output. Research on meditation postures has verified that, as Daniel Brown says, "'steadiness' does not imply a cessation of bodily activity, but a redistribution of muscle activity which counteracts the ordinary random activity ... so that gross motor activity undergoes a kind of 'settling.'"[3] This settling and steadiness help the body to quiet, while still remaining alert.

When "white noise" from random gross muscular activity is quieted, it is possible for awareness to open to more subtle levels of bodily activity—subtle activity that is experienced as a flow of energy currents. In these moments the factors of distraction are settled. Attention becomes highly refined. Concentration deepens. In this balanced state, the bodymind is not "assaulted by the pairs of opposites," as Patanjali tells us. In other words, the mind becomes secluded from the pull of the afflictions.

In *āsana*, we find a seat from which to effectively develop concentration. The noise in the field calms, and we can investigate the subtle bodies. In these settled states, the subtle roots of craving and aversion are burned away. *Sukha*, or sweetness, naturally arises. A literal translation of Patanjali's three-word *sūtra* on posture (2.46—*sthira-sukham-asanam*) is "steadiness, sweetness, posture!"

Early references to *āsana* are most likely references to *padmāsana*, which was found to be ideal both for sitting meditation and the subsequent practice of *prānāyāma*—literally, "regulation of vital energy," Patanjali's fourth "limb." All subsequent postures were spontaneous variations of this first posture.

Swami Kripalu, when initiated by his guru, was given just two practices: *padmāsana* and the *prānāyāma* known as *anuloma viloma*—the practice of "retention of breath" described by Patanjali. Swami Kripalu practiced these assiduously for years. With time, something astonishing happened: as the swami's practice deepened, dozens of new postures began to emerge spontaneously. And not just postures, but *mudrās,* or "gestures" (often gestures of the hands) and more advanced *prāṇāyāmas* as well. These were techniques in which Swami Kripalu had never had instruction. In effect, his own body instructed him in *āsana, prāṇāyāma,* and *mudrā.*

Swami Kripalu's experience probably reenacts the entire history of *hatha-yoga.* It is most likely that the multiplicity of postures was discovered in this way over and over again by meditating yogis. In order to investigate new aspects of the field of experience, their bodies spontaneously adopted new seats, new *āsanas,* new steadily held poses which opened up new aspects of the field for exploration. Just like *padmāsana,* these postures would have been practiced until they were stable and comfortable, revealing some new aspect of the field beyond craving and aversion. Each new posture provided a new base, or seat, from which to explore, to witness. A new still point in the center of the storm of sensation.

Yogis found that the mystical and ecstatic states of concentration that emerged in meditation had profound effects on the human nervous system, and they found that a physical preparation for these altered states made the process much easier to endure without losing the balance of the mind. Yogis experimented with hundreds of *āsanas, mudrās,* and *prāṇāyāmas*—which promoted purification and optimal levels of health. But this experimentation did not gather steam until well after the time of Patanjali.

Gradually, in certain parts of the *sramanic* stream, the practice of *āsana* and *prāṇāyāma* became a central focus. What emerged, then, was the science which came to be known as *hatha-yoga,* or forceful yoga. It wasn't until the fifteenth century CE that Svatmarama Yogin gathered together and published the first systematic text of the *hatha-yogis*—the *Hatha-Yoga-Pradīpikā.* This is still certainly the definitive scripture of *hatha-yoga.* It is written in *sūtra* form, much like Patanjali's *Yoga-Sūtra.* It is interesting to note, however, that while Svatmarama acknowledges the distinction between *hatha-yoga* and *rāja-yoga,* he emphatically speaks for the primacy of *rāja-yoga.*

"Those who practice only *hatha* and do not know *rāja-yoga*," says Svatmarama, "I consider such practitioners to be depriving themselves of the fruit of their endeavor."[4]

"Without *rāja-yoga*," says Svatmarama, "the earth is inauspicious. Without *rāja-yoga*, the night is inauspicious. Without *rāja-yoga*, even *mudrās* are inauspicious."[5]

STILLNESS, PURIFICATION, AND INTEGRATION

Maggie's discovery of the immovable spot—and its interesting manifestations—gives us an opportunity to explore a further by-product of seclusion—the by-product which is sometimes called "purification," or "integration." Integration is, in effect, the *downloading of* samskarās *into awareness.* And it can be dramatic, as it was for Maggie.

Remember that every action of body, speech, and mind creates a *samskāra,* or subliminal activator—a track, or a seed. Remember, too, that in the view of *rāja-yoga*, the mind and the body are the same—made of the "same stuff." Mind and body simply lie along different points in the spectrum of subtlety. The body is a gross form of consciousness. The mind is a more subtle form of consciousness. Yogis came to believe that *samskāric* tracks are laid down in all sheaths of the body—pressed into the physical, energy, and subtle bodies.

So, as we have seen, every act of body, speech, and mind is, in effect, stored in the vast storehouse of consciousness. Our *future* actions of body, speech, and mind are then influenced by these *samskāric* tracks. And in order for us to be free from the power of these subliminal activators, each *samskāra* will have to be experienced again—and fully digested (burned up!)—either now or later, in a future incarnation. Yogis found, too, that there is a hierarchy of *samskāras*—that some *samskāras* are more deeply etched than others. (Yogis have said that some *samskāras* are grooved into consciousness like "a line drawn in water"; some are grooved like "a line drawn in sand"; and some, like "a line drawn in rock.")

The most difficult *samskāras*, those etched in rock, are those to which we had the most powerful original reaction. For Maggie, for example, the experience of Georgie's death aroused powerful thoughts and emotions—fear of loss, and the terror of abandonment. These feelings were so frightening that Maggie could not bear them as a fifteen-year-old. She could not experience them without losing the balance of the mind. And so, she had to deny them. To suppress them. For Maggie, the *samskāras* of her reactions to Georgie's death were hidden in the deepest part of her consciousness.

Why did they emerge when they did, and what is the relationship of this emergence to Maggie's practice?

This is a fascinating question, and one with which yogis preoccupied themselves. Through self-study, yogis discovered something amazing: When we are in a state of non-reactivity, when we are dwelling at the still point, we are not generating any new *samskāras*. In these moments, the mind and body are still. *Nirodha*. And this stillness and non-reactivity has powerful consequences. It initiates the process of purification. Says the meditation teacher S. N. Goenka: "Every moment for the whole of our lives we have generated reactions. Now, by remaining aware and balanced, we achieve a few moments in which we do not react, do not generate any *samskāra*. Those few moments, no matter how brief, are very powerful: they set in motion the reverse process, the process of purification."[6]

When the mind is secluded, when consciousness is not preoccupied with digesting a flood of *current experience,* it begins automatically to register and digest material from the vast storehouse of *samskāric* impressions. In these moments, impressions of past experiences bubble up to the surface, and are experienced as "real"—that is to say, they are experienced just as any other current sensory input is experienced. (Remember the six sense doors!) Now the contents of the storehouse are re-experienced, one by one. The less deeply grooved *samskāras* are experienced first, the more deeply etched *samskāras* later. Here is the kicker: when they are re-experienced without reactivity—with a balance of awareness and equanimity—

they are digested, burned up, or as yogis sometimes say, "cooked"—just as digestion burns up a big meal.

As Maggie's consciousness became balanced and non-reactive, and as her Witness became more resilient (not "blown away" by powerful feelings), it was inevitable that these old impressions would resurface.

Now we can see more clearly why "seclusion" of the mind is so important in the yogic strategy. Yogis saw that even a few seconds of real concentration (real seclusion, real *dhāranā*) initiates the purification of the deeper levels of the mind. Goenka refers to this as a kind of "fasting of the spirit in order to eliminate past conditioning."[7] The deeper we go into the fasting (seclusion), the deeper the levels of *samskāra* that are surfaced. This is exactly the process Kate experienced when she found herself "fasting from gossip"—a technique which exposed the subtle intentions and motivations behind her lying.

It isn't so difficult to understand this kind of fasting—because it is so analogous to fasting at the physical level. Purification of the mind involves much the same process as purification of the body. It simply happens at a more subtle level. Both are characterized by periods of withdrawal, and by moments of intense reactivity—intense craving or aversion—followed by moments of equanimity.

We are now close to the core of yoga's technology of transformation. Because, if we are to believe yogic sages, it is in these moments of withdrawal and seclusion of the mind that the foundations of the afflictions are destroyed. Craving, aversion, greed, ignorance, hatred—these are all eradicated in states of meditative absorption.

Yoga scholar Georg Feuerstein gives a lucid description of how this occurs: "'Attenuation' [of *klesha*] is achieved by refusing these forces [greed, hatred, and ignorance] an outlet ... Their power is partly checked by sensory withdrawal and the accompanying stilling of the mind. In other words, the yogin plays the subliminal structures off against each other. By disallowing them to take effect in the conscious mind, he indirectly achieves their mutual annihilation.... When even the last subliminal activator [*samskāra*] is exterminated, the *klesha* can be said to be fully destroyed as well."[8]

As Goenka says, "To trigger this process [of purification]...we must simply refrain from any fresh reaction. Whatever might be the cause of the sensations we experience, we observe them with equanimity. The very act of generating awareness and equanimity will automatically eliminate old reactions, just as lighting a lamp will dispel darkness from the room."[9] This is the process of self-observation without judgment taken to new depths.

What happens as *samskāras* are being "downloaded," as they were for Maggie? They are reexperienced, without reactivity this time—they are seen (witnessed) and known without judgment, grasping, or aversion. As a result they are "burned up" in the heat of tapas. Concentration, it turns out, is simply a new and highly refined form of *tapas*.

And finally, we are back again, as always, to *nirodha*. Stillness in the mind draws forth those areas that are not still. This is the genius of stillness. It inexorably and naturally purifies the mind. But, of course, this can only happen when concentration, awareness, and non-reactivity have matured.

And what does this purification feel like? As Maggie discovered, the downloading of *samskāras* is not quite the same as simply *remembering* a past event or emotion. It is actually a *reexperiencing* of the undigested *samskāric* tracks. So, for Maggie, it was a reexperiencing of the scene of Georgie's death. In some ways, she did not relive it: she lived it for the first time. But this time with awareness and equanimity, and all the fruit of her years of contemplative practice.

Contemporary neuroscience has given us a series of intriguing insights into this process. This begins with a sophisticated new tool for exploring Puppy Mind itself. We now understand that Puppy Mind is reflected in brain-wave activity. Neuroscientists can now map this brain-wave activity. We can see Puppy Mind on the computer screen.

How does this work? Nerve cells in the brain communicate with each other by emitting tiny electrical impulses, and this activity can be registered as oscillations, or brain waves. These brain waves can be measured by amplifying the impulses and displaying them on a computer monitor—a method called electroencephalography, or EEG.

And what do these brain waves tell us? Well, first of all, this electrical activity in the brain is very different depending on our state of mind. When the mind is active, excited, anxious, and wakeful (Puppy Mind!), "beta-waves" predominate in the EEG. These are oscillations in the range of 13–36 waves per second. When the mind is calmer, quietly focused and recollected, these oscillations can slow to a range of 8–13 per second, a range called "alpha." Alpha waves predominate when we're conscious, aware, and centered—and they are a kind of portal into the deeper states of consciousness. They are characteristic of the waking, meditative state.

But, as yogis also discovered, there are mind-states that manifest an even slower, quieter, range of brain waves. In adults, states of "half consciousness"—between wakefulness and sleep—are characterized by "theta waves," oscillations in the range of 4–8 waves per second. Theta waves are formed deep in the brain and seem to reflect activity associated with strong emotions and dreaming states. But the brain is capable of quieting even more profoundly. In states of deep sleep, the oscillations can slow to a range of 1–4 waves per second. These are called "delta waves." These slowest patterns are associated with the deepest states of consciousness. Some researchers have said that they reflect the most subtle, intuitive aspects of the mind.

New research shows that during yoga and meditation practice most subjects experience a significant decrease in beta waves, but an increase in alpha and theta waves. Studies have shown that increased theta waves, when mixed with alpha waves, "correlate with the appearance of previously unconscious feelings, images and memories.

Brain researchers claim that a person in the high alpha/theta state is able to confront and integrate unconscious processes."[10] One researcher draws the obvious conclusion from these studies: "The meditative state, characterized by high alpha/theta activity, can bring about a release, or 'cleansing' of unconscious material."[11]

As Maggie's practice deepened, she began to systematically cultivate these slower, quieter rhythms in the mind. This led inexorably to a downloading of memory, and repressed thoughts and feelings. And, finally, because she was able to remain in a state of non-reactive self-observation, the process culminated in the emergence and immolation of some deeply grooved *samskāras*.

LIVING IN "TIME OUT OF TIME"

Maggie now entered a period of weeks during which she continued to relive repressed experiences. Out of the memory of Georgiana's death flowed countless other small memories—as if the memory of the death scene had been a kind of key. Rather like the key to Georgiana's letter box.

"It's as if I buried a part of myself with Georgie," Maggie said. "A part of me went into the ground with her.

"And now, it's all washing out. I'm coming alive again. Everything seems sacred. Alive. It's as if I've been reunited with Georgie."

For a short window of time, Maggie found postures, meditation, and *mantra* to be effortless—like riding a wave. She was drawn to the quiet. She sat as if at the still point of the turning world, and watched as her life replayed itself. There were both painful and pleasurable memories, of course, but to Maggie they were better than the inner compartmentalization in which she had lived. ("A relief to feel them. A relief to feel at all!") Her sleep and dreams were, as she said, "drenched in memory," and she often lay in bed, now, savoring these.

She saw, too, that as she got quiet and lived at the still point, the process played itself out spontaneously. As soon as she was tempted to direct it with her will, as soon as she brought grasping into the equation, the process was interrupted. The harder she reached for her sweet memories, the more elusive they became. She learned to trust the process. She learned that it would all unwind in just the right way.

Slowly, Maggie began to understand that her writing had been an attempt to reunite herself with these memories. The current novel, in fact, was, she later said, "like a big archeological dig." She discovered that in "channeling" Duncan Gregor, she was really reuniting with a split-off part of herself. She identified with him in so many ways: he was a brilliant artist who never came into his own; he was another human being on the planet who had loved Georgiana as passionately as she had; he had lived free of the restraints of the often-stilted society in which Maggie had grown up—a position in life which Maggie also strived for. In discovering Duncan Gregor's voice, she actually found a part of her own voice. Or, rather, a part of The Voice, which she had split off.

Remarkably, Maggie was not undone by all this "purification." In fact, there was a new settled quality to her. She was less driven, more vulnerable, more openhearted. I noticed over the months to come that she had more time for our friendship. I nestled closer to her in these months, and she to me.

Paradoxically, Maggie's grasping, her wanting, her striving and pushing, had been both the *road* to this reunion with split-off parts, and an *obstacle* to it. Her real reunion, with herself and with her experience of Georgiana, all only tumbled out when her grasping had been momentarily stilled through practice. It emerged as she stayed present at the center of the storm of thoughts, feelings, and memories.

—

As the drama of Maggie's discoveries unfolded, I was profoundly surprised by several things. First of all, as a psychotherapist, I would have expected more drama, more catharsis. But it became clear to me that Maggie was not really experiencing the phenomenon that therapists today call "traumatic reexperiencing." Indeed, where was the trauma in it? Rather, for Maggie it was a reexperiencing that emerged naturally when her mind had developed enough awareness and equanimity to digest it. There were, of course, plenty of tears, and deeply felt sadness and loss. But Maggie insisted that she was not depressed or undone. And, indeed, she was not. She talked, rather, about "a sweet kind of sadness."

Was it really just yoga and meditation that provided her with the new source of equanimity? I don't think so. I came to understand, later, that Maggie's maturation came also as a result of her new web of relationships—which included me and our band of friends. Maggie had, for the first time since Georgiana's death, a network of relationships in which she felt safely held and soothed—comforted, supported, upheld. I would come to understand that Maggie had relied not just upon her own developing Witness, but on the witness consciousness of our entire group. Just as Sigmund Freud "loaned" his patients his ego when they needed it, our group loaned its members the group witness consciousness.

Frank Lloyd Wright said, "We create our houses and then they create us." Likewise, we create our web of relationships, and then they create us. It was only out of this safe and sane web of relationships that the new Maggie was being born. And the new me. And Jake, Susan, Rudi, and Kate.

Practice was important, of course. Postures. Meditation. *Mantra.* We all continued to practice—and deeply. But with this experience of Maggie's revelation, I began to wonder just how much of the real juice of transformation came about through the growing bonds and collective intelligence and wisdom of our group—rather than the practices we did on the mat, and on the meditation cushion. Certainly they potentiated each other in some mysterious way. Perhaps this would become clearer as we continued to work together.

One other thing surprised me about Maggie's experience: she never, throughout the whole course of this adventure, spoke about the death of her parents. She never, at least in my hearing, consciously connected the loss of Georgiana to the loss of her parents when she was just three years old. She never uttered their names.

It was clear to me that this *samskāra* was even more deeply buried—still safely tucked away until she could bear knowing it. A graduate school mentor of mine once said, "There are some things you never get over." I wondered if Maggie would ever, in this lifetime, rediscover inside herself the loss of her parents. For surely, it was all in there. Perhaps this would have to wait for a future year, or a future life.

BREATH, TRUST, AND THE TRANSMUTATION OF HUNGER

HUNGRY GHOSTS GOBBLING AIR

My late-afternoon yoga class was practicing a simple alternate nostril breathing technique. It was already dark outside, and the first light snow of the season was falling. There were only a dozen people in the room. I had taught the class a breathing practice called *nādī-shodhana* (or purifying breath), and though most of the students had caught on right away, Susan was struggling. She was overworking it, as usual—huffing and puffing. Others were beginning to notice. Jake (ever aversive to noise) looked at me with a cold and plaintive stare.

I tried to catch Susan's eye. But no. Her eyes were closed, and she was bearing down on her practice with all her might. She was closing and opening the nostrils correctly—with the thumb and third and fourth fingers of her right hand. Back and forth, back and forth, huff and puff, huff and puff. But her practice had none of the subtlety of beautiful *prāṇāyāma*.

I interrupted my own practice for a while and watched. Susan was gobbling air. I was used to seeing students hold their breath. But Susan had brought in an interesting new twist. Hunger for air—a strange kind of overindulgence.

Susan's voracious appetite included not just food, but all types of experience. She was always moving, driven—eager for the next mo-

206

ment, for what it might bring. She was, as a result, time-bound, rushed, and slightly frantic—always leaning into the next moment. She could not trust that life itself would feed her. That breath would feed her.

As I watched more closely, I discovered something curious: though the drama of huffing and puffing made it appear that Susan was breathing deeply, she actually was not. She was not breathing down into the lower lobes of the lungs. The wave of breath was not going all the way down into her belly. Her diaphragm was held tightly, and though her chest was moving, her abdomen was not. She was gobbling breath, yes. But it was obvious that it was not satisfying. Why?

Susan was exhibiting a subtle form of hyperventilation syndrome. She was breathing by using the thorax rather than the diaphragm—a condition that results in chronically overinflated lungs. This simple breathing irregularity can chronically activate the body's fight-or-flight response, resulting in a sense of being ill-at-ease in the body.

The lesson? Breathing deeply is not necessarily the same as breathing fully and effectively. Truly effective breathing involves long, slow exhalation and natural (not forced or excessive) inhalation.

Susan, did you know that you were breathing like that?" I asked.

Susan and I were sitting together on a stack of pillows at the back of the room after class. A small group of students was practicing postures quietly on the other side of the room.

For a moment, Susan looked wounded. "I was afraid this class would be too advanced for me," she said.

"No, Susan. It's not that at all. It's just that there is something here we could explore."

We talked for a while, and Susan began to relax. I reflected back to her precisely what I had seen in her breathing. She got interested in what I had to say.

"Would you like to investigate this a little bit more?"

Susan nodded her head. (This was the upside of Susan's hunger—

she was an excellent student; in the pursuit of learning she was willing to risk.) I had her lie down on the floor in supine position, in what is sometimes called corpse pose.

I had Susan put her hands on her belly. I put on some soothing music—a low, quiet drone—and lit a couple of candles. The Dancing Shiva was shimmering on the altar behind us.

I instructed Susan to place her hands palms down on her belly, to let them be heavy, and to breathe down into her belly as if her breath could meet the touch of her hands there.

"Feel the warmth of your hands on your belly. Feel the breath down in the core of the body. Feel it in your back. And in your sides. Let yourself relax."

Susan lay for a few moments like that—her body completely still. I covered her with a soft blue blanket, and then, with her permission, I gently held the back of her head.

"Oh, keep doing that. That's wonderful," she said, purring. I massaged her neck for a moment.

Susan began to relax. She was soothed. She told me later that she felt held and safe—and that this feeling changed the way she was breathing.

I could still see tightness, though. Susan's ribs seemed locked, and her diaphragm held rigidly. Her belly was moving, but her sides and back were not.

I continued to coach her. "Just let your body breathe naturally. Trust the breath. It's OK however it emerges. Don't attempt to guide or force the breath in any way. Just be with it as it arises."

Before long, Susan's breathing shifted. Her breath became soft. Quiet. Her ribs unlocked. Subtle waves of sensation were rising and falling throughout her body. Susan's belly, abdomen, and pelvis were pulsing with the breath.

"Um-hum," she mumbled almost inaudibly.

Then, as if momentarily frightened that this pleasure would end, she opened her eyes. "Stay right where you are," she said. "That is so soothing."

Susan, reassured, began to let the weight of her head release into my hands. She rested like that for a while. The candles flickered. The soft drone of the music was calming. A smiling Swami Kripalu looked down on us from his perch on the wall behind us.

Finally, when Susan seemed calmly absorbed in the breath, I pulled my hands from beneath her head. I put a meditation cushion close to her body, and sat cross-legged in meditation pose several feet from her side. I had determined to let her lie there as long as she wanted to.

A few minutes after I withdrew my hands, I watched as Susan's body changed. I could see a wave of trembling begin in her belly. Her breathing became more ragged again as she resisted the wave of feeling.

"It's OK, Susan," I said softly. "I'm right here. Stay with yourself. Trust the energy and let it move."

Susan began to choke. Energy began to move in her body now. Her body began to shake softly and jerk. She surrendered to the wave of breath, and was riding this wave.

"Stay with it," I coached. "Allow the body to breathe as it will. Relax. Just feel." Finally, a wave of sobbing emerged. Then subsided. Then arose again.

Susan reached out, wanting to touch me. I stayed next to her. "Stay with yourself, Susan. It's OK. I'm here." She could bear to stay with the sobbing for a few moments. Then she tried to stop it again. Tried to get off the wave of breath.

"Stay with the breath, Susan. Trust it."

After ten minutes or so, the waves of sobbing began to slow, becoming more internal. Finally, the waves subsided altogether. After a few minutes, Susan sat up and blew her nose. Then she took a seated posture next to me and closed her eyes.

Now, Susan was breathing normally, and more fully than I'd ever seen her breathe. For the first time, it looked as though her breath was really breathing her. The wave of emotion had cleansed her breathing—like a rainstorm clears the air.

Susan and I sat next to each other for another twenty minutes—meditating. By now, everyone else had left the room. Susan's breathing was effortless and quiet. She was perfectly still.

Susan and I talked for a while afterward. She shared with me her surprise that I would want to be with her in this way. She was terrified that she might have overwhelmed me—that her need might have "disgusted" me, or pushed me away; terrified that too many moments like this would lose her my friendship.

"Susan, I don't need you to be any particular way," I said. "I'm interested in how you *are*. How you *really* are." She was, I think, beginning to see that this was true.

I asked her what had triggered the wave of sobbing.

"I don't know. It was like there was this huge gaping hole inside me. Like a cavern. It was terrifying. At times, the hole was full of something heavy. Lead. Cannonballs. A big weight. I felt both empty and horribly full.

"Then, after I cried, I felt loneliness in that cavern. And my mind was full of images of my family. You know how in my family everyone is in your face all the time? At the same time, I realized we're so alone. For the first time, it seemed OK to feel this aloneness. And I knew you were right there next to me."

Susan's pattern of breathing was both a manifestation of, and a defense against these feelings of emptiness. It was an emptiness she had not previously been able to bear. The whole Goldstein clan, indeed, was in flight from this same experience of emptiness and aloneness. And so they preoccupied themselves with finding ways of feeling full. As a result, they blocked their sense of moment-to-moment aliveness. They entered into an unconscious conspiracy to avoid this aliveness at any cost, because feeling alive meant directly experiencing this gaping hole. The way Susan's family loved one another, in fact, was to help each other avoid life. This was their unwritten contract—to distract each other from a life that seemed unbearable.

IMPLICIT MEMORY AND DYSREGULATION OF BREATH

The ancient yogi seekers discovered that all of the secrets of resistance to life can be discovered in the breath. The way we breathe tells us everything about the way we live. When the mind is disturbed, the breath is disturbed. In book one of the *Yoga-Sūtra*, Patanjali describes many of the symptoms of affliction in the mind and body.

> *Sickness, apathy, doubt, carelessness, laziness, sexual indulgence, delusion, lack of progress, and inconstancy are all distractions that, by stirring up consciousness, act as barriers to stillness.*
> *When they do, one may experience distress, depression, or the inability to maintain steadiness of posture or breathing.*
> (1.30–31)

Dysregulation of the breath, or what yogis sometimes call "hard breathing," is an inevitable side effect of afflicted mind. The precise form of this dysregulation is very telling. The breath will tell us when we're angry. The breath will tell us when we're craving. The breath will tell us when we're lying, cheating, and stealing. The breath will tell us when there is any hint of *duhkha* present at all.

Yogis discovered as many varieties of breathing disturbances as Inuit discovered snow. In their book *Vivation*, authors Jim Leonard and Phil Laut have a particularly colorful list of these forms of "hard breathing":

congestion of the sinuses; constriction, tension and excessive closing of the larynx; chronic inflammation of the bronchi; spasms of the smooth muscle of the bronchi (asthma); inhibited use of the diaphragm and the external intercostal muscles, thus holding on to the exhale and interfering with the normal rhythm; chronic tension and excessive use of the internal intercostal muscles, thus forcing the exhale and interfering with the normal rhythm; the bunching of the various fascia involved . . .[1]

For the most part (as in Susan's case), disturbances to breath are unconscious. Each of us develops characteristic styles of breathing that chronically hold and pattern breath so that unbearable aspects of our emotional body are held out of awareness. *Samskāras* are patterned into the subtlest processes of breath.

Yogis understood that disturbances to the breath are subtle, and that in order to perceive them at all, one must study them closely. Susan was an interesting case. As I studied her pattern, it appeared that while she was excessively focused on the in-breath (gobbling air), she had a hard time letting go of the out-breath. Her diaphragm was constricted, and the wave of breath did not penetrate down into the pelvic bowl and the lower half of the body. She was doing some strange combination of over-breathing and holding her breath. As a result, she was constantly on the edge of her seat, waiting for something bad to happen. The Goldstein clan was a frozen tribe: waiting to exhale.

Susan's symptoms were aspects of what is now sometimes called hyperventilation syndrome. Hyperventilation means breathing excessively fast, or breathing too much air too quickly for the actual conditions in which we find ourselves. Trying to breathe too deeply, and too fast, releases carbon dioxide quickly. As a result, the arteries and vessels carrying blood to our cells constrict, and the oxygen in our blood is unable to reach the cells in sufficient quantity. This includes the carotid arteries, which carry blood to the brain. The red blood cells become "sticky" (hemoglobin holds more tightly to oxygen molecules) and are slow to release oxygen into the cells. The lack of sufficient oxygen going into the cells then activates the sympathetic nervous system, which makes us more tense, irritable, tight, and constricted.

"Complete breathing" is a very different animal. In a complete breath, we let the diaphragm pass through its entire range of motion in a free and natural way. In full breathing—sometimes called natural, or diaphragmatic breathing—the abdomen releases during inhalation, making a soft round belly, like the belly we see on so many statues of meditating yogis. But it is not just the belly that expands. When we're breathing fully, we breathe into all the spaces of the body—back, sides, ribs, belly, pelvis, legs. The movement of the inbreath enlivens even the spine.

Full, relaxed breathing includes a long, slow exhalation as well. This is important, for it is precisely this relaxed exhalation that activates the parasympathetic nervous system, what we today call the "relaxation response."[2]

When the breath is fully open, relaxed, and free, all aspects of the breathing system—lungs, diaphragm, muscles of the rib cage, and chest—are unconstricted in their movement, and the breath naturally finds a slow, steady rhythm. Though physiology texts state that the average breath rate for adults is twelve to fifteen breaths a minute, many serious practitioners of yoga breathe at a much slower rate. A study published in *The Lancet* suggests that a breath rate of six breaths a minute has certain benefits that higher frequencies do not have—and found that patients who slow their breathing down to this rate through breathing exercises have higher levels of blood oxygen and perform better on exercise tests.[3] Yogis, likewise, found that a healthy "at rest" breathing rate is between six and eight breaths per minute.

Besides hyperventilation, it turned out that Susan had a host of other breath-related irregularities: Her mouth and jaw were chronically tight. Her throat felt constricted—as if there were constantly a "lump" there. When she sobbed, as she had with me, she felt these constrictions release.

Susan was the picture of the Hungry Ghost—with much of her energy stuck in the top of her body, unable to penetrate the block at the throat (the teeny neck). The wave of breath and energy could not penetrate into her pelvis and abdomen. The feelings there were just too dangerous, too overwhelming. From the neck down, Susan did not fully inhabit her body. She was, indeed, living like a ghost in the world. How did this come about? Susan's patterns of breathing were formed long ago, probably in infancy, as a result of the fear, anxiety, and repressed hunger that so characterized her family life. But the patterns had now become divorced from their original causes, and had a life of their own—what psychologists call "functional autonomy."

As a result, Susan's pattern of breathing was restimulating her anxiety, fear, and longing. The past was alive in the present through this unconscious pattern. Eugene O'Neill described this form of suffering: "There is no present or future. Only the past repeating itself over and over again."[4]

In other words, the breathing dysregulation *itself* was holding Susan's memories of a painful childhood, a traumatic family life. Psychologists sometimes call this form of physiologically-based memory an implicit memory. Unlike an explicit memory, implicit memory does not carry with it any sense of something being recalled. It is, rather, a kind of habitual, automatic, mechanized process that holds the memory without the emotional facts of the memory ever becoming fully conscious.

Implicit memory is the way the nervous system has learned to relate to the environment. Remember the cats and the stripes? Whatever the sources of Susan's original breathing inhibition were (and Susan knew a lot about them through her analysis with Dr. Brenner), nevertheless here they were, today—alive in the body and the breath.

Implicit memories are laid down through a process called procedural learning—a learning of processes that becomes habitual, and reactions that become automatic and mechanized. This contemporary discovery appears to be a Western representation of some of the functions of *samskāra*: Habit. Automatization. Mechanization. The ruts in the road. Increasingly, Western-trained therapists are seeing, as yogis did two thousand years ago, that the results of procedural learning can only be effectively disrupted by what some call a "bottom-up" approach—direct physiological retraining. Insight is relatively ineffective in deconstructing habitual behavior.

Western psychologists have found that there are two primary ways of disrupting the results of procedural learning. They are, not surprisingly, the very two approaches taken by yogis.[5]

First, simply call attention to the process—without judgment of any kind. This, as we have seen, naturally begins to disrupt the automaticity of the pattern.

And second, engage in activities that intentionally disrupt the pattern, and engage in relearning more effective, natural, healthy behaviors. Intentionally reshape the way the nervous system relates to the environment.

In our investigations of her breathing patterns, Susan and I would explore both approaches.

THE SELF-REGULATING BREATH

Patanjali's approach to working with the breath is simplicity itself. Remember the mother of all knots in the shoelace? Disturbed breathing is precisely this kind of knot. And the antidote is the same: Stop. Watch. Observe without judgment, without reaction. Allow awareness to become absorbed in the breath, *just as it is.*

When breath becomes the object of this kind of attention, a small miracle happens: the breath naturally settles. Patanjali says it like this:

As the movement patterns of each breath—inhalation, exhalation, lull—are observed as to duration, number, and area of focus, breath becomes spacious and subtle. (2.50)

In other words, as we bring awareness to every aspect of the breath—inhale, exhale, lull—the breath automatically begins to reregulate itself. In this technique, there is no attempt to manipulate the breath or to impose another pattern on it. Just notice exactly how it is.

This is simply a further manifestation of the yogic principles we have been investigating all along: concentration on the breath moves consciousness toward meditative absorption, with all the attendant effects of calm and interiorization. In the case of breath, concentration (and the resulting absorption) has another interesting effect. Absorption begins automatically to reregulate the breath—to move the breath toward its most subtle, healthy, and balanced version. In other words, the breath is a self-regulating function!

As author Chip Hartranft says in his commentary on Patanjali,

> Whatever aspect of the breath one observes—its length, quantity, or region of activity—the effect is to make the unconscious conscious. Its rhythms no longer dictated by internal commotion, the observed breath begins to soften and spread out in each of its phases.[6]

Breathing therapists have noticed this phenomenon as well. They have found that simply teaching patients to bring their awareness back again and again to their breathing automatically leads them to self-correct deficient breathing patterns.

Psychotherapists have learned the same lesson, but have developed a different language for describing what happens—describing it instead in terms of procedural learning. Says one prominent teacher of this technique: "Observe, rather than interpret, what takes place—especially the body's automatic responses—and repeatedly call attention to it. This in itself tends to disrupt the automaticity with which procedural learning ordinarily is expressed."[7]

In the weeks that followed our *prānāyāma* lesson, I challenged Susan: notice the breath. While you're in the car on the way to pick up Monica, simply bring your awareness to the breath. While you're walking the dog, check it out: how, precisely, are you breathing right now? While you're sitting staring at your computer screen—stop, and see how you're breathing.

"One more thing," I said. "As soon as you remember to notice your breath, also soften your belly."

Authors and meditation teachers Stephen and Ondrea Levine developed a simple and remarkably effective approach to the breath. "Develop the habit of soft belly," they say. "Just soften your belly. As soon as you relax your belly, you begin to breathe more deeply. You become conscious of breathing."[8]

So, I taught Susan the simplest *prānāyāma* in the world. "Soften your belly."

I said to Susan, in effect: Don't worry about advanced breathing, or manipulating the breath in any way whatsoever. That is for later, perhaps. *Sramanas* developed a complex and subtle repertoire of breathing practices and exercises meant to disrupt pattern and restore full and natural breathing—and these advanced techniques are taught today in many yoga traditions. But Susan simply needed to learn how to trust her own natural breathing. There was so much for her to learn just by watching the way the breath emerges.

"Could you learn to be present right now with exactly the way it is?" I asked Susan. "If it's tight, observe that. Feel it. If it's ragged, observe that. Be with it. How is it, exactly? Can you ride the wave of breath precisely as it is?"

———

I also taught Susan a technique to help with her practice of conscious breathing—a technique that we teach to most of our students at Kripalu Center. It was the same technique I had been applying with her the evening of our "breathing breakthrough" in the Sunset Room.

It's called BRFWA, or Breathe. Relax. Feel. Watch. Allow.

Breathe   Soften the belly, and bring your awareness to the breath. The body responds immediately. The wave of breath begins to flow into all parts of the body.

Relax   Full breathing automatically initiates relaxation. In order to deepen this effect, it can be useful to coach yourself. "Relax." You can consciously relax the muscles: The face. The brow. The belly.

Feel   Actively begin to investigate the wave of feeling generated by this relaxation. Where in your body do you feel sensation, energy, movement? Investigate. Move toward the sensations and feelings, rather than away from them.

Watch   As your thoughts quiet down and you enter more fully into your sensations, you may notice a witnessing awareness beneath, or "inside," your experience. Allow yourself to identify with this Witness. The Witness stands at the center of experience, and is able to be *with* the experience, the sensation, the feeling, but not overwhelmed by it.

Allow   Now, coach yourself to allow the wave of feeling to wash through you. No need to block anything. It's all safe. It will not destroy you. It will not annihilate you. It will not hurt others. Stay with it. Stay with yourself.

———

It didn't take Susan long to discover the surprising power in this practice. It allowed her to stop trying so hard. It allowed her to learn to trust the natural wisdom of the body. She could let go of effort rather than produce more. And for Susan, in almost every way, less was more.

After a while, I found Susan experimenting with this technique in yoga class. Sometimes, she would spread out her blue blanket at the back of class, lie down, and simply become attentive to her breathing. She felt soothed just listening to the teacher's voice. She felt soothed just feeling the class around her. Here, she felt safe enough to experience her own body. Susan found that she loved to be alone in the presence of others. She knew that in this environment, no one would intrude upon her experience—as her family did. For the first time, she experienced a nonintrusive presence. She drank it in.

Increasingly, Susan could reenact the scene of our first breathing lesson. But now she could coach herself. It helped her to do this in the context of the class, because she felt safely held and soothed in their presence, as she had in mine that evening many months earlier. In our first breathing session, I had "loaned" Susan my witness. Now, the witness was awakened within her.

Susan learned that when she was relaxed and present, and when anxiety and fear had drawn back like the tide, her breath became soft, subtle, and effortless. Indeed, yogis found that when consciousness is not colored by *duhkha*, the breath is subtle indeed.

In the *Yoga-Sūtra*, Patanjali mentions this state of quiet, and declares it to be a preparation for the deepest meditative states. In his second *sūtra* on *prānāyāma*, as we have seen, Patanjali mentions the three movements of breath (inhalation, exhalation, lull). Now he tells us about a fourth pattern and its remarkable effect on consciousness.

> *As realization dawns, the distinction between breathing in and*
> *   out falls away.*
> *Then the veil lifts from the mind's luminosity.*
> *And the mind is now fit for concentration.* (2.51–53)

The mind and body are now prepared to enter into the deeper stages of meditation practice—with all their attendant powers and possibilities.

CRAVING OR SAVORING?

Susan and I walked up to the orchard. It was a cold day in December, and the sky was steely gray. We found our usual spot at the top of the orchard, and sat on some rocks, with Kripalu and Lake Mahkeenac spread out before us. For a while, we sat and munched on peanut-butter cookies—and sipped tea from my stainless steel thermos.

Susan and I were both pensive. It had been almost a year and a half since our first picnic on the ridge together as a group. Remarkably, it had been a year since Susan's dramatic near slip in the Stop & Shop parking lot. Perhaps our perch high above the lake prompted long thoughts in each of us—thoughts of our time together as a group, thoughts of our practice and its effects on our lives. Or perhaps the approaching holidays had prompted this introspection. I knew that Susan would soon be heading to New York, to spend Hanukkah with her mother and father.

Susan said to me, "You know what's funny? I feel things more now than I used to."

She looked at me seriously. "I feel my hunger."

Susan declared this as if it had occurred to her for the first time. She continued, now directing a long gaze out over the winter-bare Berkshire Hills: "Strangely, with all those compulsive eating problems, I realize now that I never really felt hungry. Just compelled. Driven. Obsessed."

She laughed as she turned back to me. "You know—I used to think obsession was a feeling. But now that I'm actually feeling things, I see that it's not really a feeling at all. For me it was actually a way to block feelings."

She nibbled on the cookie. "Now I taste food, too."

Susan was exactly right. Her cravings had been "acted out." Not felt. And now she was beginning to see one of the central problems with this acting out: acting out behavior splits us off from the feelings driving the behavior. Acting out means that we're lost in the chain of thought, feeling, reaction, action. We've momentarily lost the battle for freedom. We're automatons.

For Susan, a central goal in her practice of yoga (and also in her psychotherapy treatment with Dr. Brenner) was to bring these oral longings and hunger into awareness—to slow down the obsessive thoughts and compulsive actions that for so many years had tumbled inexorably out of her complex chaining reactions. It was obvious to me that she was beginning to interrupt them earlier and earlier by simply feeling them.

Susan was discovering that hunger and need are just hunger and need. She did not have to feel so afraid or ashamed of them. They did not make her a monster. She was not going to devour anyone. She saw, more and more, that she was an ordinary person, having ordinary feelings.

Susan's credo in this work had become the one she spoke shortly after her near slip a year earlier: "No matter what the feeling, it's always better to feel it."

Susan had begun to discover a crucial difference between *craving* and *savoring*. In craving, we vainly attempt to possess the object, to devour it, to have it. In savoring, we find pleasure in simply knowing the object.

With this discovery, Susan was approaching one of the most liberating insights in the wisdom tradition of yoga—an insight that clarifies our confused relationship with the object world. Yogis saw that human beings wish to devour, to possess, to *have* objects of pleasure—people, places, and things. They saw, too, that objects cannot really be possessed. However, objects *can* be known. And it turns out that it is *knowing* the object that creates happiness.

We might say that "savoring" is the happiness created through the simple act of knowing an object. This savoring creates a different relationship with objects. But it also creates a different relationship with time. In the experience of savoring there is no time pressure. There is no pressure for more. There is no pressure to possess the object. "The life of sensation is the life of greed," says Annie Dillard. "It requires more and more. The life of the spirit requires less and less; time is ample and its passage sweet."[9]

Contemporary neuroscience is beginning to help us more fully understand this very difference between savoring and craving. It seems that these two processes are on different circuits in the brain. Neuroscientists have found that all forms of craving involve abnormalities in the production of powerful brain chemicals called endorphins and dopamine. Interestingly, these abnormalities are generic to all forms of craving—craving for food, for sex, for shopping, gambling, and for highly addictive ritualized behaviors of all kinds.

When experiencing an addictive craving, the brain releases massive amounts of endorphins. For a compulsive gambler, for example, this endorphin rush can be stimulated just by thinking about the behavior—thinking about the gambling tables, or the racetrack. The endorphin rush brought on by thoughts of the behavior is so pleasant that we want more of it. So, we imagine ourselves at the gambling table. This repetition of thoughts strengthens craving. The next step in the process, however, creates an addictive spiral: it turns out that endorphins stimulate the activity of the high-octane neurotransmitter dopamine. As dopamine floods the system—in the midst of this addictive hit—the number of receptor sites sensitive to dopamine decrease. This process is called downregulation.

With downregulation, we find that we're less sensitive to the thoughts of a night at the tables. We're dulled to it. Just thinking about a night at the gambling tables does not create such a rush anymore. In order to get the hit, we have to actually *do* the behavior. We have to actually do the teeniest bit of gambling. That will give us the rush. But after a while, just doing "the teeniest bit of gambling" doesn't give us the same rush, either. Now, we have to do it more, harder—and with higher stakes. A gambling spree.

Here is one apt description of this increasingly well-understood process: "The absence of a pleasurable sensation in conditions that were formerly sufficient can cause a mild feeling of let-down after receptors have been down-regulated. The increased requirement for dopamine to maintain the same electrical activity is the basis of physiological tolerance and withdrawal associated with addiction."[10]

This means, simply, that the more of the substance (or the object) we *get*, the more we *need* in order to replicate the hit of brain chemicals. Once we are caught in this addictive loop, we find that it is harder and harder to actually enjoy a formerly stimulating experience or object. Now the cycle of craving and grasping is more deeply conditioned (the *samskāra* is more deeply grooved). We want more and more. But we enjoy less and less. So in the ramping up of the process of craving, the circuitry of wanting is strengthened, and the parallel circuitry of liking, or savoring, is concomitantly decreased.

Eventually, we end up in the Hungry Ghost realm—with those huge stomachs and mouths, and very teeny necks. We feel empty and hungry all the time. We can never really feel full. Any fullness we do feel is the fullness of *duhkha*—of unsatisfactoriness.

Nonetheless, there is good news in these neuroscientific discoveries. Because the obverse appears to be true, as well: the more we practice liking and savoring—what I have called "knowing" the object—the more the circuitry of craving is weakened. Why? As there is less dopamine being pumped into the brain, there are eventually more receptor sites for this neurotransmitter. Upregulation! The brain becomes more and more sensitive to pleasurable sensation. We enjoy more and more. But we crave less and less. This fantastic discovery again lends support to Patanjali's view that we can practice the positive, or non-afflicted, states, and thereby increase them.

Susan was slowly learning to organize her experience of life around savoring her natural breathing—and, likewise, around savoring food rather than craving it. Slowly, across the months, I watched her make this shift—the shift to the wave of breath, to the present moment. Slowly, her war with her body was coming to an end. She was learning to trust life.

When hunger is our frame of reference, says psychologist and author Mark Epstein, "the body is experienced as an alien entity that has to be kept satisfied, the way an anxious mother might experience a new baby. When awareness is shifted from appetite to breath, the anxieties about not being enough are automatically attenuated. Just as a nursing mother learns to trust that her body will respond to her infant with milk, so meditators who shift to a breath-based foundation learn to surrender into the ebb and flow of their own breath."[11]

When we begin to discover, explore, and identify with the breathing body, a shift happens. We have a direct, moment-by-moment awareness of ourselves as breathing beings. Our relationship to time is changed: we no longer run breathlessly after it, but simply stay with it, breath by breath. And as we identify with the subtle breathing body, we begin to see the subtle body of the world, pulsing with the same life force that initiates our breathing.

Then, as Patanjali says it, "The covering of light is removed."

Part Five

MEDITATIVE TRANSFORMATIONS

OF

SELF

ONE of the best stories of the early Christian desert hermits goes like this: "Abbot Lot came to Abbot Joseph and said: Father, according as I am able, I keep my little rule, and my little fast, my prayer, meditation and contemplative silence; and according as I am able, I strive to cleanse my heart of thoughts: Now what more should I do? The elder rose up in reply and stretched out his hands to heaven, and his fingers became like ten lamps of fire. He said: Why not be totally changed into fire?"

—Annie Dillard, *For the Time Being*

RUDI

Living at Ease in the World

IT HAD always been difficult for me to get a handle on Rudi Sawyer's personal history, for he talked so little about his past, his parents, and his upbringing. As far as I could tell, this did not seem to be out of any aversion to his past. He denied there was anything traumatic there whatsoever, and I believed him. It seemed more the case that he had learned to live happily in the present, and his personal history had surprisingly little draw on him.

Through casual questioning, however, Rudi's friends and I had pieced together some of the puzzle. Rudi's father had been a high school science teacher in a small town in Michigan—and his mother a home economics teacher. He seems to have been, himself, something of a science geek. In the one picture I saw of him in his high school years, he was all teeth and glasses: big black-framed glasses and a huge grin.

Rudi won the state competition in the science fair two years in a row (I saw the big blue ribbons once, gathering dust on the wall of his storeroom) and apparently as a result, he won a scholarship to one of Michigan's better liberal arts colleges. He excelled in math and became a rising star in computer science.

Rudi is still vague about how he got to India. As far as we could tell, his study of science led him into an interest in philosophy and metaphysics. In college, he sent away for audiotapes of Alan Watts's compelling talks on Eastern philosophy. (He still keeps this collection, along with his Ram Dass tapes, in a big cupboard at Acorn Cottage.) He spent the summer after his senior year in India traveling from ashram to ashram with two buddies from the Midwest.

His buddies came home at the end of the summer, both sick. But Rudi stayed. He had met his own remarkable teacher—an obscure, half-naked yogi who wanted no American disciples and kept trying to send Rudi home. Rudi fell in love with this teacher, though most other Americans shied away because of the rigorous discipline in his ashram. With some amount of arm-twisting, we could occasionally get Rudi to tell stories of his ashram days: he was up in the wee hours every morning, practicing yoga, meditation, and *prāṇāyāma*. He worked at the lowliest jobs—cleaning toilets and floors. He seems to have thrived. He learned to chant, to meditate, and to do *yoga-āsana*. Most of all, he seems to have just been in love with his teacher. He stayed at the ashram for four years.

Finally, Rudi's sister was diagnosed with breast cancer, and Rudi came home. As Rudi's mother told us wistfully one afternoon while she and his father were visiting, "He was never the same after that."

The year after he returned home, Rudi got a job working for IBM in New York. His contemplative training and practice had honed his already impressive intelligence, and he became known as a programming and software genius.

Though Rudi was adept at his computer work, it was not what he longed to do. He never aspired to the big career with IBM that he could certainly have had. When Rudi had finally put together a modest amount of savings, he retired to live quietly in the Berkshires—where he knew Ed Harrington (a retired IBM executive, and current owner of the old estate of which Acorn Cottage is still a part).

Rudi lived quietly at Acorn Cottage, which he had outfitted with the latest computer gadgetry, and sheathed in books and religious icons of all sorts. He took up gardening, and soon mastered the indigenous Berkshire flora—becoming the preferred gardening guru for many of the great estates in the Berkshires. Whenever possible, he liked to be outside, in nature.

Rudi was extremely knowledgeable about yoga, and especially the sometimes toe-curling subtleties of yoga philosophy. Much of his learning was from his time at the ashram, where he had studied the important yoga scriptures with his teacher. Now, he was more interested in living yoga than studying it. He lived simply. He heated with wood that he cut and split himself. He grew his own vegetables in a garden out by the old tennis courts. And, like Thoreau, his life in the woods kept getting simpler and simpler with each passing year. ("Simplify, simplify," said Thoreau. "Most everything is a distraction.")

Rudi did not like to teach. From the beginning of our friendship, he made it clear that he was a reluctant mentor, but a very willing friend. He was reclusive and preferred to avoid crowds and socializing. But he was also generous, and hugely fun to hang out with. He loved nothing better than to cook for friends, and even in the winter he could be found cooking on the outdoor grill—which was always set up in the kitchen garden just behind the cottage.

Rudi, it seemed, had now devoted his life to the art of living. Though he worked a lot, his work, as he described it, almost always seemed like play. He had, from my point of view at the time, astonishingly little ambition. He was unfailingly generous with his time, energy, and money, and would stop any project midstream to help whoever knocked at his door. It seemed he was never doing anything that couldn't be interrupted for a friend.

Rudi, more than anyone I had ever met, seemed not to be trying to get anywhere in the world. He had, apparently, already arrived. How had he done that, I wondered? Had he always been like that?

Several times, I explored this line of questioning with Rudi. Had he always been so happy? Yes, he said. He thought he had always been happy. Was it his practice, his relationship with Swami, that helped him to be so content?

Perhaps. I don't know, said Rudi. If he had ever been different, he had no memory of it now.

I preferred to think that this was a man who had truly been cooked in the fire of yoga, and had been cooked almost to perfection. He was at ease in the world. He was at ease with himself.

When one is dedicating one's life to a practice, one looks around to see what its fruits might be. How have others—others greater than oneself—been matured, or developed by this practice? Where does devoted practice lead? Might it lead to a life without undue ambition for achievement? A life lived, as Don Juan would say, as if nothing had been accomplished and nothing was left undone? Might it lead to a generous life? A happy life?

More than anyone else, I used Rudi as an example of where yoga might lead.

Chapter 13

THE VISION OF SAMENESS

REVELATIONS FROM THE SEED

Rudi knelt next to the cast-iron stove, piling several more pieces of oak onto the fire, which had died down considerably as we ate dinner. Maggie and Jake huddled closer to the stove for warmth. Susan, puttering quietly in the kitchen, had zipped up her fleece, and Kate, seemingly oblivious of temperature, was mesmerized by an album of Jake's childhood photos that she'd found on the bookshelf.

It was a bitter cold night in late January. The sky was clear and pocked with stars. The moisture had frozen in our nostrils as we had each crunched our way over the snowpack to Acorn Cottage. A new moon shimmered blue and cold just at the horizon.

Now, with Rudi's masterful touch, the fire exploded with a roar that was more felt than heard, and the cabin warmed up quickly. We all settled into the mismatched collection of chairs around the fire, with cups of hot mulled cider and molasses cookies Susan had brought directly from her oven.

"Well," said Maggie, addressing herself to Jake. "Tell us."

A week earlier, Jake had returned from a thirty day yoga and meditation retreat in California. He was eager to tell the story, which he now recounted in detail. He spoke methodically, as he might speak while building a case in a courtroom.

"At the beginning of the retreat, I told the meditation teacher about my practice of loving kindness meditation—and my aversion to sitting. She suggested that I continue the *metta* practice on retreat for at least the first week—and that I continue to mix in a large amount of walking practice with my sitting."

This, I thought, seemed a sound idea, since Jake had used both *metta* and walking meditation so successfully to concentrate his mind. Why not deepen those concentrative skills?

"Well, I did the *metta*, and I did get concentrated, of course. 'May you be happy, may you be healthy, may you have ease of well-being.' In the first several days, I ran through all the objects—myself, my benefactor, friend, neutral person, and then, of course, the enemy.

"But something surprising happened right away. I noticed that Mom didn't come up as 'the enemy' much anymore. It was strange: she didn't really fit into any of the old categories. But her image was still compelling. So by the third day, I was using her exclusively as the object of my concentration, and sending her the phrases."

We were now a perfectly quiet circle, the whole group, sitting around the fire and leaning in toward Jake's story.

Jake continued. The *metta* technique was working well for him. In practicing hour after hour, and directing his attention repeatedly back to the image of his mother—both sitting and walking—he was developing deep states of concentration. His teacher was recommending that he stay with this practice. After five or six more days, astonishing things began to happen.

"My perception of Mom's image began to change," Jake said, squinting his eyes slightly as he remembered. "Her image got huge, it got tiny. It disappeared into a pinpoint." As his concentration deepened even more, Jake began to perceive the image as what his teacher called a "seed"—a highly condensed image.

"Even more," he went on, "I discovered that this seed contained the entire history of my relationship with Fiona. Damn. As I sat with her image, the seed began to open. The whole history of our life together poured out. Just kind of spontaneously downloaded itself. It was, like, almost year by year."

Jake described in detail how his mind began to automatically download every "byte" associated with his mother, not so much as memory, but as if he were reliving the experience—or in some cases as if he were living it for the first time. Things were revealed about his relationship with Fiona of which he had previously had no conscious knowledge. The process continued day after day, and he seemed to have no control over it.

"Now something wild happened," said Jake. "At one point there began to emerge from the seed a progression of images of Mom's fore-bears. One by one the images came forth and revealed themselves to me—my grandparents, their parents, their parents before them. And each of them revealed themselves as also a complex seed. Seeds inside seeds—condensed images of entire lives and historic times."

I saw Susan give Maggie a doubting look.

"Here's the amazing thing. Just since I've been home I've been on the phone with Mom. These people really existed."

I myself had experienced something similar on a long retreat, so I knew firsthand the experience Jake was describing. Others were more skeptical.

Jake continued his storytelling, undeterred. Over the course of the ensuing weeks, Jake's feelings of loving kindness and genuine well-wishing toward his mother exploded. He felt waves of energy flowing outward from his heart toward his mother's.

"My body was so full of love, I thought it would explode. In fact, the movement of energy was so strong, it actually scared me. I felt at one point that Mom must be receiving it somehow in the cells of her body. I thought of whales who communicate across thousands of miles of water by means of subtle sounds. I visualized Mom walking through the grocery store, and receiving this energy wallop. I was afraid it might knock her down."

Jake's narrative had hypnotized us. The room was still, but for the crackling of the fire, and the now-increasing howl of a stiff wind blowing around the roof and walls of the cottage.

Jake went on to describe other altered states—side effects of his concentrated mind. At one point, the seed itself became tiny, and began to turn into light. A steady, pulsing flow of white light emanated from the seed, which seemed to be deep within him, and then, eventually, became him. He was the seed. The seed was him. He experienced himself as pure light, and all other traces of self disappeared.

Jake was holding the most intriguing piece for last. "Here's the most amazing thing. I discovered that there were tracks coming back the other way."

Susan knit her brow. "What?"

Rudi got it. "It means that Fiona had been praying for Jake, too. Jake found the tracks of Fiona's prayers coming back toward him."

"She has been praying for me. Praying for me for years," said Jake.

"Of course, she hasn't been praying for the right things, exactly. I mean she's been praying, I assume, that I'll get married, give up yoga. Whatever. Be a good dog. Get the Devil outta me. But I don't think it matters. It's the spirit of well-wishing itself that makes the tracks."

Jake later discovered that, indeed, Fiona had her own prayer group of Catholic ladies: the St. Mary Society. They had all been praying for Jake for years.

Jake was pensive as he summed up: "It's like there's this whole new place inside from which I love Mom completely. This isn't to say I don't see who she is realistically. I mean, really, I think I see her now more clearly than ever. But this experience seems to have burned away the ambivalence that has been there forever. I know she's felt the difference in our relationship, too—even though she doesn't know anything about my mystical experience. But I can feel this new thing happening between us."

Jake's meditation practice had taken him into extraordinary new territory: the state of *dhyāna*.

DHYĀNA: KNOWING THE OBJECT

As the aiming and staying capacities of the mind mature, we may penetrate momentarily into the next phase of concentration—which
Patanjali calls *dhyāna,* or meditative absorption. This phase repre-
sents a profound deepening of the earlier stage of concentration,
dhāranā. (Remember that in *dhāranā,* "concentration locks consciousness on a single area.") Now this concentrated state deepens
into absorption.

> **In meditative absorption** [dhyāna], *the entire perceptual flow
> is aligned with that object.* (3.2)

In this *sūtra,* Patanjali uses the key word *ekatānatā* (here translated
as "flow"), which means "extending continuously or unbrokenly."
"This continuity," says yoga scholar Taimni in his highly regarded commentary, "may be compared to the continuity of the flow of water in a
river or that of oil being poured from one vessel into another."[1]

When we penetrate into the state of *dhyāna,* a sense of easy flow
will saturate our experience. In this new phase of concentration there
is a marked quality of effortlessness, a sense of receptivity to a natural
process, and an experience of union with the object of our concentration. Taimni's image of oil being poured from vessel to vessel is apt,
because in this phase the mind "streams" into the object. The mind
experiences a visceral, alive connection with the object, and seems
capable now of penetrating to its very core.

Yogis discovered that with the onset of *dhyāna,* some startlingly
new features arise in consciousness. First of all, of course, there is the
achievement of a new quality of steadiness *(sthira).* Once stabilized,
the yogi can hold his concentration for long periods of time.

But also, there is a remarkable change in the mind's *perception* of
the object. As the mind becomes more one-pointed, the object itself
seems to become more subtle. Consciousness now becomes absorbed
in the *pure perceptual features of the object*—without reactivity, but

also without elaboration, association, or judgment. Yogis experiencing *dhyāna* are primarily attending to and absorbed in the "bare" experience of the object—its outlines, colors, shades, and movement.

Psychologist Daniel Brown describes this experience as characterized by a lack of thinking or recognizable perceptual patterns. "The yogi," he says, "has stopped the mind, at least in the sense of its so-called 'higher operations': thinking and pattern recognition. The yogi keeps his awareness at the more subtle level of the actual moment of occurrence or immediate impact of a thought or of a sensory stimulus."[2]

This gives rise to what is sometimes called "bare attention." All associations and comments of the mind are pared away from consciousness. Brown continues: "The meditation period is experienced as a succession of discrete events: pulses, flashes, vibrations, or movements without specific pattern or form. . . . Though mental and bodily events occur moment-by-moment in uninterrupted succession, attention remains fixed on each discrete moment. Awareness of one event is immediately followed by awareness of another without break for the duration of the sitting period, or for as long as this level of concentration remains."[3]

When the meditator has reached this point of skillfulness, something new arises. As attention becomes "bare," not only does the internal object dominate the stream of consciousness but the object itself also undergoes changes, and becomes increasingly unstable— just as Fiona's image did for Jake. It loses its solidity, its hard edges. It may seem, for example, as large as the ocean or as small as a mustard seed. The object changes size or shape. What once seemed fixed is now experienced as an image in constant flux.

After sustained practice, subject-object separation disappears altogether. The subject becomes immersed in the object. All that exists at this point is the object as illumined by and revealed to consciousness. The mind's awareness of itself has disappeared.

Taimni describes this process: "Patanjali calls the disappearance of the mind's awareness of itself as *svarūpa sunyam iva*. In this state, 'the mind's *own form* or essential nature disappears, as it were...' With the disappearance of the mental *svarūpa*, a faculty higher than the intellect comes into play, and the perception of the reality hidden behind the object takes place through the instrumentality of this faculty which perceives by becoming one with the object of perception. The perceiver, the object of perception and perception become fused in one state."[4]

Now there arises a mystical identification with the intended object. At this stage of practice, *an object can be known by the mind without the use of sensory activity.* Luminous mind perceives the object, and penetrates it—in effect, becomes one with it—in a way that sensory activity would only inhibit. Mircea Eliade, in his pivotal book *Yoga: Immortality and Freedom*, describes this event, "Instead of knowing through forms (*rūpa*) and mental states (*citta-vritti*) as formerly, the yogin now contemplates the essence (*tattva*) of all objects directly."[5]

The knowledge gained from this experience is a new kind of knowledge altogether. "Thenceforth," Eliade continues, "the yogin will no longer be 'distracted' or 'troubled' by the activity of the senses, by sensory activity, by memory, etc. All activity is suspended."[6]

When concentration becomes this refined, the object emerges in an entirely new form—described by Jake's meditation teacher as the "seed." The initial encounters with this "seed" are striking, for this seed is charged with new and highly condensed information about the object. The seed contains an astonishingly subtle summation of information from all the sense systems—smell, taste, touch, form—as well as subtle attributes of the object which have never before been discernible through ordinary perceptual processes.

Eliade gives us the classic and unrivaled description of the new kind of "knowing" that emerges along with the seed. He describes how, at the deepest stages of absorption, yogis actually penetrate and "assimilate" the objects of attention with the newly refined and skillful mind. Here is Eliade's description of the unfolding of the seed in a yogic meditation on fire:

"As an example, we cite the yogic meditation on the subject of fire, as it is taught today (the meditation begins with concentration, *dhārana*, on some glowing coals placed before the yogin). Not only does it reveal to the yogin the phenomenon of combustion and its deeper meaning; it allows him, in addition: (1) to identify the physiochemical process taking place in the coal with the process of combustion that occurs in the human body; (2) to identify the fire before him with the fire of the sun, etc.; (3) to unify the several contents of all these fires, in order to obtain a vision of existence as fire; (4) to penetrate within this cosmic process, now on the astral plane (the sun), now on the physiological plane (the human body), and finally even on the plane of infinitesimals (the seed of fire); (5) to reduce all these planes to a modality common to them all—that is, *prakriti* as fire; (6) to 'master' the inner fire, by virtue of *prānāyāma*, suspension of respiration (respiration=vital fire); (7) finally, through a new 'penetration,' to extend this 'mastery' to the glowing coals before him, for, if the process of combustion is exactly the same from one limit of the universe to the other, any partial mastery of the phenomenon infallibly leads to its 'master' in toto, etc."[7]

Here, Eliade captures the quality of insight that is revealed as the seed opens its secrets to the mind of the meditator. It is an experience which almost certainly eludes the power of words to describe.

Jake had described some very sophisticated meditative events with great precision and accuracy. His understanding of these events clearly came from direct experience, for he had no theoretical knowledge of these things whatsoever. He had never read or studied any of the scriptures that describe them, nor had he been even vaguely interested in doing so. His experience of the special kind of knowing that comes with *dhyāna* emerged inexorably from practice—just as it had for yogis for thousands of years.

COALESCENCE: THE MYSTIC UNION

Rudi was poking the fire, trying to resuscitate it one final time. Jake had finished his story, and Kate and Susan had already decamped—citing the late hour and Kate's early morning yoga class. Now, Jake was finishing up the last of the cider, and Maggie and I were ready to bundle up for the trek home through the snow.

Jake seemed preoccupied. Was he perhaps not finished?

Maggie noticed it, too. "Jake, what is it?"

"Well. Something else happened there at the retreat. But I don't feel like I can even express it in words."

I put my jacket back on its hook near the door, and sat down near the fire next to Jake.

Jake began quietly: "After my mind had explored the 'seed,' you know, like I described it, then . . . well . . . I don't know. I had a kind of flash of understanding or something."

His eyes were focused toward the ceiling as he strained to find words.

"Everything kind of dissolved into light."

Jake's eyes lowered, and met mine. "I have felt so happy ever since. Nothing upsets me. It's like I know something. But I don't really know what it is I know."

Jake had experienced what yogis would call a preliminary glimpse of *samādhi*—a more advanced stage of absorption than *dhyāna*.

I looked at Jake and nodded. I understood his problem in communicating the experience of *samādhi*. It is an experience that is notorious for being inexplicable. Language relies on categories, and the very nature of this experience is that it transcends all categories of name and form. The great yogic saint Ramakrishna struggled with this same problem. He would say to his disciples, "I wish very much to tell you about it (this state) but I cannot. Somebody shuts my mouth."[8]

Nonetheless, *yogi-sramanas* have made many attempts to describe this state to the extent that words will allow.

When consciousness becomes stilled, the play of *samskāras* is temporarily suspended. This means, simply, that all facets of ordinary mind are in abeyance. There is no conceptualization, and the object (whether it be a "gross" external object, or a "subtle" internal object) is known directly, beyond name and form. Patanjali calls this "integration," or *samādhi.*

> *When only the essential nature of the object shines forth, as if formless, integration has arisen.* (3.3)

In *samādhi,* the boundaries of Time and Space which ordinarily separate one object from another collapse. Knowing is instant, direct, and immediate. There is union between subject and object. No seam is left showing.

In Western mystical traditions, this is known as the *coincidentium oppositorium:* the mystic union. In yoga it is called *samādhi,* or, literally, "putting together." "With this experience of *samādhi,*" says Chip Hartranft, "'I' and the world have been 'put together.'"[9] It is the state that mystics in all traditions penetrate over and over again. Initially, it is experienced as a kind of altered state, as it was for Jake. Then, with repeated penetrations, it begins to alter the very traits of consciousness, so that ordinary mind—the entire psycho-mental structure—is deconstructed. Each time awareness penetrates this state of *samādhi,* *samskāras* are permanently burned up, leaving the mind freer from its bondage to conditioning, and free to know the bare experience of the moment.

Jake's sense of closeness to this state would wear off, I knew, but his mind would never be the same.

In the yoga tradition, one important (and fascinating) characteristic of this state is called *samāpatti*—meaning coalescence, or coincidence. In this state of coalescence, the usual distinctions between self, object, and the process of perception itself all disappear. Patanjali describes it:

> As the patterning of consciousness subsides, a transparent way of seeing, called coalescence, saturates consciousness; like a jewel, it reflects equally whatever lies before it— whether subject, object, or act of perceiving. (1.41)

As coalescence emerges, objects are no longer perceived as separate. And as they are directly known, they are found to be made of the "same stuff" as everything else in the created world. All created things are seen to have the same properties, the same nature.

In *samāpatti*, one realizes that *the self who experiences belongs to the same domain as the experience.* No longer does the sense of self set one apart from the rest of nature. This experience of coalescence permanently changes the mind. Having had it, one knows—immediately, directly, not conceptually—that all aspects of the created world have the same nature, the same essence (*tattva*).

This experience is sometimes called "the vision of sameness." It gives rise to a new and effortless quality of loving kindness toward the self and toward all beings. The knowledge of "sameness" burns the roots of craving. Since one knows oneself to be One with all created things, all craving for objects is destroyed. We are already the same as the object. We are made of the same stuff. We no longer need to possess the object. We *are* the object. So with coalescence comes a profound transformation of our relationship with the object world. As a result of coalescence, violence and hatred are no longer possible. The afflictions are further extinguished.

Jake looked for a long time into the fire. "The world looks different. Changed. But I know it's me that is changed."

Jake was neither holding on to this state, nor pushing it away. In the postmeditation experience he was simply savoring it. It would wane, of course, but its echo would always be there as a touchstone. The world of people, places, and things would never look the same. "Jake" and "the world" had been put together.

We sat together in silence as the crackling of the fire died, until the room became almost dark—illumined only by the moonlight washing through the windows, coloring everything in silver.

THE LAW OF COMPLEMENTARITY

Maggie and I slowly crunched our way home over the brittle snow-pack. The wind that had earlier been howling around Acorn Cottage had now died down to a whisper. The night was clear and the sky was still lit with stars. Again, our breath froze in our nostrils. From the lawn of Acorn Cottage, we could see the hulking silhouette of the old mansion. Everything was eerily alive, but utterly silent. There was a mystery to the night. I wondered if Maggie felt it as well.

As we walked wordlessly home together, I thought of Thoreau's walks on similarly frigid New England nights, when he heard new depths to the silence of winter.

I am disturbed by the sound of my steps on the frozen ground. I wish to hear the silence of the night, for the silence is something positive and to be heard. I cannot walk with my ears covered. I must stand still and listen with open ears, far from the noises of the village that the night may make its impression on me. A fertile and eloquent silence. Sometimes the silence is merely negative, an arid and barren waste in which I shudder, where no ambrosia grows. I must hear the whispering of myriad voices. Silence alone is worthy to be heard. Silence is of various depths and fertility, like soil. Now it is a mere Sahara, where men perish of hunger and thirst, now a fertile bottom, or prairie of the West. As I leave the village, drawing nearer to the woods, I listen from time to time to hear the hounds of Silence baying at the Moon,—to know if they are on the track of any game. If there's no Diana in the night, what is it worth? The silence rings; it is musical and thrills me. A night in which the silence was audible, I heard the unspeakable.[10]

As we walked, I thought about a central truth of yoga that Thoreau discovered in his two years at Walden Pond: the more of our own interior life we discover, the more deeply we feel the interior life of other beings—and of the world.

In the yogic view, the microcosm and the macrocosm are one and the same. The universe is organized around increasingly subtle layers of reality, as we have seen, from the most gross outward physical reality all the way to the so-called Unmanifest Realms. The human organism is organized in exactly the same way. They are both holograms of the same reality. The inner and outer worlds are inextricably linked. When we see deeply into our self, we also see deeply into the world.

Yogis called this the Law of Complementarity: whatever is found in the human organism is also found in the universal organism. The whole world is inside, says the poet Kabir. All seven oceans are inside, and hundreds of millions of stars. Through penetrating our own internal sheaths, we also penetrate the sheaths of the universe.

Open the door into your self, and you've opened the corresponding door into the world. This is the basis for all of the extraordinary powers described in the third chapter of the *Yoga-Sūtra*. It is the basis for "insight into the past and future"; for "insight into the language of all beings"; for "insight about the subtle, hidden, and distant." Patanjali uses the third chapter of his treatise to describe the myriad ways in which knowing our own mind opens us to the minds of others, and to the subtle internal structures of the universe: Time and Space and Mind and Matter.

It was only when we got to Maggie's house that I realized she had not been absorbed in contemplating these same mysteries on the walk home. As I would discover, she was preoccupied with an altogether different kind of mystery.

As we approached the front door, Maggie asked me to come in for a moment. I declined, at first, but she insisted. "I have something for you," she said.

As we stood in the foyer, she handed me a thin and elegant envelope—slit open across the top, and obviously containing a letter of some sort. Maggie was barely suppressing a smile. "Take it out."

I pulled the ivory vellum stationery out of the envelope, and scanned it. It was signed by a well-known literary agent from a big New York agency.

> We would be very pleased to represent your fine novel, Ms. Winslow. In fact, I know several editors who I'm quite sure will be interested.

Now, Maggie was grinning from ear to ear.

Chapter 14

SHIVA'S DANCE:
INSIGHT AND DISSOLUTION

THE ECSTASY OF THE DHARMA CLOUD

It was a clear day in early April. Rudi and I were helping a crew of volunteers remove an old elm that had fallen over the main road to Kripalu. Rudi, dressed in his overalls and work boots, looked like he was born to hold a power saw in his hands. A Herman Melville for the twenty-first century.

When I called Rudi in the wee hours that morning to ask for his help with the tree emergency, he had not hesitated. "Of course. I'll be right there."

Rudi was unfailingly generous with his time, energy, and the moderate resources he had. He was, I think, the most authentically generous person I had ever known. I was continually surprised by this particular character trait—perhaps because of my own selfishness. Even though I would offer my time (sometimes even happily) I did still usually have a sense that what I was doing was more important, and I would quietly be eager to get back to it. Not so for Rudi. When he was with you, he was with you. Your work was his work.

Rudi had achieved remarkable things in his life: He was well read and knowledgeable about arcane Hindu philosophy (and I knew what a mammoth feat this really was). He was uncommonly knowledgeable about the flora of the Berkshires, and the special techniques for gardening in our challenging climate. But Rudi had no need to have his brilliance reflected back to him. In psychological language, we might say that Rudi seemed utterly without narcissism. He was not driven even in the slightest fashion by the illusory Firebird.

With Rudi's help, we made quick work of the elm. We had it cut and stacked in five hours that morning. Afterward, Rudi and I sat under a cloudy sky on the front terrace of Kripalu, gazing off at the Berkshire Hills, and sipping hot chocolate provided by the Kripalu kitchen.

I took the opportunity to ask Rudi something I'd been wondering about for weeks.

"Rudi. When you were in India with Swamiji—did you go all the way to the end of the path? Did he send you home because he thought you were already cooked?"

Rudi howled, and laughed so hard that he spilled hot chocolate on his overalls. "Oh, Swamiji would get a kick out of that question.

"No, no, no. All of Swami's students were more advanced than I was. In fact, Swami sent me home and told me just to focus on living a simple life, and practicing the *yamas*. That's all. His instructions were totally non-sexy. I was a kindergarten student for him."

Rudi had told me before that the Indian students made much quicker headway in the final stages of practice than did the Westerners at the ashram. But I also knew enough about his experiences in India to know that he had practiced some of the more advanced stages of meditation with Swami and his students.

I wanted to push him on this point. I was grappling with the last part of the path of *rāja-yoga* for my book. I knew intellectually about the insights that come toward the end of the path—what Patanjali calls the "vision of discernment," or *viveka-khyāti*—and the resulting experience of the "shower of phenomena," or *dharma-megha-samādhi* (a highly refined form of the *samādhi* we examined in the last chapter). I had read many of the commentaries, to be sure. But I had never experienced these things myself. And I didn't really know anyone who had—except, possibly, for Rudi.

However, getting Rudi to talk about esoteric aspects of practice was not so easy. Bragging about achievements on the path was something his teacher had cautioned him never to do. So I asked him straight out, "Did you experience *dharma-megha-samādhi?*"

He thought for a moment, and his gaze became distant. "Yeah," he said hesitantly. "It's not a big deal, really, when you get there. It just seems natural. At a certain point in practice, you see that all things arise and pass away moment by moment in a kind of hail of phenomena."

For a moment, Rudi became absorbed in the question. It was almost as though just talking about the state of *dharma-megha-samādhi* began to initiate it. It was known to be the highest state of ecstasy in the path of classical yoga—and was often compared to seeing the world as a kind of "shower" of phenomena. *Megha* means "cloud," and *dharma-megha-samādhi* is sometimes translated as "the ecstasy of the *dharma* cloud." It is the precursor of final liberation—the penultimate insight.

"It's amazing," Rudi continued, putting down his cup of hot chocolate, now, and facing me. I could tell he was about to give me a serious answer. "Your heightened perception of phenomena slows down time," he said. "So everything moves in slow motion. It's like seeing a movie, but seeing it in individual frames. You see the succession of momentary events as they each arise and pass away. They don't blur together like the movie does when it's going at regular speed. You see it all in mind-boggling detail."

Then he added, choosing his words carefully and gazing off into the middle distance, "Of course, behind that rain of phenomenal experience abides Pure Awareness. The Witness. This is what Patanjali means in his third *sūtra*: 'Then, pure awareness can abide in its very nature.' You see that behind the whole drama, and the flux of the created world, is just pure knowing."

Rudi turned back to me. "Once you see this, it changes you. You know that everything created is impermanent. Rising and passing away in every moment. But all with the same essence. You differentiate between consciousness, or the mind—which is made of the same stuff as the rest of the created world—and the Witness which is Pure Awareness."

INSIGHT AND DISSOLUTION

Rudi's description of *dharma-megha-samādhi* does not make sense until it is put into the context of all the earlier stages of yoga—and especially into the context of the increasing refinement of concentration that characterizes the preceding stages of the path.

In the process of mastering all of the stages of concentration, meditative absorption, and integration, the mind becomes a highly attuned instrument. Our capacity to aim toward, stay with, and penetrate the object matures—first with gross objects, then with subtle objects. Now, with this attainment, something remarkable begins to happen. The concentrated mind begins to explore itself! In effect, the mind takes itself as its own object of study.

This is an important moment, and an inevitable one if the meditator persists. The mind matured by concentration training begins to systematically examine the ways in which all phenomena—thoughts, feelings, and sensations—arise and pass away in the stream of consciousness, and the ways in which consciousness itself is created moment by moment. This process follows inexorably upon the heels of deep states of concentration.

If concentration practice can be likened to tying the wild puppy of the mind to a post—tying the mind to an object—then this next meditative event involves releasing the puppy from his tether, and allowing him to roam freely in the field. The puppy, now equanimous and focused, sets about "knowing" the field. He sniffs around. He pokes his nose into holes. What wild animals come and go? How does the land lie? How does the ground smell? What is this field of mind really like?

This new phase of meditation depends on an altogether new and different attentional strategy: rather than *narrowing* the stream of attention (as in concentration), we now learn to methodically *widen* it, to observe the endless fluctuation of thoughts, feelings, images, and sensations. We see precisely how patterns arise in the field of consciousness. We familiarize ourselves with the chaining of thoughts, feelings, impulses, and actions at the most minute level.

In this phase of practice, the meditator learns to attend to as many mental and physical events as possible, exactly as they arise, moment to moment. In this way, the meditator sees precisely how the world of ordinary experience and the self are actually constructed. How do these patterns fit together to give me a unified sense of self? As Rudi said, it is very much like slowing down the frames of a movie to see how the illusion of solidity is created. With practice, we begin to see individual frames!

Yogis found that this investigative capacity of the mind emerges naturally (and inevitably) once the mind becomes calm and quiet. This examination of the mind's own workings is actually the final aim of concentration training. As Daniel Brown says, "Just as a scientist may painstakingly construct a sensitive electronic instrument to measure some process, likewise, the meditator has carefully prepared himself through the refinement and steadying of attention with its accompanying shifts in levels of perception in order to gain insight into the fundamental workings of the mind."[1]

We now see that *dhāranā, dhyāna,* and *samādhi* are really three phases of one continuous process. Eventually, the advanced practitioner learns to move rapidly from one to the next. Patanjali gives these three phases one name—*samyama,* or "perfect discipline."

Concentration, absorption, and integration regarding a single object compose the perfect discipline of consciousness. (3.4)

Once Patanjali has laid out the training in concentration, he instructs the practitioner to use the resultant attentional skills to explore all phenomena. He instructs the practitioner to use the "perfect discipline" of concentrated mind to explore the entire field of mind and matter. He instructs the practitioner to release the now-trained puppy from his tether, and explore!

In the end stages of the path, this "perfect discipline" is applied first to a series of increasingly subtle interior objects—like the breath and the energy bodies—and then to an examination of consciousness itself. Much of Patanjali's third chapter, which is widely believed to be only about the attainment of supernormal powers, actually contains his instructions for a systematic examination of the field of experience. As it turns out, supernormal powers and the careful investigation of the field of experience are intimately linked.

The process of investigating the field can, at times, be more than a little terrifying. Indeed, some Buddhist traditions call aspects of these investigative practices "the experiences of terror." Why? Because as we examine experience closely, we discover that the world is not at all as it appears to be. The concentrated mind is capable of perceiving mental phenomena previously too minute or fleeting to be noticed. Suddenly, the most subtle workings of the interior world become visible! Familiarization with the chaining of mental events effectively deconstructs our ordinary way of seeing. We now see the flaws and biasing factors inherent in Ordinary Mind. We begin, finally, to see the very roots of ignorance—or *avidyā*. We see that ordinary perception is inherently deluded.

The meditator now begins to see that all aspects of the created world (*prakriti*) arise and pass away continually. All created phenomena are of their very nature impermanent and fleeting. "A bubble in a stream," as the scriptures have it.

When experience is broken down into its component parts, alas, it is impossible to find any "self" within the created world. The entire world of mind and matter reveals itself to be only patterns arising because of causes and conditions. The psycho-mental structure that we think of as "me" is not really a "self-under-its-own-power" at all. We see that any attempt to hold on to the stream of experience, to claim a self, or to identify with a pattern only leads to suffering, to *duhkha*—just as attempting to hold on to a rope which is being pulled through your hands inevitably leads to rope burn.

Yogis at this stage of practice see through what are sometimes called the Four Erroneous Beliefs:

1. The belief in the permanence of objects
2. The belief in the ultimate reality of the body
3. The belief that our state of suffering is really happiness
4. The belief that our bodies, minds, and feelings are our True Self

Says Patanjali:

> *Not seeing things as they are* [avidyā] *is the field where the other causes of suffering germinate, whether dormant, activated, intercepted, or weakened.*
> *Lacking this wisdom, one mistakes that which is impermanent, impure, distressing, or empty of self for permanence, purity, happiness, and self.* (2.4–5)

Repeated penetration into these insights begins to deconstruct the unconscious ideas we have about self (the ideal ego), and the belief in permanence, self, and object-happiness (the misperception that happiness results from our relationships with objects). The ideas we have about our own permanence and immortality are dissolved. Meditators see that the world of ordinary experience and the self are actually constructions, compound in nature, rather than "real things" in and of themselves.

As the now highly-refined consciousness sees through the Erroneous

Beliefs, *samskāra* and *vāsanā* are burned away—no longer just warded off, as in the earlier concentration phases. As we know the truth of impermanence, we are unable to cling to life; we are unable to cling to any solid sense of Me and Mine whatsoever; we are unable to identify with the passing show of attraction and aversion. Finally, as this process proceeds, the most subtle biasing factors in perception—the roots of ignorance—are completely eradicated.

The meditator now sees, beyond any doubt, that the Erroneous Beliefs obscure the true nature of the Self. Our involvement with them obscures the Seer, the Unborn, Uncreated, Eternal, that is not compound, and that exists beyond Time and Space and is not subject to cause and effect.

At the conclusion of this phase of practice, meditators begin to break the perceptual process down into its irreducible parts. They see thousands of discrete events arising and passing away in each millisecond. Patanjali calls this event *dharma-megha-samādhi.* It is his description of the most momentary vision of phenomena that he believes humanly possible. At this stage of practice, phenomena are seen to be like a rainstorm, but a rainstorm in which each discrete raindrop is perceived by consciousness.

Yogis discover behind this shower of phenomena an abiding pure awareness, unborn and unchanging. Meditators see that the world of ordinary experience and the self are actually constructions, rather than "real things" in and of themselves. Describing these highly refined final insights, Patanjali says:

> *Focusing with perfect discipline on the succession of moments in time yields insight born of discrimination.*
> *This insight allows one to tell things apart that, through similarities of origin, feature, or position, had seemed continuous.*
> *In this way discriminative insight deconstructs all of the phenomenal world's objects and conditions, setting them apart from pure awareness.*

*Once the luminosity and transparency of consciousness have
become distilled as pure awareness, they can reflect the freedom of awareness back to itself.* (3.53–56)

We are finally at the very heart of the strivers' discovery about the
dilemma of human beings—the very dilemma which I introduced at
the beginning of this book:

~ The ordinary reality in which almost all human beings live is but
an elaborate construction based on subtle but important errors in
perception (*avidyā*—or ignorance).
~ These chronic errors in perception become fetters (*klesha*—or afflictions) which lead us to act in ways that create chronic unhappiness
for ourselves and others.

This central argument is laid out early in the second book of the
Yoga-Sūtra. But, alas, it is not comprehensible until most of the
stages of the path have been mastered. Only late in the game can we
grasp the complex meaning of Patanjali's word "ignorance" (*avidyā*).
And for this reason, though most commentaries introduce *avidyā*
early on, I have left it until this late point in our investigation. We're
finally able to appreciate its genius. Patanjali says very simply, "The
causes of suffering are not seeing things as they are."

Not seeing things as they are!

The insight phase of practice fully exposes the nature of our ignorance. This can be at times difficult and destablizing. Learning to acknowledge, experience, and bear reality can be fragmenting, and can
cause considerable anxiety. What Jungian analyst Marion Woodman
calls "standing in the naked truth" can be terrifying indeed.

As a result, there must develop a delicate interplay between the "experiences of delight" and the "experiences of dissolution." The experience of fragmentation and anxiety requires a repeated return to concentration, and the persistent and systematic cultivation of equanimity. The final insights develop inevitably as we refine first one strategy and then the other—first concentration and then insight. And with increasing skillfulness, the final stages of the path emerge.

SHIVA: DANCING AT THE STILL POINT

As Rudi and I sat finishing our hot chocolate, the sun began to burn through the dense cover of clouds. Volunteers were cleaning up winter-rotted leaves from the flower beds and the rock garden behind us on the terrace in front of Kripalu—and I noticed that they had changed the position of the big six-foot bronze statue of Dancing Shiva. He now looked commandingly out over Lake Mahkeenac.

As the light glanced off the newly positioned statue, I felt a jolt of recognition. Shiva is an embodiment of this very experience of *dharma-megha-samādhi*! He is a representation of the consciousness that perceives the dissolution and re-creation of the phenomenal world in every instant. Shiva is a being who has seen through the Four Erroneous Beliefs. His wild dance of abandon—so wonderfully displayed in statues of the Dancing Shiva—is an evocation of a life lived in the full knowledge of impermanence and insubstantiality.

Liberation from the fetters demands a radical appreciation of impermanence. Not a theoretical understanding. Not a metaphysical understanding. But direct knowledge of the profound nature of the insubstantiality of all things. All phenomena arise and pass away, arise and pass away, moment by moment.

Nowhere in the yoga tradition is this confrontation with impermanence more dramatically revealed than in the stories of Shiva—the god of death and transformation who has threaded his way mysteriously through this story of contemporary yogis.

It was no accident that Jake, in the summer of his breakdown, became fascinated with the energies of this deity. The ancient rascal-god Shiva often became the favored friend of the *sramana*, precisely because Shiva was so fearless in his confrontation with the realities of death and impermanence.

Perhaps the most well-known of the many tales of Shiva is the story of his wild dance of death called the *tandava*. He performs this dance of death and transfiguration at the center of a traditional Indian cremation ground. It was precisely an icon of this Dancing Shiva that Jake had been distributing during the summer of his breakdown, now almost two years earlier. Jake had no idea, in those early days, how fully those little statues represented his own experience.

In the legend of the *tandava*, the ancient storytellers recount Shiva's visit to a group of priests and wise men gathered in a charnel ground. Though sages by contemporary standards, these holy men are still unaware of their own ignorance—they are still in bondage to the Four Erroneous Beliefs. They are tied to their own forms of doctrine and dogma, clinging to beliefs and views about I, Me, and Mine. They still separate the world into categories. As a result, they cannot recognize Shiva—who lives outside categories.

The sages begin to taunt this stranger in the charnel ground—attempting to drive him away from their "holy circle." Shiva is unmoved. This, of course, drives the sages crazy. They set a ferocious tiger upon him. Shiva skins the tiger alive and puts its hide around his waist. The sages, now completely beside themselves, set a serpent upon him. Shiva puts the serpent around his neck—incorporating this symbol of evil into his own power.

Clearly this Shiva plays by new rules. He is capable of embracing all of the categories of form. He is not in thrall to the "pairs of opposites"—good and evil, inside and outside. Finally, the sages send a black dwarf, called "forgetfulness," to defeat him. The demonic dwarf—named *Muyalaka*—symbolizes the forgetfulness of reality, the snares of illusion.

Shiva, whose patience has run out, determines to show the sages his true nature—and their own. He puts his foot on the crouching figure of "forgetfulness," and begins a wild cosmic dance which extends throughout the universe. As the story is told, all the deities come from the divine abodes to watch the spectacle. As Shiva dances, he beats his drum—a steady beat which builds in speed until it finally emits a blinding light. And as this yogic Lord-of-the-Dance spins, the world gradually begins to dissolve.

Now, as the world of form dissolves, Shiva gives the gods and the sages (and all who can bear to watch without flinching) a direct experience of the hail of phenomena—the ecstasy of the *dharma* cloud. His dance exposes the way in which our ordinary experience of the object world is nothing more than a construct of consciousness.

Finally, as the dance concludes, the world has dissolved into light.

Then—in perhaps his most surprising trick—Shiva restores the world out of nothingness.

Shiva's dance is the dance of yoga. It takes place beyond name and form, beyond doctrine and dogma, beyond I, Me, and Mine. To enter into this dance is to participate in the energies of the universe—integrating the conventional separation between heaven and hell, pain and pleasure, gain and loss. Shiva lives inside and outside, nowhere and everywhere. He lives in time and out of time. He lives at one and the same time in both the Manifest and the Unmanifest Realms.

Living as Shiva always brings us an experience of time out of time. Thoreau caught the spirit of this view: "The life of a wise man is most of all extemporaneous, for he lives out of an eternity which includes all time. All questions rely on the present for their solution. Time measures nothing but itself."[2]

NATURE'S FIRST GREEN

After finishing our hot chocolate, Rudi and I sauntered down the sloping lawn from Kripalu toward Lake Mahkeenac. Spring's subtle harbingers were everywhere—in the almost surreal golden eruptions of the willows down by the lake; in the thickening red of the sumac saplings in the power line cut. "Nature's first green is gold,"[3] said Robert Frost, referring to the early golden eruptions of willows in spring. The poet noticed, above all, their fleeting nature.

> Nature's first green is gold,
> Her hardest hue to hold.
> Her early leaf's a flower;
> But only so an hour.

Most of the snow cover had melted in the heat of the morning sun, and I could begin to smell the earth again. Birds were singing for the first time in months. After the first hundred yards of our walk, I took off my fleece. Rudi was already down to his red tie-dyed T-shirt.

Thoreau often said that he delighted most in transitional seasons. The change of seasons, he said, put him close to the soul of time, which was always melting away. Actually, for him, nature was almost entirely about transition. He began to sniff out spring in mid-February and he could feel fall in his bones in the middle of July. On this particular winter-spring afternoon, I knew what he meant. The day demanded that we listen carefully: smell, touch, breathe—lean in. Everywhere the layers of winter had been pulled back to expose the germinating spring underneath.

Rudi was quiet on our walk. He was usually quiet, in fact. And I loved this about him. In his quiet was all the space in the world just to be. Rudi had a quality of happiness that I had not encountered before. It was not the happiness that is the opposite of sadness. For Rudi's happiness had a good deal of sadness in it. It was, I guess, the happiness that embraces sadness.

An old Christian monk friend of mine once told me that a true contemplative is "one who lives with a broken heart." It took me a long time to understand this. Finally, I got it: a heart that is open to the world must be willing to be broken at any time. This brokenness produces the kind of grief that expands the heart so that it can love more and more. I think Rudi might have lived with this kind of broken heart.

The more I got to know Rudi, the more fascinated I became with him. He was one of the only human beings I knew who was simply not chasing any form of illusion. Whatever grasping he surely once had, had been transmuted into some more refined form of longing. For Rudi did have longing. In fact, he was almost all longing. Longing for God, for life, for knowing the world.

Rudi came closer to being enlightened, I think, than any being I will ever meet. And yet, he was also in so many ways just like the rest of us. He spent a third of his time fiddling with his computers and playing online. He got angry. He overate. Sometimes at our dinner parties he drank too much. Rudi was no saint. He did not give off white light.

What was clear, though, about Rudi, is that in his personality there was very little coloration of narcissism. Rudi was not on a quest for any illusory form of the Yellow-Crested Firebird whatsoever. He was, rather, on a quest for Reality. He seemed to love things just the way they were.

Were these exceptional qualities in Rudi the result of yoga?

I suspected that they were. I hoped that they were. I hoped that it was just possible that my own neurotic suffering—my own patterns and cravings and aversions and delusions—could eventually be softened through the practice of yoga, the way I thought maybe Rudi's had been. I hoped that my own deepest internal longings could manifest something as beautiful in the world as Rudi had manifested.

And, indeed, my own experience had given me reason to hope that all of this was possible. As we have seen repeatedly throughout this investigation, practicing the wisdom of yoga transforms consciousness by means of an ingenious two-phase process. First, the ego ideal—our longing for idealized mental, physical, and emotional states—is assuaged and to some extent satisfied in deep states of concentration. And then, the ideal ego is deconstructed through insight practices—practices which, as we have seen, reveal precisely how internalized representations of I, Me, and Mine are constructed.[4] This two-winged process seems to transmute the hunt for the Firebird into a different kind of longing: a longing for being itself, a longing to live fully in the face of death. It seems to transmute an ordinary life of quiet desperation into a life of simple presence.

In the two years since my sabbatical, I had continued to study the wisdom of *rāja-yoga*. And I had begun to piece together the mystery of this two-stage process in more detail—the transmutation of the ego ideal, and the systematic dismantling of the ideal ego.

As we have seen, the ego ideal is transformed through the repeated experiences of equanimity, steadiness, rapture, and bliss created in the states of *dhāranā, dhyāna,* and *samādhi.* In these states of absorption, grasping after the idealized internal representation of happiness is repeatedly gratified, as we actually experience happiness again and again.

To say this another way: the representations of the ego ideal are satisfied by the contentment that arises when the mind is secluded from the pull of the afflictions. Even in Eastern literature, these experiences of absorption are seen to gratify the longing to feel safely held and soothed—the longing, one might say, to feel held by the lost, or fantasized good mother. In the course of mastering these practices, the Paradise Lost for which we search becomes Paradise Regained. In these states, we feel held, and we experience authentic contentment, harmony, and wholeness. These become experiences to which we can reliably return—on the meditation cushion, the yoga mat, or even in daily life. The experiences of delight produced by deep states of concentration leave us with a kind of steadiness, and eventually a sense of indestructibility. *Sthira!*

As a result of repeated penetrations into these satisfying states, the grasping inherent in the early ego ideal goes through a profound transformation. Grasping becomes transmuted into a more refined kind of longing. This longing is different from grasping, because it no longer reaches out of the moment. It simply wants to know itself, and to know life as it is. Being and becoming have been merged, and we live in the world (as Rudi did, I think) with beginner's mind, seeing every moment fresh—with nothing accomplished and nothing left undone. Our relationship with the object world has been trued up: we see through the suffering inherent in wanting to *possess* people, places, and things; and we understand the true delight in simply *knowing* these objects, and knowing them to be made of the same stuff as your own "self."

As we proceed along the path of yoga, the fate of the ideal ego is very different than that of the ego ideal. The "steadiness" of mind that arises as an inevitable by-product of *dhāranā, dhyāna,* and *samādhi,* allows us to tolerate a close inspection of the secretly held ideas about the nature of the self—our secret belief in our immortality, indestructibility, permanence, and power. In later stages of practice, the mind begins to investigate itself, as we have seen—culminating in *dharma-megha-samādhi* and *viveka-khyāti.* Through this investigation, we begin to see all the ways in which the mind itself creates the illusion of substantiality. Repeated inspection of the mind reveals the grandiose images of self to be illusory. We see how the "self" is constructed moment to moment, and, once exposed, the process of "self-making" is attenuated, and finally ended. Moment by moment experience is no longer filtered through unconscious beliefs about how things *should* be. The yogi knows the phenomenal world as it is. The deeply buried ideal ego is exposed, and seen through, and the slippery internal representations of the ideal ego are seen for what they always were—an illusion.

Once I came to understand this process, I could see how this very progression of events had likely changed Rudi. Perhaps it was yoga that allowed him to shed any obsessive involvement with the drama of his personal history. Perhaps it was yoga that helped Rudi to become a human being who lived in the present. Rudi's relaxed, present-centered orientation marked him as different—as eccentric in our culture. Those of us who knew him recognized this. At the same time, we knew him to be in every way like us. We were, we could see, "made of the same stuff."

After wandering together in silence for an hour or so, Rudi and I found a big piece of slate in the middle of a clearing just on the shore of the lake. Sitting in the sun, with Rudi sprawled out nearby, I had an almost unbearably sweet meditation—fifteen minutes of bliss. As I opened my eyes again, I noticed that I wanted to hang on to this state of well-being—to continue to savor the spectacular beauty of the day through it. But underneath the bliss arose a feeling of melancholy— of profound sadness—which at first I tried to push away. This never works, of course. Finally, I let the sadness come in.

Once I stopped resisting it, I understood the melancholy instantly. Everything would soon change with our group of friends. Maggie's new agent had been as good as his word, and had procured Maggie a remarkably good contract for her novel—which would be published by a major house in September. I had no idea how this would change our friendship. I secretly (and selfishly) worried that I would no longer have Maggie to myself, and feared that this would be a very big loss in my life. Things would change, too, with Kate and Jake: within the next two months, Kate would be flying back to the Midwest, to begin her life there anew without Ward. Jake had been involved with his new girlfriend, Maria, for almost six months now, and was spending more and more time in Boston. It was clear to me: life was about to radically change.

As we lounged on the rock, I asked Rudi, "Are you feeling sad about Kate and Jake?"

He looked at me and smiled—nodding his head.

For the past two years we had each been part of a rare and privileged event: a small, dedicated group of practitioners had banded together to support one another in living. We couldn't have planned such a thing if we'd tried—and of course we hadn't really tried. It just happened.

It is usually assumed that contemplative practice is a quintessentially solitary endeavor. In fact, it is highly social. The search for truth is a much more collaborative process than most of us realize. And where would I ever find such collaborators again?

Rudi and I talked for a while by the shore of Lake Mahkeenac, with the soft waves rippling at our feet. When we finally parted company, Rudi gave me a hug, lifting me off the ground. I felt his scratchy beard and the strength of his frame. Rudi headed back through the woods toward Acorn Cottage for dinner with Jake and Maria. I headed home in the other direction—lingering for a while at the top of the hill, where I watched two red-tailed hawks circle the lake.

> *Nature's first green is gold,*
> *Her hardest hue to hold.*
> *Her early leaf's a flower;*
> *But only so an hour.*
> *Then leaf subsides to leaf.*
> *So Eden sank to grief,*
> *So dawn goes down to day.*
> *Nothing gold can stay.*

Chapter 15

THE END OF STRIVING

THE GREAT DELUSION

"He hated the manuscript."

"What?" exclaimed Maggie.

I had just returned from Boston, where I'd met with my editor, Robert. He had said it all as nicely as anyone possibly could have: The manuscript of my *Beginner's Guide* was too technical. Too mystical. Too sprawling. And "incomprehensible to the mainstream reader."

Robert and I had sat together in a hushed corner of the Ritz Carlton dining room, carefully looking through the tall white stack of manuscript pages. Waiters moved unobtrusively around the plushly carpeted room.

By the time I'd finished my walnut and endive salad, my anxiety had begun to grow. I could feel what was coming. When the stuffed sole finally arrived, I had lost my appetite altogether.

"This just isn't it, yet, Steve," Robert had finally concluded, swirling an olive over the edge of his martini glass. I felt momentarily short of breath.

Over chocolate hazelnut torte, Robert gave me his suggestions for restructuring and rewriting the book. I looked up at Maggie as I told her this part of the story: "His plan would take at least a year—full time. Probably more."

"Hmm," said Maggie, rather vaguely.

"On the drive back to the Berkshires, I felt insane. Two and a half years of work. Shit."

Maggie and I were walking up and down her back lawn as we talked. Maggie stopped to pull some weeds away from a struggling rosebush. "I thought it was rather good," she said, in what I hoped was deliberate understatement. (Maggie, whose first three novels had been turned down, had learned through bitter experience to be sanguine about rejection. But in the wake of her current publishing success, I think she may have felt shy about discussing my failure.)

"Well," I said, shaking my head slowly, and now slightly irritated with Maggie, "I thought it was at least moving in the right direction."

At nine thirty that evening I was still restless. My thoughts were racing, unable to land anywhere at all comfortable. Would I try to rewrite it? Maybe I should just let it go and move on? I got up and walked the two miles to Acorn Cottage—mostly for the air, I told myself, but really, I think, hoping that Rudi might be home. As I approached, I saw the lights.

Rudi did not tell me what I wanted to hear.

"You've been bollixed up with all those old commentaries, and Sanskrit scholarship, and fine points of yoga metaphysics, and stuff. You have to admit—the book was pretty technical."

I felt my face grow hot.

"Why didn't you tell me this before?"

Rudi shook his head. "Stephen. I've told you this in so many ways. You haven't been listening. You had to find out for yourself."

We sat for a moment in silence.

Finally, Rudi leaned forward in his chair. "I'm just saying, maybe your editor is right. He probably knows something about the yoga of editing."

Rudi got up for a moment to turn off the gas under the kettle. He fumbled with some tea bags and mugs. But then he turned around to address me, finishing his thought. "Look: it's possible that not that many people will really be interested in your wrestling match with the *Yoga-Sūtra*. Let's face it. Most people don't give a whiz about Patanjali anyway. They just want to learn how to live."

"But, Rudi, you spent years studying these same treatises. You told me that you had also written your own commentary on the *Yoga-Sūtra* at the ashram. Was that a waste of time?"

"No. And I'm not saying it was a waste of time for you, either. It's been your struggle. There has to be struggle. And the reason for the struggle is to help you see what matters.

"You and I both needed to dig into those scriptures," Rudi continued. "Hey, it's our path. But in the end, we all have to write our own scriptures, don't we? Your commentary does *you* more good than it does anyone else. Really, your life is your scripture."

I felt angry with Rudi, as I had with Maggie. Still, I could recognize the truth in what he was saying.

Finally, after we settled in with mugs of tea, and had sat again in silence for a few moments, Rudi said something that hit squarely home. "Look. You understand these complex pieces of yoga metaphysics pretty well. But that's not the hard part. The hard part is living them. Now you've just got to figure out how to live in the world in such a way that you're really putting them into practice. That's a different ball game. And a much more interesting one."

Funny. In recent weeks I had been thinking some of the same things myself. As the book project drew to a close, I had felt the whole thing collapsing under its own weight. It got heavier and heavier. It was chock full of grasping for scholarly respectability. Clinging. *Duhkha*. And, yes, boring.

Now, Rudi's questions reverberated for me. I knew they were the right ones: How could I live in the world without grasping and clinging? How could I live more simply? How could I live in the genius of Patanjali's stillness? Thoreau had done it. And Merton. And Castaneda. And Dillard. Perhaps I could, too.

Rudi and I spent the rest of the evening talking. We ended with a starlit walk into the pasture behind the old tennis courts. As we passed the old stump that Jake had used as a makeshift altar, we both paused. "You know," Rudi said, "you think you're guiding the process. But you're not. You're not guiding the process of your writing, any more than you're guiding the process of your awakening. The truth is, you don't have a clue what the failure of this book means. It's probably a success hiding out as a failure."

Later on, as I walked home from Acorn Cottage, I felt calmer. When I got to the cemetery, I lay down on the knoll near the Winslow obelisk, and looked up at the stars.

I realized, in a flash of sanity, that I really didn't know. I didn't know what to do. I didn't know whether my editor was right. I didn't know how to write the book.

I said it out loud: "I don't know."

I felt an immediate wave of relief. I felt my belly relax. I could breathe again.

Then I remembered. Almost all of my epiphanies over the previous fifteen years had been this same one: I don't know. Over and over again in life, I keep coming to this same crossroads. I keep having to learn to let go of needing to be the one who knows. I keep having to let go of trying to master life through thinking about it—through perfecting my explanation of it. And every time, the result is the same. Relief. Like relaxing into a river whose current I have been resisting with all my might.

I repeated the words over and over again like a mantra: "I don't know."

As I lay on my back in the cool grass, I looked at the Milky Way. The sky was clear, and in the black of the cemetery the stars seemed close at hand.

"The ten thousand things are just as they are," I said to myself, quoting the Fifth Zen Patriarch.

The belief that we are somehow guiding our lives really is The

Great Delusion. Life is constantly unmasking this delusion. Life inevitably reveals the humble poseur behind the artificially enlarged image of the Wizard of Oz.

For a moment, lying on my back in the cemetery, I was in right relationship with life. I was not in charge. I felt a prayer come through me and rise straight up to the Milky Way: "Thy Will, O Lord. Not mine."

SURRENDER

Later that night, lying in bed, I realized that the whole day had been a Shiva meltdown. These immolations are a central factor in waking up. They are often, as Rudi suggested, good news masquerading as bad.

"How does enlightenment happen?" asks the "crazy wisdom" yogi and teacher Bhagwan Shree Rajneesh. "It happens to a seeker when he drops his seeking. It happens to one who has searched with his total potential and has failed, utterly failed. In that failure, the first ray of light. And then it takes you by surprise! When you are completely feeling hopeless, when you are thinking to forget all about enlightenment, when the search has stopped, when even the desire to be enlightened has left you, suddenly it is there...and therewith the matter is settled."[1]

In these moments of surrender, we fall into a gap. And in that gap, we see unequivocally that our various Managers and sub-personalities cannot take us where we long to go. We see that ordinary mind is finally powerless over suffering and delusion.

But if our Managers are not guiding our journeys, then who is? Is our journey guided at all? The answer from the *sramanic* point of view is, yes—our journeys are guided. But they cannot be pushed from below—guided by willpower and force, and the big plans and schemes of our minds. Our journeys are pulled from above. Pulled from the power of Divine mind—or what Patanjali calls *īshvara*, the Lord.

Says Western-born author and psychologist Swami Ajaya, "Development does not proceed from the bottom up like building a house, but from the top down, as consciousness calls us forward into being. We grow upside down, as it were. A person's growth is directed by his future."[2]

If the first movement of the spiritual life is a realization of our entrapment and powerlessness, then the next movement is one of surrender to a higher consciousness. And with this surrender comes a flood of light, as it did for me, along with an intimation of Grace. Finally we are open to the wisdom of a power greater than ourselves. We are available to an altogether new kind of guidance—a guidance that is ineffable, yes, but at the same time more real than rain.

It is surprising to many yoga students that any experience of the Divine plays a role in Patanjali's exposition. But there it is: Patanjali includes the practice of *ishvara-pranidhāna*—or, literally—"surrender to the Lord of the yogis," or "surrender to the Divine ideal"—in his exposition of the path of yoga. In fact, *ishvara-pranidhāna* is a centerpiece of Patanjali's view—appearing both in his succinct description of *yoga-kriyā* (yogic action) at the beginning of chapter two, as well as in his Eight-Limbed yoga in the second half of chapter two. There is no way to miss it.

My students regularly rebel at finding a hint of God here in the world of yoga. Many have come to the spirituality of the East precisely to get away from God—certainly from the long-bearded, all-knowing Father in Heaven who both guides and admonishes from on high. Or from the inscrutable God of the Job story in the Old Testament—who allows his faithful servant Job to suffer every kind of crushing loss, apparently without intervening.

Students of Buddhism who come to study yoga are shocked to find Divinity here as well. But Buddhists are often shocked for different reasons. The Buddha was agnostic about God. Though he taught about beings in the heaven realms, he demurred on all questions about the existence of God—just as he passed on metaphysical questions of any kind. Indeed, the explicit introduction of any kind of "Lord" is one of the most profound differences between the tradition of *rāja-yoga* and Buddhism.

Who, or what, then, is this Lord, this *īshvara*? Contemporary seekers will find this God of the yogis to be a radical reframe of our Western notions.

First of all, as I've said, Patanjali was not steering his work according to ideas, doctrines, or metaphysical speculations, but by the *direct and immediate experience of yogis.* This certainly included his own experience. *Īshvara* is (as is everything else in the *Yoga-Sūtra*) an experiential fact. Not a metaphysical speculation. It seems likely that yogis in the *sramanic* stream just kept coming up with an experience of "the Lord," over and over again—so consistently that Patanjali simply had to include it in his treatise on yoga.

Īshvara, the Lord described by Patanjali, is not created and cannot be destroyed, but is, rather, the great Unborn, Unchanging, Eternal that exists beyond time and space. He is not subject to cause and effect—nor to any of the laws of ordinary mind. *Īshvara* has never been entangled with the afflictions in any way. His power comes through the purity of awareness. He is, in fact, nothing but Pure Awareness—the seeing without a Seer. Patanjali's God is the Witness behind the Witness—the seed inside the seed.

This Lord of Patanjali's is not so easy for us to fathom. He is not exactly the kind of God to whom we bow down. Nor, indeed, is *īshvara* even really a "he" or a "she" or an "it" of any kind. This Lord is simply the power of Pure Knowing. Rather than bow down to this power, we align ourselves with it. We attune to it. Patanjali's phrase, *īshvara-pranidhāna,* means "aligning oneself with *īshvara*"—yoking every aspect of conscious life to the perspective of Pure Awareness. Patanjali describes the role of "the Lord" in our awakening:

> *Realization may also come if one is oriented toward the ideal of pure awareness,* īshvara.

> *Īshvara is a distinct, incorruptible form of pure awareness, utterly independent of cause and effect, and lacking any store of latent impressions.*
>
> *Its independence makes this awareness an incomparable source of omniscience.*
>
> *Existing beyond time, īshvara was also the ideal of the ancients.* (1.23–6)

This Lord is a kind of gravitational force—into whose orbit we must eventually come. At first, though, of course, we resist—preferring the allure of our own grand plans and schemes, preferring the elusive quest for the Firebird. Finally, though, there is nothing to do but surrender. St. Augustine said it: "My heart is restless until it finds its rest in Thee." Most of the rest of Augustine's view of God does not fit the yogic view, however, for Augustine's God most definitely *does* enter into causality and time. *Īshvara* does *not*. *Īshvara* is, rather, a kind of planet around whom our true orbit lies.

Eliade describes a "metaphysical sympathy"[3] between the yogi and *īshvara* that inspires the yogi to a kind of *imitatio dei*—an imitation of the Divine mind. Georg Feuerstein describes *īshvara* as "the archetypal yogin who 'instructs' by his sheer being."[4] *Īshvara* has also been described as a kind of Divine Mirror, in which we might turn to catch a glimpse of Reality—and the possibility of freedom.

Descriptions of this "Lord" vary widely, but most commentators agree: As we allow ourselves to be pulled into the orbit of *īshvara*, our true nature is slowly and ineluctably revealed.

Over and over again, practicing yogis describe the trajectory of their experience as moving toward a surrender to *īshvara*, moving into the orbit of the Divine mind and will. The plodding day-to-day practice of the yogi is seen as a way of preparing consciousness to receive this experience, and of preparing the body and mind to be overwhelmed by it. It is a process of preparing the Managers and sub-personalities to be humbled. Rajneesh struggles to articulate the view of the *sramanas*—and we see that it is very hard to do without personifying this Lord:

> God *is*. There is no question of God's being. The question is, we cannot see Him. We don't have eyes. All the meditations and the prayers and the purifications only help you, make you capable of seeing. Once you can see, you will be surprised—it has always been there. Day in, day out, year in, year out, it was showering on you, but you were not sensitive enough to catch hold of it, you were not empty enough to be filled by it. You were too much full of your own ego.[5]

The practice of yoga leads inexorably to the direct realization of an unseen power that pulls on us, guides us, draws us onward toward full integration. The longing we feel in the presence of this power is the outward and visible sign of its reality, just as the unique orbit of planets is the proof of the existence of other unseen masses and forces. "For now, we see through a glass darkly," says St. Paul. "But then face-to-face." Then we know ourselves to be made in the image and likeness of this Pure Awareness. Then there are no distinctions between self and other, known and unknown. And what was present at the Beginning is fully realized in the End:

> *Yoga is to still the patterning of consciousness.*
> *Then pure awareness can abide in its very nature.* (1.2–3)

GUIDANCE

One afternoon several weeks later, I went back to Acorn Cottage to talk with Rudi again. I found him trimming back the lilacs around the tennis court. The bushes had bloomed extravagantly this year, but all of the blossoms had now gone by, and Rudi was determined to prune them back so that he'd have another bumper crop next year. He gave me a long-handled pruning tool, and showed me how and where to trim. We worked together in the sun for the next hour or so.

Between snips, I told Rudi about my experience in the cemetery after leaving his house the night of my book rejection.

"And also . . . I've been praying again," I said.

"Uh huh." Rudi nodded as he reached deep into the gnarly base of an ancient lilac branch.

"It's strange. It's like the prayers just arise spontaneously," I said.

I thought for a minute about how to explain this to Rudi. "I'm lying in bed early in the morning. Very still. And these prayers emerge all by themselves. They're like prayers for guidance. But almost beyond words."

Rudi stopped, and I could tell he was thinking about what I'd said.

"'The spirit prays through us with sighs too deep for words,'" he said, quoting St. Paul.

Standing in full sun, Rudi wiped his brow with the back of his dirty work glove, leaving a smudge of dirt on his forehead. A smile began to creep across his wide face.

"You know what?" he said, with some mischief in his voice.

"What?" I said, brushing some twigs off my shoulder.

"You're screwed."

Rudi laughed out loud, now—with some glee—and pulled at his beard.

I looked at him quizzically.

"You'll never be able to steer your life the way you used to. Your new steering mechanism has been activated," he said, still chuckling.

"It's wireless," he continued, clearly enjoying his own metaphor, "and tied into a current of energy and intelligence beyond anything you can imagine."

Rudi picked up one of the particularly large branches he had cut, and began methodically snipping it into smaller pieces. He spoke as he worked: "You have to get used to this new way of steering. It's different. You just have to navigate closer to the ground."

As we worked together in silence, a cool breeze shimmered the leaves of the lilac bushes. In those moments of closeness with Rudi, I felt happy. I realized that in the most fundamental way, everything was really absolutely OK. Something had altered inside me. I realized that subtly, almost imperceptibly, my view of the world had changed.

What was the nature of this change? Just for those seconds, I could see it clearly: I was contented. Contented with life just as it was. I mused on this for a while as I snipped: How had this change come about? Through what doorway had it entered? Was it because of practice? Enough moments on the yoga mat in states of concentration when I felt held and soothed down to my very bones? Enough moments on the meditation cushion, when my mind settled into bliss? Enough times sitting next to Maggie and Jake and Rudi and Susan and Kate and seeing that we are all exactly alike inside? Did the change even have anything to do with yoga? Or was it just living life? I really don't know.

As I pared away at the lilac branches, it came to me. I realized that I was living that new view that Rudi had spoken of. That for the first time I really knew—knew in the deepest part of my mind—that I do *not* have to bend life to my will. Willpower is the caveman approach to life. I could let go of the need to dominate things, and watch how they unfold instead.

How had I arrived here? Was it a result of an understanding of the laws of karma? An understanding that all things arise and pass away as a result of causes and conditions? Or was it my belief in a higher power who guides my life, so that my Manager does not have to be in charge of the really important things?

Yoga should come with a warning: these practices will change your life. The deepest desires of our Managers, and our other sub-personalities, will be shot to hell. But the outcomes will be more spectacular than anything we can imagine.

Now Rudi pointed his pruning tool at me and said: "Just because you've discovered this, don't expect that the world will understand, you know, or love you for it. Don't expect that it will make your book work.

You might end up a loser. Like me." Rudi laughed, and said with emphasis: "Cause after all—Shiva just wants to melt you down, boy."

Then he stopped again, and said in a more serious tone, "Winning and losing are more tied together than you think. For me, being a loser is being a winner. I have time and quiet. I have peace of mind. I have freedom."

We were both sweating now, with the exertion of the trimming, and Rudi handed me his quart bottle of water.

"Ah, what the heck. If you're tuned to God's channel, you've got everything you need. Every step of the way you'll get unseen help."

Rudi gathered up a big armful of brush to carry to the woodpile behind the house. He motioned with his head, and I began to pick up another load. I moved along behind him toward the mammoth pile of brush we were creating just beyond Acorn Cottage.

Rudi looked back over his shoulder and smiled. "Just see if you can get out of your own way."

APPENDIX A

Yoga and Buddhism

Throughout *The Wisdom of Yoga,* readers who are knowledgeable about Buddhism will have noticed some remarkable similarities between the views and practices of *rāja-yoga* and those of Buddhism—and particularly the views of Theravada Buddhism, sometimes called the "teaching of the elders." (The Theravada school of Buddhism derives its scriptural inspiration from the Pali Canon, which scholars generally agree contains the earliest surviving record of the Buddha's teachings.)

Indeed, the similarities between the *Yoga-Sūtra* and the teachings of the Pali Canon are in some instances so striking that they may surprise, or even confuse, the Buddhist reader. There are obvious historical reasons why these two paths should so resemble each other. After all, Siddhartha Gautama, the Buddha-to-be, became a yogi when he left his father's palace to "go forth" in pursuit of liberation. When he renounced his life of ease, the young prince joined the great *sramanic* stream of practice and inquiry. He sought out and studied with the greatest yogis of his day—including approximately five years of study with the well-known yogis Alara Kalama and Uddaka Ramaputta. Under their tutelage, the young aspirant studied the most sophisticated yogic meditation techniques then known—earlier versions of the techniques which Patanjali would later describe as the various stages of *dhāranā* and *dhyāna,* and which Buddhist teaching describes as the *jhanas* (concentrations).

Siddhartha Gautama quickly mastered the most refined yogic knowledge of his time, and soon left his meditation teachers to practice in the forest with a group of five other yoga adepts interested in investigating even more advanced austerities. This phase of his practice led to the dramatic part of the story with which most of us are familiar: when the young Buddha-to-be was near death, he gave up his extreme practice of asceticism, and accepted a bowl of milk from the farm girl Sujata. Siddhartha then resolved to sit under the *bodhi* tree until he attained enlightenment. His practice under the *bodhi* tree did, indeed, lead him to a complete extinguishment of the "fetters" (*kleshas,* or afflictions)—an experience he would call "waking up." In the process of "waking up," the Buddha mastered entirely new aspects of meditative technique. After his enlightenment, he taught these techniques widely. His unique contributions to the meditative culture of his time were contained in the final two stages of his Eight Fold Path—Right Concentration, as described in the scripture called the *Anapanasati Sutta,* and Right Mindfulness, as described in the *Satipatthana Sutta.*

The Buddha's teaching contributed enormously to the understanding of meditation in the *sramanic* stream at large—though not all yogis adopted the Buddha's views. Nonetheless, the Buddha's contributions to yoga were so profound that for more than a thousand years after he lived, his teachings flourished in India, side-by-side with other schools of yogic discipline, and other views about the goals of meditation practice.

In Patanjali's time (probably about the second century of the Common Era), Indian culture was saturated with Buddhist views and practices. By about 400 CE, only two hundred years after Patanjali, in fact, many of the most accomplished yogis of the day studied at the great Buddhist university called Nalanda. In this era, yogis and Buddhists drank from a common stream of philosophy and practice. So it is not surprising that Patanjali's *Yoga-Sūtra* relies, at times, on views and techniques developed by a Buddhist culture. Yogis and Buddhists appear to have argued about (and sometimes exchanged) views and practices liberally for almost a thousand years—from the time of the Buddha (563 BCE–483 BCE) until at least the middle of the first millennium of the Common Era.

The systems of *rāja-yoga* and Buddhism are similar in a number of important ways:

1. Both traditions were interested primarily in two aspects of the human dilemma: the problem of suffering, and the problem of seeing reality clearly. They developed a similar series of techniques for attenuating suffering and

for seeing clearly. In both cases these techniques employed a three-pronged process: First, the cultivation of so-called skillful behavior—behaviors which attenuate suffering for self and other. In yoga these were called *yama* and *niyama;* in Buddhism they were called *sila.* Second, the cultivation of deep states of concentration. In yoga these were called *dhāranā* and *dhyāna.* In Buddhism, they were called *samādhi* (right effort, concentration, and mindfulness). And third, the use of highly concentrated mental states to investigate the ways in which the "self" is constructed, moment by moment. In both traditions, this direct investigation of the mind and body led to liberating insights. In yoga these insights arose as *samyama,* or "perfect discipline" (*dhāranā, dhyāna,* and *samādhi*) was applied to "individual mind moments"; in Buddhism, they arose from a series of insight, or wisdom, practices like *vipassana.*

2. Both traditions acknowledged that so-called "ordinary reality" is but an elaborate construction—and that this construction is replete with erroneous ideas. In particular, these constructions confuse perceiver, the act of perception, and the perceived. (This view, by the way, is similar to Western constructivist theories of perception, which acknowledge that the ordinary view of reality is merely a rough approximation—and that it is significantly distorted in many respects.) Yogis observed that these errors result in the Four Erroneous Beliefs (the belief in the permanence of objects, the belief in the ultimate reality of the body, the belief that suffering is really happiness, the belief that our bodies and minds are our True Self). Buddhists observed that these errors obscure the so-called Three Marks of Existence (*anicca,* the truth of impermanence; *annata,* the truth of no-Self; and *duhkha,* the truth of suffering).

3. Both Buddhists and yogis agree that when confused thinking is ended, through direct and systematic investigation of phenomena, our view of external reality is permanently altered, and confusion and suffering are ended. In yoga, this is called *kaivalya* (emancipation) and in Buddhism, *nirvana* (the "unbinding" of constructions). Of course, *kaivalya* and *nirvana* appear to "mean" very different things in the context of the views that surrounded them, but the actual *experience* of these states, as they are described by adepts, is very similar.

4. Both paths proceeded in remarkably similar ways to untie the knot of confused perception. Both Buddhists and yogis recognize the similarity (and in some cases identity) of a number of central pillars of "view" (or description of reality)—including *nirodha* (cessation), *klesha* (affliction), *karma* (action), *samvega* (vehemence), *samādhi* (concentration), *prajñā* (intuitive

wisdom), and *samskāra* (subliminal activator). Each one of these central pillars of "view" will be investigated in this book, and in some cases where it is necessary to keep the yogic "view" distinct from the Buddhist "view" I will add a note to the reader.

5. Finally, both traditions share an emphasis on a direct, immediate investigation of reality. Both systems reject an emphasis on metaphysics, and hold themselves to be existential practice traditions—oriented toward solving the two central linked problems of distorted perception and suffering. They share an emphasis on self-study, self-reliance, and self-liberation. We might say that these paths share a profoundly similar flavor.

We have established some of the commonalities between *rāja-yoga* and Buddhism. However, though they are fewer than commonly believed, nevertheless there *are* several fundamental disagreements between Patanjali's view and that of the Buddha. The two most important differences are these:

1. Patanjali finds an abiding "pure awareness" that remains when all conditioned aspects of the psycho-mental structure have been deconstructed with practice. (Yogic thinkers have described this as a Self, which, of course, the mind finds nearly impossible to avoid personifying on some level.) The Buddha, on the other hand, believed that the body was *manomaya,* imbued with mind, and that all aspects of consciousness arise and pass away with the objects of consciousness. So, when ordinary mind is deconstructed, there is no abiding pure awareness of any kind. The Buddha could find no lasting Self that knows things—only things that, in the aggregate, *feel like a Self who knows.*

2. The Buddha saw all mental states to be linked with *vedana* or sensation (feeling), and believed that a true insight into the profound impermanence of these states could not be developed without a direct investigation of this linkage. This view appears nowhere in Patanajali's *Yoga-Sūtra.* This absence of an explicit technique linking bodily sensations to mental states in the *Yoga-Sūtra* is perhaps the most important practical difference between the traditions. Although this is indeed a big difference in their rhetoric—and the linkage is really not explicitly described by Patanjali in anything like the detail of the Buddha's teaching on Dependent Origination—nonetheless this linkage seems to be taken almost as a given in Patanjali, and is hinted at on numerous occasions, for example *Yoga-Sūtra* 2.10–2.11.

In spite of these important differences, the similarities are extensive. The Eight-Limbed Path offered by Patanjali is remarkably similar to the Buddha's earlier Eight Fold Path. But if the similarities between *rāja-yoga* and Buddhism are so profound, why is this fact not more widely appreciated? Indeed, why have generations of yoga scholars and practitioners alike seen them as so profoundly distinct?

Perhaps the major source of this problem issues from the vast commentarial literature on the *Yoga-Sūtra*. Patanjali's treatise was written in such a terse, aphoristic style that its readers have always had to rely on commentary to flesh out its meaning. One assumes that Patanjali himself offered this commentary to his students. But Patanjali did not leave us with any written record of his own commentary. If he did leave us with such a commentary, it appears to have been lost. Only the spare 196 *sutras* themselves remain. So in the absence of an original commentary, thousands of other scholars and adepts (perhaps less well-qualified than Patanjali) have leapt into the gap.

For two thousand years, a wide variety of commentators have conflated Patanjali's yoga with views that are quite different from those held by Patanjali and his colleagues. These include, most important, *Sāmkhya* philosophy—with which yoga is erroneously believed to be identical—but also *Vedānta, Advaita Vedānta,* and even *Tantra.*

A case in point (and perhaps the most important case) is the earliest extant commentary on the *Yoga-Sūtra,* called the *Yoga-Bhāshya* ("Discussion on Yoga"). This commentary was probably composed by a sage named Vyasa in the fifth century CE. It quickly became an influential interpretation of the *Yoga-Sūtra.* Georg Feuerstein, America's most influential yoga scholar, points out in his *Shambhala Encyclopedia of Yoga* (p. 343; Shambhala, 1997) that "Vyasa's work is the basis for all subsequent exegetical efforts in Classical Yoga." Feuerstein goes on to say that Vyasa's commentary is based not on pure classical yoga views, but on those of the *Sāmkhya* teacher Vindhyasvasin—views and practices which differed considerably from Patanjali.

A quick review of the current state of the commentarial literature will reveal the puzzling fact that almost *all* commentaries used by contemporary readers are profoundly influenced by non-classical views. *How to Know God,* for example, an influential contemporary translation and commentary by Christopher Isherwood and Swami Prabhavananda, though beautiful and poetic, does not give a truly yogic view of the *Yoga-Sūtra,* but rather a

Vedantist view. (The Vedantic view that the individual soul, or *atman*, is One with the ground of being, the Absolute, or *Brahman*, appears nowhere at all in the *Yoga-Sūtra*.) Patanjali was not a Vedantist. Indeed, almost all influential commentaries are written from a *Vedāntist, Advaita-Vedāntist, Sāmkhya*, or even *Tantric* view. And all of these views differ considerably from the view of classical yoga—*rāja-yoga*. As a result, readers are simply unfamiliar with the authentic views that underlie the *Yoga-Sūtra* —and that share so much in common with Buddhist views.

In constructing my own commentary on the *Yoga-Sūtra*, I have pared it down to its most elementary bones. My commentary focuses principally on the second chapter of the *Yoga-Sūtra*, (and the beginning of the third) in which Patanjali articulates his Eight-Limbed Path. This kind of treatment is meant for a mainstream Western audience, and purely as an introduction to Patanjali's brilliant treatise. More advanced yogis will want to investigate a translation and commentary that fleshes out the path more fully than a strictly mainstream audience could easily tolerate.

Nonetheless, though my commentary is "mainstreamed," I have tried to maintain an authentic and intellectually precise rendering of Patanjali—written from the view of *rāja-yoga* practice. This has not been easy, for there are few translations and commentaries that support this view. There is, however, one exemplary translation and commentary written from the classical point of view. This is Chip Hartranft's work, *The Yoga-Sūtra of Patanjali*, published by Shambhala Press. I have used his translation throughout, and am indebted to Chip and to Shambhala Press for their generosity in allowing me to use their work.

In addition, I have relied on the only serious comparative study of Buddhism and *rāja-yoga* done by a Western scholar trained both as a psychologist and a meditator—the study done by Harvard psychologist Daniel Brown, and published along with Ken Wilber's work in *Transformations of Consciousness* (Shambhala, 1986). This study, entitled "The Stages of Meditation in Cross Cultural Perspective," gives a careful account of the classical yoga view. I've also relied on the helpful *A Re-Appraisal of Patanjali's Yoga-Sūtras in the Light of the Buddha's Teaching*, by S. N. Tandon, and published by the Vipassana Research Institute (Dhammagiri, 1995). Tandon's study gives us a careful analysis of the distinctions between the Buddhist view and that of classical yoga. I've relied, as well, on the valuable contribution made by Professor Joshi in his book, *Discerning the Buddha: A Study of Buddhism and of the Brahmanical Hindu Attitude to It* (New Delhi: Munshiram Manoharlal Publishers, 1983). Joshi clearly identifies the common development of *rāja-yoga* and Buddhism in the *sramanic* stream of practice.

Just because *rāja-yoga* and Buddhism share similar views and practices is not, of course, a reason to conflate and confuse them. I do think it useful to remain aware of the important areas of disagreement, and to remain precise in noting the distinctions between the two traditions.

The reader will have noticed my occasional use of quotes from Buddhist sources, American teachers of Buddhism, and the words of the Buddha himself (through scripture). And also, my occasional use of ideas and practices that have been more fully investigated by the Buddhist meditation tradition than by the yoga meditation tradition itself.

Why use Buddhist sources in a book on yoga? Alas, the path laid out so clearly in the *Yoga-Sūtra* is a path of meditation, and yet, many of the most refined meditation practices described by Patanjali are not taught in today's yoga tradition as it has come to us in the West. One assumes that they *were* taught in Patanjali's time. When they are taught today, however, at least in America, they are more often taught by Buddhist teachers.

The practice of *metta*—loving kindness meditation—is a case in point. Even though *maitri*, or "friendliness" (toward all Beings) is mentioned in the *Yoga-Sūtra* (see chapter ten), and clearly seen by Patanjali as an important aid in practice, most of us involved in the yoga tradition in America have learned the formal practices of *metta* meditation from Buddhist teachers. As a result, many practitioners (probably on both sides of the aisle, if there is an aisle) believe them to be exclusively Buddhist.

Another case in point is the whole spectrum of "insight" practices. Though these are clearly present in Patanjali's treatment of meditation practice *(samyama* on mind moments—see chapter fourteen), insight practice is rarely taught in the yoga traditions in America. Once again, American yogis have learned these insight practices from Buddhist teachers.

In summing up, I would say that I use Buddhist sources to describe common views and practices when distinct yogic sources are not available, or are less compelling. The Buddhist tradition emphasized scholarship and preservation of the teachings in a way never true of the yoga tradition—which has always been more fragmented, less cohesive, and less interested in preservation of texts and scholarship.

———

Finally, I would say that these overlapping areas of view and practice that we have examined only serve to point out, once again, that classical yoga and Buddhism are sister traditions. They have traded ideas and practices back and forth for two thousand years, and continue to do so. For most of us, this is not a problem. I would go even further. I believe that these two great traditions will experience a rapprochement in the West, which will integrate them in a new fashion. We are already seeing evidence of this: postures (*āsana*) and breathing practices (*prāṇāyāma*) have found their way into many Buddhist meditation retreats. Meditation practices from Buddhism have found their way into many yoga studios. The process has begun. I wish not to confuse the issue, but also I do not wish to resist a healthy rapprochement.

APPENDIX B

The Yoga-Sūtra *in English*

translated by Chip Hartranft

Chapter 1. Integration

1 Now, the teachings of yoga.
2 Yoga is to still the patterning of consciousness.
3 Then pure awareness can abide in its very nature.
4 Otherwise awareness takes itself to be the patterns of consciousness.
5 There are five types of patterns, including both hurtful and benign.
6 They are right perception, misperception, conceptualization, deep sleep, and remembering.
7 Right perception arises from direct observation, inference, or the words of others.
8 Misperception is false knowledge, not based on what actually is.
9 Conceptualization is based on linguistic knowledge, not contact with real things.
10 Deep sleep is a pattern grounded in the perception that nothing exists.
11 Remembering is the retention of experiences.
12 Both practice and nonreaction are required to still the patterning of consciousness.
13 Practice is the sustained effort to rest in that stillness.
14 This practice becomes firmly rooted when it is cultivated skillfully and continuously for a long time.
15 As for nonreaction, one can recognize that it has been fully achieved when no attachment arises in regard to anything at all, whether perceived directly or learned.
16 When the ultimate level of nonreaction has been reached, pure awareness

can clearly see itself as independent from the fundamental qualities of nature.

17　At first the stilling process is accompanied by four kinds of cognition: analytical thinking, insight, bliss, and feeling like a self.

18　Later, after one practices steadily to bring all thought to a standstill, these four kinds of cognition fall away, leaving only a store of latent impressions in the depth memory.

19　These latent impressions incline one to be reborn after one leaves the body at death and is dissolved in nature.

20　For all others, faith, energy, mindfulness, integration, and wisdom form the path to realization.

21　For those who seek liberation wholeheartedly, realization is near.

22　How near depends on whether the practice is mild, moderate, or intense.

23　Realization may also come if one is oriented toward the ideal of pure awareness, *īshvara*.

24　*Īshvara* is a distinct, incorruptible form of pure awareness, utterly independent of cause and effect, and lacking any store of latent impressions.

25　Its independence makes this awareness an incomparable source of omniscience.

26　Existing beyond time, *īshvara* was also the ideal of the ancients.

27　*Īshvara* is represented by a sound, *om*.

28　Through repetition its meaning becomes clear.

29　Then interiorization develops and obstacles fall away.

30　Sickness, apathy, doubt, carelessness, laziness, sexual indulgence, delusion, lack of progress, and inconstancy are all distractions that, by stirring up consciousness, act as barriers to stillness.

31　When they do, one may experience distress, depression, or the inability to maintain steadiness of posture or breathing.

32　One can subdue these distractions by working with any one of the following principles of practice.

33　Consciousness settles as one radiates friendliness, compassion, delight, and equanimity toward all things, whether pleasant or painful, good or bad.

34　Or by pausing after breath flows in or out.

35　Or by steadily observing as new sensations materialize.

36　Or when experiencing thoughts that are luminous and free of sorrow.

37　Or by focusing on things that do not inspire attachment.

38　Or by reflecting on insights culled from sleep and dreaming.

39　Or through meditative absorption in any desired object.

40　One can become fully absorbed in any object, whether vast or infinitesimal.

41　As the patterning of consciousness subsides, a transparent way of seeing, called coalescence, saturates consciousness; like a jewel, it reflects equally whatever lies before it—whether subject, object, or act of perceiving.

42 So long as conceptual or linguistic knowledge pervades this transparency, it is called coalescence with thought.

43 At the next stage, called coalescence beyond thought, objects cease to be colored by memory; now formless, only their essential nature shines forth.

44 In the same way, coalesced contemplation of subtle objects is described as reflective or reflection-free.

45 Subtle objects can be traced back to their origin in undifferentiated nature.

46 These four kinds of coalesced contemplation—with thought, beyond thought, reflective, reflection-free—are called integration that bears seeds of latent impressions.

47 In the lucidity of coalesced, reflection-free contemplation, the nature of the self becomes clear.

48 The wisdom that arises in that lucidity is unerring.

49 Unlike insights acquired through inference or teachings, this wisdom has as its object the actual distinction between pure awareness and consciousness.

50 It generates latent impressions that prevent the activation of other impressions.

51 When even these cease to arise and the patterning of consciousness is completely stilled, integration bears no further seeds.

Chapter 2. The Path to Realization

1 Yogic action has three components—discipline, self-study, and orientation toward the ideal of pure awareness.

2 Its purposes are to disarm the causes of suffering and achieve integration.

3 The causes of suffering are not seeing things as they are, the sense of "I," attachment, aversion, and clinging to life.

4 Not seeing things as they are is the field where the other causes of suffering germinate, whether dormant, activated, intercepted, or weakened.

5 Lacking this wisdom, one mistakes that which is impermanent, impure, distressing, or empty of self for permanence, purity, happiness, and self.

6 The sense of "I" ascribes selfhood to pure awareness by identifying it with the senses.

7 Attachment is a residue of pleasant experience.

8 Aversion is a residue of suffering.

9 Clinging to life is instinctive and self-perpetuating, even for the wise.

10 In their subtle form, these causes of suffering are subdued by seeing where they come from.

11 In their gross form, as patterns of consciousness, they are subdued through meditative absorption.

12 The causes of suffering are the root source of actions; each action deposits

latent impressions deep in the mind, to be activated and experienced later in this birth or lie hidden awaiting a future one.

13 So long as this root source exists, its contents will ripen into a birth, a life, and experience.

14 This life will be marked by delight or anguish, in proportion to those good or bad actions that created its store of latent impressions.

15 The wise see suffering in all experience, whether from the anguish of impermanence or from latent impressions laden with suffering or from incessant conflict as the fundamental qualities of nature vie for ascendancy.

16 But suffering that has not yet arisen can be prevented.

17 The preventable cause of all this suffering is the apparent indivisibility of pure awareness and what it regards.

18 What awareness regards, namely the phenomenal world, embodies the qualities of luminosity, activity, and inertia; it includes oneself, composed of both elements and the senses; and it is the ground for both sensual experience and liberation.

19 All orders of being—undifferentiated, differentiated, indistinct, distinct — are manifestations of the fundamental qualities of nature.

20 Pure awareness is just seeing itself; although pure, it usually appears to operate through the perceiving mind.

21 In essence, the phenomenal world exists to reveal this truth.

22 Once that happens, the phenomenal world no longer appears as such, though it continues to exist as a common reality for everyone else.

23 It is by virtue of the apparent indivisibility of awareness and the phenomenal world that the latter seems to possess the former's powers.

24 Not seeing things as they are is the cause of this phenomenon.

25 With realization, the appearance of indivisibility vanishes, revealing that awareness is free and untouched by phenomena.

26 The apparent indivisibility of seeing and the seen can be eradicated by cultivating uninterrupted discrimination between awareness and what it regards.

27 At the ultimate level of discrimination, wisdom extends to all seven aspects of nature.

28 When the components of yoga are practiced, impurities dwindle; then the light of understanding can shine forth, illuminating the way to discriminative awareness.

29 The eight components of yoga are external discipline, internal discipline, posture, breath regulation, withdrawal of the senses, concentration, meditative absorption, and integration.

30 The five external disciplines are not harming, truthfulness, not stealing, celibacy, and not being acquisitive.

31 These universals, transcending birth, place, era, or circumstance, constitute the great vow of yoga.

32 The five internal disciplines are bodily purification, contentment, intense
discipline, self-study, and dedication to the ideal of yoga.

33 Unwholesome thoughts can be neutralized by cultivating wholesome
ones.

34 We ourselves may act upon unwholesome thoughts, such as wanting to
harm someone, or we may cause or condone them in others; unwholesome thoughts may arise from greed, anger, or delusion; they may be
mild, moderate, or extreme; but they never cease to ripen into ignorance
and suffering. This is why one must cultivate wholesome thoughts.

35 Being firmly grounded in nonviolence creates an atmosphere in which
others can let go of their hostility.

36 For those grounded in truthfulness, every action and its consequences are
imbued with truth.

37 For those who have no inclination to steal, the truly precious is at hand.

38 The chaste acquire vitality.

39 Freedom from wanting unlocks the real purpose of existence.

40 With bodily purification, one's body ceases to be compelling, likewise contact with others.

41 Purification also brings about clarity, happiness, concentration, mastery of
the senses, and capacity for self-awareness.

42 Contentment brings unsurpassed joy.

43 As intense discipline burns up impurities, the body and its senses become
supremely refined.

44 Self-study deepens communion with one's personal deity.

45 Through orientation toward the ideal of pure awareness, one can achieve
integration.

46 The postures of meditation should embody steadiness and ease.

47 This occurs as all effort relaxes and coalescence arises, revealing that the
body and the infinite universe are indivisible.

48 Then one is no longer disturbed by the play of opposites.

49 With effort relaxing, the flow of inhalation and exhalation can be brought
to a standstill; this is called breath regulation.

50 As the movement patterns of each breath—inhalation, exhalation, lull—
are observed as to duration, number, and area of focus, breath becomes
spacious and subtle.

51 As realization dawns, the distinction between breathing in and out falls
away.

52 Then the veil lifts from the mind's luminosity.

53 And the mind is now fit for concentration.

54 When consciousness interiorizes by uncoupling from external objects, the senses do likewise; this is called withdrawal of the senses.

55 Then the senses reside utterly in the service of realization.

Chapter 3. The Extraordinary Powers

1 Concentration locks consciousness on a single area.

2 In meditative absorption, the entire perceptual flow is aligned with that object.

3 When only the essential nature of the object shines forth, as if formless, integration has arisen.

4 Concentration, absorption, and integration regarding a single object compose the perfect discipline of consciousness.

5 Once the perfect discipline of consciousness is mastered, wisdom dawns.

6 Perfect discipline is mastered in stages.

7 These three components—concentration, absorption, and integration—are more interiorized than the preceding five.

8 Even these three are external to integration that bears no seeds.

9 The transformation toward total stillness occurs as new latent impressions fostering cessation arise to prevent the activation of distractive, stored ones and moments of stillness begin to permeate consciousness.

10 These latent impressions help consciousness flow from one tranquil moment to the next.

11 Consciousness is transformed toward integration as distractions dwindle and focus arises.

12 In other words, consciousness is transformed toward focus as continuity develops between arising and subsiding perceptions.

13 Consciousness evolves along the same three lines—form, time span, and condition—as the elements and the senses.

14 The substrate is unchanged, whether before, during, or after it takes a given form.

15 These transformations appear to unfold the way they do because consciousness is a succession of distinct patterns.

16 Observing these three axes of change—form, time span, and condition—with perfect discipline yields insight into the past and future.

17 Word, meaning, and perception tend to get lumped together, each confused with the others; focusing on the distinctions between them with perfect discipline yields insight into the language of all beings.

18 Directly observing latent impressions with perfect discipline yields insight into previous births.

19 Focusing with perfect discipline on the perceptions of another yields insight into that person's consciousness.

20 But not insight regarding the object of those perceptions, since the object itself is not actually present in that person's consciousness.

21 When the body's form is observed with perfect discipline, it becomes invisible: the eye is disengaged from incoming light, and the power to perceive is suspended.

22 Likewise, through perfect discipline other percepts—sound, smell, taste, touch—can be made to disappear.

23 The effects of action may be immediate or slow in coming; observing one's actions with perfect discipline, or studying omens, yields insight into death.

24 Focusing with perfect discipline on friendliness, compassion, delight, and equanimity, one is imbued with their energies.

25 Focusing with perfect discipline on the powers of an elephant or other entities, one acquires those powers.

26 Being absorbed in the play of the mind's luminosity yields insight about the subtle, hidden, and distant.

27 Focusing with perfect discipline on the sun yields insight about the universe.

28 Focusing with perfect discipline on the moon yields insight about the stars' positions.

29 Focusing with perfect discipline on the polestar yields insight about the stars' movements.

30 Focusing with perfect discipline on the navel energy center yields insight about the organization of the body.

31 Focusing with perfect discipline on the pit of the throat eradicates hunger and thirst.

32 Focusing with perfect discipline on the "tortoise channel," one cultivates steadiness.

33 Focusing with perfect discipline on the light in the crown of the head, one acquires the perspective of the perfected ones.

34 Or, all these accomplishments may be realized in a flash of spontaneous illumination.

35 Focusing with perfect discipline on the heart, one understands the nature of consciousness.

36 Experience consists of perceptions in which the luminous aspect of the phenomenal world is mistaken for absolutely pure awareness. Focusing with perfect discipline on the different properties of each yields insight into the nature of pure awareness.

37 Following this insight, the senses—hearing, feeling, seeing, tasting, smelling—may suddenly be enhanced.

38 These sensory gifts may feel like attainments, but they distract one from integration.

39 By relaxing one's attachment to the body, and becoming profoundly sensitive to its currents, consciousness can enter another's body.

40 By mastering the flow of energy in the head and neck, one can walk through water, mud, thorns, and other obstacles without touching down but rather floating over them.

41 By mastering the flow of energy through the solar plexus, one becomes radiant.

42 By focusing with perfect discipline on the way sound travels through the ether, one acquires divine hearing.

43 By focusing with perfect discipline on the body's relationship to the ether and developing coalesced contemplation on the lightness of cotton, one can travel through space.

44 When consciousness completely disengages from externals—the "great disembodiment"—then the veil lifts from the mind's luminosity.

45 By observing the aspects of matter—gross, subtle, intrinsic, relational, purposive—with perfect discipline, one masters the elements.

46 Then extraordinary faculties appear, including the power to shrink to the size of an atom, as the body attains perfection, transcending physical law.

47 This perfection includes beauty, grace, strength, and the firmness of a diamond.

48 By observing the various aspects of the sense organs—their processes of perception, intrinsic natures, identification as self, interconnectedness, purposes—with perfect discipline, one masters them.

49 Then, free from the constraints of their organs, the senses perceive with the quickness of the mind, no longer in the sway of the phenomenal world.

50 Once one just sees the distinction between pure awareness and the luminous aspect of the phenomenal world, all conditions are known and mastered.

51 When one is unattached even to this omniscience and mastery, the seeds of suffering wither and awareness knows it stands alone.

52 Even if the exalted beckon, one must avoid attachment and pride, or suffering will recur.

53 Focusing with perfect discipline on the succession of moments in time yields insight born of discrimination.

54 This insight allows one to tell things apart that, through similarities of origin, feature, or position, had seemed continuous.

55 In this way discriminative insight deconstructs all of the phenomenal world's objects and conditions, setting them apart from pure awareness.

56 Once the luminosity and transparency of consciousness have become as distilled as pure awareness, they can reflect the freedom of awareness back to itself.

Chapter 4. Freedom

1 The attainments brought about by integration may also arise at birth, through the use of herbs, from intonations, or through austerity.

2 Being delivered into a new form comes about when natural forces overflow.

3 The transformation into this form or that is not driven by the causes proximate to it, just oriented by them, the way a farmer diverts a stream for irrigation.

4 Feeling like a self is the frame that orients consciousness toward individuation.

5 A succession of consciousness, generating a vast array of distinctive perceptions, appears to consolidate into one individual consciousness.

6 Once consciousness is fixed in meditative absorption, it no longer contributes to the store of latent impressions.

7 The actions of a realized yoga transcend good and evil, whereas the actions of others may be good or evil or both.

8 Each action comes to fruition by coloring latent impressions according to its quality—good, evil, or both.

9 Because the depth memory and its latent impressions are of a piece, their dynamic of cause and effect flows uninterruptedly across the demarcations of birth, place, and time.

10 They have always existed, because the will to exist is eternal.

11 Since its cause, effect, basis, and object are inseparable, a latent impression disappears when they do.

12 The past and future are immanent in an object, existing as different sectors in the same flow of experiential forms.

13 The characteristics of these sectors, whether manifest or subtle, are imparted by the fundamental qualities of nature.

14 Their transformations tend to blur together, imbuing each new object with a quality of substantiality.

15 People perceive the same object differently, as each person's perception follows a separate path from another's.

16 But the object is not dependent on either of those perceptions; if it were, what would happen to it when nobody was looking?

17 An object is known only by a consciousness it has colored; otherwise it is not known.

18 Patterns of consciousness are always known by pure awareness, their ultimate, unchanging witness.

19 Consciousness is seen not by its own light but by awareness.

20 Furthermore, consciousness and its object cannot be perceived at once.

21 If consciousness were perceived by itself instead of by awareness, the chain of such perceptions would regress infinitely, imploding memory.

22 Once it is stilled, though, consciousness comes to resemble unchanging awareness and can reflect itself being perceived.

23 Then consciousness can be colored by both awareness and the phenomenal world, thereby fulfilling all its purposes.

24 Even when colored by countless latent traits, consciousness, like all compound phenomena, has another purpose—to serve awareness.

25 As soon as one can distinguish between consciousness and awareness, the ongoing construction of the self ceases.

26 Consciousness, now oriented to this distinction, can gravitate toward freedom—the fully integrated knowledge that awareness is independent of nature.

27 Any gaps in discriminating awareness allow distracting thoughts to emerge from the store of latent impressions.

28 These distractions can be subdued, as the causes of suffering were, by tracing them back to their origin, or through meditative absorption.

29 One who regards even the most exalted states disinterestedly, discriminating continuously between pure awareness and the phenomenal world, enters the final stage of integration, in which nature is seen to be a cloud of irreducible experiential forms.

30 This realization extinguishes both the causes of suffering and the cycle of cause and effect.

31 Once all the layers and imperfections concealing truth have been washed away, insight is boundless, with little left to know.

32 Then the seamless flow of reality, its transformations colored by the fundamental qualities, begins to break down, fulfilling the true mission of consciousness.

33 One can see that the flow is actually a series of discrete events, each corresponding to the merest instant of time, in which one form becomes another.

34 Freedom is at hand when the fundamental qualities of nature, each of their transformations witnessed at the moment of its inception, are recognized as irrelevant to pure awareness; it stands alone, grounded in its very nature, the power of pure seeing. That is all.

GLOSSARY OF PRINCIPAL SANSKRIT WORDS

A Note on Language

The *Yoga-Sūtra* is written in Sanskrit, one of the oldest Indo-European languages in use in the world today. It is the "classical" language of India, and it is still taught in schools and households there, though its use is primarily liturgical, religious, and scholarly.

I have adopted a simplified system of transliteration of Sanskrit words to the Roman alphabet. Ordinarily, scholars use a number of diacritical marks to indicate Sanskrit sounds—and of these I have retained only the macron, which is a dash over the *a, i,* and *u,* indicating that a vowel is to be lengthened in pronunciation.

A more complete guide to pronunciation of Sanskrit words can be found in *The Yoga-Sūtra of Patanjali* (Shambhala, 2003) by Chip Hartranft, as well as *The Shambhala Encyclopedia of Yoga* (Shambhala, 1997), by Georg Feuerstein. Both texts are cited frequently in this book.

aklishta: Actions not resulting in bondage, benign actions; untroubled.

āsana: Posture, seat; the third limb of Patanjali's Eight-Limbed Path.

ashta-anga-yoga: Literally, "eight-limbed yoga"; refers to the Eight-Limbed Path prescribed by Patanjali in the *Yoga-Sūtra.*

asmitā: The sense of "I," or "self-feeling." One of the five *kleshas,* or afflictions, enumerated in the *Yoga-Sūtra.*

avidyā: Lack of wisdom, ignorance of one's true nature, not seeing things as they are, one of Patanjali's five *kleshas.*

citta: Consciousness

dhāranā: Concentration, binding consciousness to a single focus; the sixth limb of Patanjali's Eight-Limbed Path.

dharma-megha-samādhi: Ecstasy of the dharma cloud; the penultimate insight, and the highest form of *samādhi*.

dhyāna: Meditative absorption, the seventh limb of Patanjali's Eight-Limbed Path.

drashtri: Seer, witness, pure awareness.

duhkha: Pervasive unsatisfactoriness, distress, suffering.

dvesha: Aversion, hatred; one of the five *kleshas* enumerated by Patanjali.

ekatānatā: Extending continuously, unbroken concentration.

hatha-yoga: Literally, "forceful yoga," refers to the extensive repertoire of practices and techniques for self-realization through the body; most fully detailed in the *Hatha-Yoga-Pradīpikā* (fourteenth century CE) and the *Shiva-Samhitā* (eighteenth century CE).

īshvara: The power of pure awareness; the ideal of pure awareness; "the Lord."

īshvara-pranidhāna: Surrender to *īshvara*, dedication or devotion to *īshvara*, surrender to "the Lord."

karma: Action; the "laws of karma" refer to the laws of cause and effect: every action has an effect, and every effect has a cause.

klesha: Affliction, cause of suffering, poison; Patanjali enumerates five afflictions: *avidyā, asmitā, rāga, dvesha,* and *abhinivesha.*

klishta: Actions resulting in bondage.

kosha: Sheath, casing, increasingly subtle levels of reality; in Upanishadic teachings, often refers to five sheaths: *anna-maya, prāna-maya, mano-maya, vijnāna-maya,* and *ānanda-maya.*

maitrī: Friendliness

marga: The way, or the path; originally referred to the hunter's path—came to be associated with hunting for one's true nature.

metta: Loving kindness

moha: Delusion

mudrā: Gesture, often with the hands, performed as a part of posture practice, or in the course of rituals; also, literally, "seal," aspects of advanced posture practice.

nāma: Name

nirodha: Stilling, cessation, restriction.

niyama: Observance, internal discipline.

padmāsana: Lotus Pose, perhaps the earliest *āsana*, and an often-used posture for meditation.

prānāyāma: Breath regulation; energy (or breath) extension.

pratyāhāra: Withdrawal of the senses, the fifth limb of the Eight-Limbed Path.

purusha: Pure awareness; "knowing" without a "knower."

rāga: Craving, grasping, clinging, attachment, greed; one of the five afflictions enumerated by Patanjali.

rāja-yoga: The "royal way" or the "exalted way," referring to the system of yoga described by Patanjali in the *Yoga-Sūtra;* also sometimes called classical yoga.

rūpa: Form

samādhi: Oneness, integration; the final stage of Patanjali's Eight-Limbed Path.

samāpatti: Coalescence, coincidence—as in "bringing together"; ecstatic identification with the object of contemplation.

samskāra: Subliminal activator; imprints left on consciousness by actions and volitions.

samyama: Perfect discipline—the seamless practice of *dhāranā, dhyāna,* and *samādhi.*

samvega: A state of disillusionment with mundane life that leads to a vehement and urgent search for truth, and an emergence from suffering, delusion, and confusion.

satya: Truthfulness; one of the five yamas prescribed by Patanjali.

Shiva: One of the three principal deities of the Hindu tradition (along with Brahma and Vishnu); in this context, he is associated with transformation and purification, and the death or destruction that brings new life. Also seen as the god of yogis, par excellence—he combines supernormal powers of asceticism with wild excess.

Shiva natarajā: Shiva in his form as "Lord of the Dance"; commonly depicted dancing in a ring of fire—symbolizing the destruction and re-creation of the universe.

siddhis: Supernormal powers; attainments.

sramana: Striver, seeker, wandering renunciate, pilgrim, ascetic.

sukha: Sweetness, happiness, ease, joy.

sūkshma: Subtle

tapas: Discipline, austerity, "heat," asceticism; one of the five niyamas described by Patanjali.

tattva: Literally, "thusness," a category of existence, a principle of nature.

vāsanā: A linked grouping of subliminal activators, character traits, habits, patterns.

vidyā: Knowledge, especially knowledge of one's true nature.

yama: Restraint, the first limb of the Eight-Limbed Path; also refers to Yāma, "the restrainer," or the Hindu god of death.

yoga-kriyā: Yogic actions, or actions that "yoke" us to the process of self-realization.

NOTES

Epigraph

Annie Dillard, *For the Time Being* (New York: Alfred A. Knopf, 1999) p. 88.

Introduction

1. Mircea Eliade, Editor in Chief, *The Encyclopedia of Religion* (London: MacMillan Publishing Company, 1987) Vol. I, p. 224. Eliade is referring to Heidegger's view that history's real power lies in its lessons for the present and future.

2. *Hatha-yoga* means, literally, "forceful yoga," and refers to the sophisticated development of physical practices which supported self-realization through the perfection of the body. A ninth century CE sage named Goraksha is often praised as the "father" of *hatha-yoga*, but the most important manuals on *hatha-yoga* were not written until the middle of the second millennium CE. These include the *Hatha-Yoga-Pradīpikā*, written by Svatmarama Yogin in the mid-fourteenth century CE, and the *Gheranda-Samhitā*, written by the yogi Gheranda in the late seventeenth century CE.

3. Breuer and Freud, translated and edited by James Strachey, *Studies on Hysteria* (New York: Basic Books, 1957) p. 305. Freud seems to have made statements like this on more than one occasion. When asked by a patient if he thinks his symptoms can really be altered, Freud says, "...you will be able to convince yourself that much will be gained if we succeed in transforming your hysterical misery into common unhappiness."

4. Quoted in Richard Faulds (ed.), *Sayings of Swami Kripalu* (Greenville, VT: Peaceable Kingdom Books, 2004) pp. 54 and 56.

Prologue Epigraph

Matsuo Basho, quoted in Richard Lewis, *The Way of Silence: The Prose and Poetry of Basho* (New York: Dial Press, 1970) p. 82.

Prologue

1. The Upanishads were esoteric, gnostic scriptures, which comprise the wisdom teachings of the Vedantic tradition. The earliest Upanishads were probably written before 1500 BCE, but the form became highly developed in the middle centuries of the first millennium BCE.

2. The Sanskrit word *sramana* derives from *srama* which means "to exert effort, or labor," or "to perform austerities." One who performs these acts of mortification or austerity is therefore *sramana*. In first century BCE India, the word came to connote wandering monks, or pilgrims. *The Soka-Gakkai Dictionary of Buddhism* (Tokyo: Soka Gakkai, 2002) translates this as "a seeker of the way," and says, "In India, the word originally referred to any ascetic, recluse, mendicant, or other religious practitioner who renounced secular life and left home to seek the truth." I considered using the term "seeker" as a translation for *sramana*, but it lacks the strength and freshness of "striver." The term *sramana* was clearly a designation for people who were putting their lives on the line, literally, either through extreme austerities, or through wandering around in the forest totally exposed to the elements. "Striver," the literal translation, retains more of the sense of radical renunciation characteristic of these wandering ascetics.

3. Shamanism refers to those methods—found in many cultures—for developing supernormal mental, physical, and spiritual potentials. It often involves a kind of magico-religious use of altered states of consciousness—sometimes through ritual, or intensive practices of various kinds, and sometimes through the use of psychotropic drugs. These altered states often include intentional journeys to unseen worlds ordinarily accessible only through dream-states, myth, and near-death experiences.

4. Buddha's quote about questions not leading to edification has two interrelated sources. The first one comes from the *Sabbasava Sutta* (*Majjhima Nikaya #2; The Middle Length Discourses of the Buddha*, translated by Bhikkhu Nanamoli and Bhikkhu Bodhi [Somerville, MA: Wisdom Publications, 1995]) p. 93: "This speculative view, bhikkhus, is called the thicket of views, the wilderness of views, the contortion of views, the vacillation of views, the fetter of views...A well-taught noble disciple...understands what things are fit for attention and what things are unfit for attention." The second source comes from sutta #63, also from the *Majjhima Nikaya* (*Culamalunkya Sutta*) p. 536: "Why have I left it undeclared (questions about whether the world is eternal or not;

whether the world is infinite or not, etc.). Because it is unbeneficial, it does not belong to the fundamentals of the holy life, it does not lead to disenchantment, to dispassion, to cessation, to peace, to direct knowledge, to enlightenment, to Nibbana. That is why I have left it undeclared."

5. Mircea Eliade, *The Encyclopedia of Religion,* Vol. W, p. 393.

6. Marcel Proust, quoted in Jon Kabat-Zinn, *Coming to Our Senses* (New York: Hyperion, 2005) p. 196.

7. Ralph Waldo Emerson, quoted in Robert D. Richardson, Jr., *Emerson: The Mind on Fire* (Los Angeles: University of California Press, 1995) p. 283.

8. Annie Dillard, *For the Time Being* (New York: Alfred A. Knopf, 1999) p. 88.

Part One Epigraph

Henry David Thoreau, *Walden: And Other Writings,* edited, with an introduction by Brooks Atkinson (New York: Modern Library, 1965) p. 7.

Jake's Story

1. For an excellent, more scholarly, investigation of ego ideal and ideal ego, see Mark Epstein's "Meditative Transformations of Narcissism," in *The Journal of Transpersonal Psychology,* 1986, Vol. 18, No. 2, pp. 143–158. My treatment of this material draws heavily on Epstein's article (though my interpretation of ego ideal and ideal ego differs somewhat from his), and I am indebted to him for his brilliant analysis of the role of meditation in the attenuation of narcissism.

2. Epstein, "Meditative Transformations . . ." p. 146.

Chapter 1

1. Patanjali uses the term *samveganam* at *YS* 1.21, "For those who seek liberation *wholeheartedly*, realization is near." Here, the word means "with vehemence." In this section, I rely primarily on Buddhist sources for a description of the state of *samvega*, because, although Patanjali uses the term, accessible yogic sources are slim, and much less interesting than Buddhist sources.

2. Thanissaro Bhikkhu, "The Buddhist Teachings on Samvega and Pasada," Hindu Website, http://hinduwebsite.com/buddhism/essays/samvega. htm, p. 2.

3. Andrew Olendzki, "Dharma Dictionary: Nibbida" published in the Fall 2003 issue of *Buddhadharma.*

4. I heard Chögyam Trungpa Rinpoche say this in a lecture in the late 1970s.

5. Carlos Castaneda, *Journey to Ixtlan: The Lessons of Don Juan* (New York: Washington Square Press, 1972) p. xiii.

6. Thomas Merton, ed., Jonathan Montaldo, *Dialogues With Silence* (New York: Harper Collins, 2001) p. xiii.

7. David Wagoner, *Traveling Light* (Champaign: University of Illinois Press, 1999) p. 10.

8. David Chadwick, *Thank You and OK! An American Zen Failure in Japan* (New York: Penguin, 1994) p. 110.

9. Franz Kafka, quoted by Lama Surya Das, www.beliefnet.com/story/7/story_7291.html; also, in Paul Goodman, *Kafka's Prayer* (New York: Vanguard Press, 1947) p. 12.

10. Castaneda, *Journey*, p. 34.

Chapter 2

1. Eliade, *Encylopedia*, Vol. I, p. 507.

2. Michael Washburn, *The Ego and the Dynamic Ground: A Transpersonal Theory of Human Development* (Albany: State University of New York Press, 1995) p. 161.

3. Given in a lecture at Kripalu, at the first conference on Yoga and Buddhism: December 2001.

4. Eliade, *Encyclopedia*, Vol. I, p. 506.

5. Ibid., p. 506.

6. I heard Ram Dass tell this story during a talk at Omega Institute in the early 1990s. It was a story that he repeated on many occasions when he was teaching about "the witness."

Chapter 3

1. Georg Feuerstein, *The Shambhala Encyclopedia of Yoga* (Boston: Shambhala Publications, 2000) p. 94.

2. In referring to states of grasping and aversion, Patanjali uses different words in different *sūtras*. At 2.34, he uses *lobha* and *krodha,* which mean "greed" and "anger" respectively. At 2.3, in his important list of the five *kleshas*, he uses *rāga* and *dvesha,* which mean "wanting" (or craving or grasping) and "aversion." To simplify, and to maintain consistency with his list of *kleshas*, I've used *rāga* and *dvesha* throughout when referring to craving and aversion.

3. Bhagwan Shree Rajneesh, *Yoga: The Science of the Soul* (Oregon: Rajneesh Foundation International, 1976), Vol. I, p. 26.

Part Two Epigraph

Kabir, *The Kabir Book,* translated by Robert Bly (Boston: Beacon Books: 1971) p. 6.

Chapter 4

1. The Sanskrit word *mantra* comes from the root *man,* "to think." Therefore, as Georg Feuerstein tells us, a mantra is "a thought or intention expressed as sound ... (it) denotes 'prayer,' 'hymn,' 'spell,' 'counsel,' and 'plan.' In Yogic contexts, mantra stands for numinous phonemes that may or may not have commu-

nicable meaning." Georg Feuerstein, *The Shambhala Encyclopedia of Yoga* (Boston: Shambhala Publications, 2000) p. 180.

2. Ibid., p. 104. See Feuerstein for a more complete rendering.

3. Ibid., p. 135.

4. Ibid., p. 135.

5. Quoted in Feuerstein, *Encyclopedia*, p. 135.

6. I. K. Taimni, *The Science of Yoga* (London: The Theosophical Publishing House, 1961) p. 277.

7. Mahasi Sayadaw, *In This Very Lifetime* (Boston: Wisdom Publications, 1992) p. 189.

8. Mark Epstein, "Meditative Transformations," p. 150.

9. Richard J. Davidson, Jon Kabat-Zinn, et al, "Alterations in Brain and Immune Function Produced by Mindfulness Meditation," *Psychosomatic Medicine,* v. 65 (4) July/August 2003, pp. 564–570.

10. Antoine Lutz, et al, "Long-term meditators self-induce high amplitude gamma synchrony during mental practice." *Proceedings of the National Academy of Sciences* (PNAS) v. 101, no 46 (Nov. 16) 2004, pp. 16369–16373.

11. William James, *The Varieties of Religious Experience* (New York: Triumph Books) p. 298. He said, "...our normal waking consciousness is but one special type of consciousness, whilst all about it, parted from it by the filmiest of screens, there lie potential forms of consciousness entirely different. We may go through life without suspecting their existence; but apply the requisite stimulus, and at a touch they are there in all their completeness."

Chapter 5

1. Ken Wilber, *Transformations of Consciousness* (Boston: Shambhala Publications, 1986) p. 70 ff. Also, Robert McDermott, *The Essential Aurobindo* (Great Barrington, MA: Lindisfarne Press, 1987).

2. Wilber, *Transformations*, p. 157.

3. Patanjali describes the qualities of the subtle world at *sūtras* 1.44, 45, and 2.10, 50 and 3.26, 45, and 4.13. At 2.19, he describes the four major phases or levels *(parvan)* of the phenomenal world:

1. *alinga* (without form, the Undifferentiate)
2. *linga-mātra* (with form, the Differentiate)
3. *avishesha* (indistinct, or Unparticularized)
4. *vishesha* (distinct, or Particularized)

The first three of these phases are all subtle *(sūkshma)* and the last is the level of apparent gross reality.

4. Annie Dillard, *For the Time Being*, p. 81.

5. For a detailed investigation of current scientific thinking about "entanglement," see Dean Radin, *Entangled Minds* (New York: Simon and Schuster, 2006).

6. http://www.poemhunter.com/francis-thompson/quotations/poet-6693/page-1/

Part Three Epigraphs
Quoted in Faulds, *Sayings of...*, p. 50
Heraclitus, *On the Universe*, Fragment 12.

Susan's Story
1. The "hungry ghost" is an archetype common to many spiritual traditions. (See http://en.wikipedia.org/wiki/Hungry_ghost.) In the yoga tradition, the most detailed description of the hungry ghost is given in an ancient treatise called the *Garuda-Pada*.

2. http://people.ucsc.edu/~todluv/fre.html

3. Geneen Roth, *Breaking Free From Emotional Eating* (New York: Plume, 2003) p. 140.

Chapter 6
1. Deepak Chopra, *Quantum Physics and Consciousness, The Emerging Mind.* Edited by Karen Shanor (Los Angeles: Renaissance Books, 2000).

2. Sylvia Boorstein, *It's Easier Than You Think* (San Francisco: Harper San Francisco, 1997) p. 16.

Chapter 7
1. This well-known quote of the Buddha comes from the "Samyutta Nikaya" (5.57) in *Numerical Discourses of the Buddha*, translated by Nyanaponika Thera and Bhikkhu Bodhi (Altamira Press, 1999). The exact quote is "I am the owner of my actions, heir of my actions, actions are the womb from which I have sprung, actions are my relations, actions are my protection. Whatever actions I do, good or bad, of these I shall become the heir."

2. Described in Deepak Chopra, *Quantum Healing* (New York: Bantam, 1989) pp. 225–226.

3. Richard C. Schwartz, *Introduction to the Internal Family Systems Model* (Oak Park: The Center for Self Leadership, 2001) p. 94. Richard Schwartz is the originator of the Internal Family Systems Model, and a pioneer in the integration of the contemplative view with Western psychology. I am greatly indebted to him for his insights about "parts," patterns, self-leadership, and witness consciousness.

4. Ibid.

Chapter 8
1. Mu Soeng, "From Anatta to Shunyata." Unpublished essay, used with permission of the author.

2. Schwartz, *Introduction*, p. 93.

3. Ibid., p. 94.

4. Mu Soeng, "From Anatta..."

5. Swami Ajaya, *Psychotherapy East and West: A Unifying Paradigm* (Honesdale, PA: The Himalayan Institute, 1997) pp. 128–9.

6. Carl Jung, quoted by Swami Ajaya, Ibid., p. 130.

7. Phillip Moffitt, in Stephen Cope, ed., *Will Yoga and Meditation Really Change My Life?* (North Adams: Storey Publications, 2001) p. 173.

8. Swami Kripalu, in Richard Faulds, ed., *Sayings of...*, pp. 48–49.

9. Quoted in Anthony Storr, *Solitude: A Return to the Self* (New York: Quality Paperback, 2001) p. 195.

Part Four Epigraph

Carlos Castaneda, *Journey to Ixtlan: The Lessons of Don Juan* (New York: Washington Square Press, 1972) p. 81.

Ibid, p. 58.

Chapter 9

1. Swami Kripalu, *Premyatra, Pilgrimage of Love*, Vol. I. (Lenox, MA: Kripalu Center for Yoga and Health, 1992) p. 41.

2. Ibid. p. 43.

3. Eliade, *Encyclopedia*, Vol. S, p. 323.

4. Swami Kripalu, *Pilgrimage of Love*, p. 44.

5. Ibid.

6. Ibid.

7. Mircea Eliade, *Yoga: Immortality and Freedom* (Princeton: Princeton University Press, 1958) p. 52.

8. Both quoted in Georg Feuerstein, *Yoga: The Technology of Ecstasy* (New York: Jeremy Tarcher, 1989) p. 185.

9. Taimni, *The Science of Yoga*, p. 240.

10. Ibid.

11. Georg Feuerstein, *The Philosophy of Classical Yoga* (Rochester, VT: Inner Traditions, 1996) p. 103.

Chapter 10

1. "Right effort" is the sixth of the eight path factors in the Noble Eightfold Path of the Buddha. Right effort is further described as the "four Right Exertions," which are elaborated in the Pali scripture called *Samyutta Nikaya* XLV.8, the *Magga-vibhanga Sutta*. See http://accesstoinsight.org/canon/sutta/samyutta/sn45-008.html.

2. Ajahn Sumedho. The author heard Sumedho give this teaching in a dharma talk at Spirit Rock Meditation Center, Woodacre, CA.

3. See, e.g., Davidson, Kabat-Zinn, "Alterations..."

4. This version of the classical *metta* phrases was developed by Buddhist teacher Sylvia Boorstein, and is used with permission.

Chapter 11

1. Bhagwan Shree Rajneesh, *Yoga: Science of the Soul,* p. 16.

2. Joseph Campbell, *Transformations of Myth Through Time* (New York: HarperPerennial, 1990) p. 116.

3. Daniel Brown, "The Stages of Meditation in Cross-Cultural Perspective," in *Transformations of Consciousness* (Boston: Shambhala Publications, 1986) p. 231.

4. Feuerstein, *Encyclopedia,* p. 122.

5. Ibid., p. 239.

6. S. N. Goenka, William Hart, *Vipassana Meditation as Taught by S. N. Goenka* (San Francisco: Harper SanFrancisco, 1987) p. 110.

7. Ibid., p. 109.

8. Feuerstein, *The Philosophy of Classical...,* p. 66.

9. Op. cit., pp. 110–111.

10. Erik Hoffmann, "Mapping the brain's activity after Kriya Yoga," *Bindu Periodical on Yoga Tantra Meditation,* Vol. 12, 2005, www.scand-yoga.org/english/bindu/bindu12/hoffman.html, p. 3.

11. Ibid.

Chapter 12

1. Jim Leonard and Phil Laut, *Vivation: The Science of Enjoying All of Your Life* (Cincinnati: The Vivation Publishing Company, 1983) p. 59.

2. Dennis Lewis, *Free Your Breath, Free Your Life* (Boston: Shambhala, 2004).

3. Ibid., p. 160.

4. Eugene O'Neill. *A Moon for the Misbegotten.* First Vintage Edition (New York: Vintage, 2000) p. 85.

5. Pat Ogden, Ph.D. In a talk at the Psychological Trauma Conference, Boston, MA, June 10, 2004.

6. Chip Hartranft, *The Yoga-Sūtra of Patanjali* (Boston: Shambhala, 2003) p. 41.

7. Jim Grigsby and David Stevens, *Neurodynamics of Personality,* (Vermont: The Guilford Press, 2001) p. 325.

8. Stephen and Ondrea Levine. These words spoken in a lecture the Levines gave jointly at Kripalu Center in 1992.

9. Annie Dillard, *The Writing Life* (New York: HarperPerennial, 1990) p. 32.

10. From the article on "Addiction" on the website of Wikipedia, http://en.wikipedia.org/wiki/Addiction, p. 5.

11. Mark Epstein, *Thoughts Without a Thinker,* p. 146.

Part Five Epigraph
Annie Dillard, *For the Time Being*, p. 180.

Chapter 13
1. Taimni, *The Science of . . .*, p. 282.
2. Daniel Brown and Jack Engler, "The Stages of Mindfulness Meditation: A Validation Study," in *Transformations of Consciousness* (Boston: Shambhala Publications, 1986) p. 198.
3. Ibid., p. 199.
4. Taimni, *The Science of . . .*, pp. 283, 284.
5. Eliade, *Yoga: Immortality . . .*, p. 69.
6. Ibid.
7. Ibid., p. 72.
8. Shri Ramakrishna, *Ramakrishna As We Saw Him* (St. Louis: Vedanta Society, 1990) p. 123.
9. Chip Hartranft, *The Yoga-Sūtra of Patanjali*, p. 18.
10. Henry David Thoreau, *"In Wildness Is the Preservation of the World": Selections and Photographs by Eliot Porter* (San Francisco: The Sierra Club, 1962). From the section on "Winter," Thoreau's journal entry of January 21, 1853.

Chapter 14
1. Brown and Engler, "The Stages of Mindfulness Meditation . . .," p. 200.
2. Robert Richardson, Jr., *Henry Thoreau: A Life of the Mind* (Berkeley: University of California Press, 1986) p. 76.
3. Robert Frost, "Nothing Gold Can Stay," *The Poetry of Robert Frost*, edited by Edward Connery Lathem (New York: Henry Holt, 1969).
4. Once again, for a more complete description of this process, see Epstein, "Meditative Transformations . . ."

Chapter 15
1. Bhagwan Shree Rajneesh, *The Secret of Secrets*, Vol. II (Oregon: Rajneesh Foundation International, 1983) p. 286.
2. Swami Ajaya, *Psychotherapy East and West*, p. 90ff.
3. Georg Feuerstein, *The Philosophy of Classical Yoga* (Vermont: Inner Traditions International, 1996) p. 12.
4. Ibid., p. 12.
5. Rajneesh, *The Secret . . .*, p. 281.

ACKNOWLEDGMENTS

It is sometimes said, "Difficult things take a long time. Impossible things take a little longer." This book, as my editor will attest, took a little longer.

And so, there are many people to thank.

First of all, I'm eager for the opportunity to thank my friends, family, and colleagues for putting up with the many eccentricities that seem to emerge when one is working on a big book—things like unacceptable amounts of social withdrawal and unreliability, boring and endless hand-wringing about the progress of the manuscript, and generally an embarrassing degree of authorial self-absorption.

Many of the aforesaid friends, family, and colleagues made significant contributions to the progress of the work—including, especially, my twin sister, Sandra Stieglitz, who is a tireless reader and champion; Atma Jo Ann Leavitt, who stuck with me through four years of dinners at the Love Dog Café and deep conversations about the structure of the book and the nature of life; Adam Mastoon, who is as impeccable as a designer and photographer (he's done the covers of all my books) as he is as a friend; Rick and Danna Faulds, whose generosity seems bottomless and comes with huge dollops of intelligence, honesty, and humility (a stunning combination); my longtime friend Alan Poole, whose steadiness and perspective always help to ground me; my friend and fellow author Amy Weintraub, who bravely edited several versions of this book; my dear friend and fellow practitioner Sylvia Boorstein, who has a heart as big as the world; my incomparable mentor, Mu Soeng, without whom this book would never have happened, and who graciously allowed me to dedicate this book to him in spite of his probable embarrassment; my brilliant new friend Chip Hartranft, who understands the *Yoga-Sūtra* much better than I ever will, and who graciously offered his translation for our project; and, of course, my mom, Barbara Crothers Cope, also an author, who never stopped believing in her kid, or in herself for that matter—and who wrote a book during the same period I was writing this book even though she was mostly blinded by macular degeneration.

This work would not have been possible without the generous support of Kripalu Center for Yoga and Health, in Lenox, Massachusetts—my true home, it appears, on this planet. Dinabandhu and Ila Sarley, president and chief operating officer of Kripalu, respectively, have made it their business and their life work to support the thriving of individual human beings, and to support the thriving of innovative institutions like Kripalu. They gave me the institution's unconditional artistic support throughout the project. Without this, I would have had to set up my computer under a bridge somewhere. Many others in the Kripalu community have offered invaluable support, especially Aruni Nan Futoronsky, Rasmani Debbie Orth, Grace Welker, Rudi Peirce, Sudha Carolyn Lundeen, Randal Williams, Phil Webster, Paul Protzman, and Susan Moul. I want to especially thank the incomparable Swami Shivananda Sarasvati for his always generous help with questions of Sanskrit in this project, and for graciously reading the manuscript in several of its unruly incarnations.

Finally, how could I have produced a work such as this without the close collaboration of my editor, Toni Burbank? She will probably not allow me to say all the things about her that should be said. She is fearless, determined, relentless, tireless, and as one-pointed as any meditator or yogi. She is also big-hearted and stunningly generous with her time and expertise. Every time she touched the manuscript it was vastly improved. I'm so grateful to her, and to her whole team at Bantam Dell Publishing Group (especially the excellent Julie Will), who have been gracious and generous collaborators through two big projects.

INDEX

About the Author

STEPHEN COPE is a psychotherapist, a yoga teacher, and the author of the highly acclaimed *Yoga and the Quest for the True Self*. He is currently Senior Scholar-in-Residence at Kripalu Center for Yoga and Health in Lenox, Massachusetts.

About Kripalu Center

KRIPALU CENTER is the largest retreat center for yoga and holistic living in North America, a distinction it has held for more than twenty-five years. Located in the beautiful Berkshire Mountains of western Massachusetts, Kripalu is a place to discover what it means to be fully human and fully alive through a nonsectarian and nondogmatic approach to yoga. Its renowned curriculum is based on a model of experiential learning that provides people with tools for optimal living and a wealth of opportunities to cultivate vibrant physical health, nurture emotional wellness, and draw spiritual sustenance from within and without.

For more information about Kripalu Center and its international network of more than two thousand Kripalu Yoga teachers, visit *www.kripalu.org*.